This Is Our CITY

Bob Guelker (1923-1986), Harry Keough (1927-2012),
and Bob Kehoe (1928-2017), three pioneers
of St. Louis and American soccer

Whether soccer fans or not, this book, which was
largely written during COVID-19 (coronavirus),
is also dedicated to the many people that died from
the virus. The pandemic, coincidentally, stalled
the opening season of St. Louis City SC.

SHANE STAY

THIS IS OUR
CITY

ST. LOUIS CITY SC AND THE REVIVAL
OF AMERICA'S FIRST SOCCER CAPITAL

Meyer & Meyer Sport

British Library of Cataloguing in Publication Data
A catalogue record for this book is available from the British Library

This Is Our CITY
Maidenhead: Meyer & Meyer Sport (UK) Ltd., 2023
ISBN: 978-1-78255-227-7

Aachen, Auckland, Beirut, Cairo, Cape Town, Dubai, Hägendorf, Hong Kong, Indianapolis, Maidenhead, Manila, New Delhi, Singapore, Sydney, Tehran, Vienna

Member of the World Sport Publishers' Association (WSPA), www.w-s-p-a.org

Printed by Integrated Books International
Printed in the United States of America
ISBN: 978-1-78255-227-7
Email: info@m-m-sports.com
www.thesportspublisher.com

Credits
Cover design: Isabella Frangenberg
Interior design: Anja Elsen
Layout: DiTech Publishing Services, www.ditechpubs.com
Cover photo: ©AdobeStock
Managing editor: Elizabeth Evans

CONTENTS

INTRODUCTION

ST. LOUIS: WHERE GREATNESS HAPPENS

After a long, tedious, wait—it happened. St. Louis got its MLS team. St. Louis City SC has arrived!

St. Louis is overwhelmingly familiar with professional sports franchises. As most people know, St. Louis—where the Mississippi and Missouri Rivers join—has been a flourishing sports city over the years, with the St. Louis Cardinals (second all-time in World Series titles with 11), St. Louis Blues (Stanley Cup champions, 2019), previously the St. Louis Rams (Super Bowl champions, 2000), St. Louis Hawks (NBA champions, 1958), and the Spirits of St. Louis (who didn't accomplish much other than kick starting the career of Bob Costas, who called games for KMOX radio). It's a city that has embraced traditional sports with the best of them. I like to call baseball, basketball, and football the "Big 3" of traditional American sports. St. Louis, Missouri, has thrived in each.

As for other sports, you might not think of St. Louis right away. You might not think of St. Louis and tennis in the same sentence, yet, the great champion of the Australian Open, Wimbledon, and the US Open, Jimmy Connors, hails from East St. Louis, Illinois, a Metro East suburb. In the world of "non-contact" sports, such as bowling, St. Louis has sat atop the mountain, with Pete Weber, who was born in St. Ann, leading the way. Interestingly, in the world of chess, also normally a non-contact sport,* St. Louis hosts the distinguished Saint Louis Chess Club located in the Central West End. As for bocce ball, well, St. Louis has some catching up to do.

---

*   Who are we kidding? It's an activity.

Regardless, soccer, which in recent years has turned from a non-traditional anomaly to one of America's go-to feature attractions, has gone hand-in-hand with St. Louis as no other city. It's almost law that kids play youth soccer in St. Louis, in leagues such as the CYC, Catholic Youth Council; SLYSA, St. Louis Youth Soccer Association; and SISL, Southern Illinois Soccer League. For all intents and purposes, St. Louis is known as the king of soccer. We'll elaborate on this title in due time. But hold on. There's something very interesting to discuss.

JUST LIKE A NEUTRON STAR

Years ago, in 1982, astronomers made a remarkable discovery far off in the universe—a neutron star spinning 642 times per second! Then, as reported in 2006, according to Maggie Mckee in *New Scientist*, astronomers found a neutron star rotating even faster! "The fastest-spinning neutron star ever found has been discovered in a crowded star cluster near the centre of the Milky Way, a new study reveals. The star rotates 716 times per second—faster than some theories predict is possible—and therefore may force researchers to revise their models."[1] "The previous record holder, which spins at 642 Hz, was discovered in 1982."[2] There are various neutron stars (by the way) that spin at slower, but still amazing, rates such as "...thirty-three revolutions per second,"[3] as Martin Rees pointed out. However, the report of 716 spins per second is a mind-boggling concept. To think such a thing had been sitting there, in all its brilliance, rotating at a speed that defies logic, just waiting to be discovered.

In a way, St. Louis soccer—which has a magic all its own—has been sitting there, waiting to be discovered by new soccer fans in the US and around the world. As you'll see, St. Louis soccer has been spinning off into space with fantastic teams, players, passion, results, records, organization, and high-quality for generations.

Let's start with the 1950 FIFA World Cup in which the United States miraculously defeated England in the famous 1-0 match. Five of the starting 11 US players were from St. Louis! That should be it; that should be "case closed," "thanks and good night," followed by "story's over." Five players? *Five players*? Yet there's more. Much more.

Within the world of club soccer, St. Louis teams—Seco, St. Paul, Kutis, St. Philip Di Neri, Imo's, Busch, Scott Gallagher, among others— have won a large number of national championships. In fact, St. Louis has been a leader in this regard, which we'll touch on later. For now, just remember this: In 1958, St. Louis Kutis was so good that it was called upon to play as proxy for the US national team. (Were there a couple of guest players? Sure. But that actually happened. And that's unheard of.)

In terms of Missouri high school soccer state championships, it's no contest. St. Louis leads the pack. St. Thomas Aquinas-Mercy, CBC, Vianney, St. Mary's, De Smet, and others who we'll touch on in a bit, have been the dominant schools in Missouri for decades now. Missouri, by virtue of the dense forest of talent in St. Louis, along with worthy competition from Kansas City and Cape Girardeau, is considered one of the nation's top high school soccer states. St. Louis has also contributed a substantial number of high school All-Americans.

Let's briefly talk college soccer, shall we? To this day, St. Louis University is the reigning all-time NCAA Division I champion with an amazing 10 titles. As a result, coaches Bob Guelker and Harry Keough† helped to shape American soccer. But that's not all. Many people are unaware of the incredible year 1973 in which St. Louis colleges garnered all national championships (SLU in NCAA Division I, UMSL in NCAA Division II, and Florissant Valley Community College in NJCAA Division I). When a city runs the table like that, something's going on—

---

†   Harry Keough happened to be on that famous US team in the 1950 FIFA World Cup.

something very special. Furthermore, one can't forget the 1979 NCAA Division I championship earned by SIUE (located in the Metro East suburb of Edwardsville, Illinois), coached by the aforementioned Bob Guelker, one of America's early soccer innovators.

St. Louis has been a longtime leader in American professional soccer. St. Leo's, way back in the early 1900s, is credited with being an early pioneer in professional American soccer. From the 1960s onward, the St. Louis Stars competed in the NASL with many St. Louis players in the lineup (a bold move at the time). Some notable players from the Stars era included Bob Kehoe, Pat McBride, Jim Leeker, John Pisani, Gary Rensing, Al Trost, and Dennis Vaninger. (Bob Kehoe, a St. Louis legend, was a player and coach for the Stars and also the USMNT.) With all due respect to St. Leo's, the Stars were truly the pioneers of pro soccer in St. Louis (and America at large, along with fellow NASL teams). After the Stars joined the NASL, the result was massive. Subsequently, the Stars, in part, played a crucial role in the increase of youth, high school, and collegiate players around St. Louis, and, arguably, around the country. Following the Stars came a gradual inundation of professional indoor teams that included the St. Louis Steamers, St. Louis Storm, St. Louis Ambush (1995 NPSL champions), St. Louis Illusion, and Illinois Piasa, along with the professional outdoor teams, St. Louis Knights, AC St. Louis, Saint Louis FC, and, most recently, St. Louis City SC.

Still, that's not all. How about just a handful of players that have represented the USMNT? You have Harry Keough, Bob Kehoe, Pat McBride, Al Trost, Denny Vaninger, Ty Keough, Greg Villa, Steve Pecher, Steve Trittschuh, Mark Santel, Mike Sorber, Matt McKeon, Steve Ralston, Chris Klein, Taylor Twellman, Brad Davis, Tim Ream, Josh Sargent, and many others who we'll cover in a bit.

It's been a long, interesting history. Sure, St. Louis hasn't exactly spun around 716 times per second (that would make it a neutron star and I don't think the mayor would allow such a thing, wink-wink), but, nonetheless, it's been achieving things in soccer that demand a second, third, and fourth look.

I know what you're thinking, New Jersey guy, California guy. Ye of little faith. For that matter, Liverpool guy and Munich guy might be thinking similar thoughts: *Yeah, so there's been soccer in St. Louis— what's the big deal?* Sure, your initial thought—likely laden with a vague assortment of disparate information—is a valid one. Certainly, the quality of soccer in New Jersey, D.C., California, and elsewhere throughout America, has been quite significant with respect to accomplishments and the overall growth of the sport nationwide. Though, without a doubt, regardless of how important the aforementioned places—and others— have been in the culture of American soccer, St. Louis has been the cradle, the hub, the headquarters—essentially ground zero.

MLS LAUNCHES IN 1996 WITHOUT THE KING

In brief, we've gone over the broad historical points of St. Louis soccer. Yes, we'll get into much more, later. (There's so much more!) Whether a seasoned St. Louis soccer aficionado or newcomer, one should find this very interesting. In 1996, when Major League Soccer launched its first season there were 10 teams...10 original teams. St. Louis was not one of them! This was odd. Bill McDermott—a former NCAA national soccer champion with SLU, a radio and TV announcer known as "Mr. Soccer" in St. Louis (a name bestowed on him by Bob Costas)—said, "If there's going to be a professional soccer league in the United States, it's almost mandatory that St. Louis play a part."[4] This has been the sentiment in the soccer community for ages. Yet, back in 1996, even Kansas City had a team while its neighbor and soccer stronghold, St. Louis, didn't. This was *very* odd. And everyone knew it. Well, let's just say, anyone that knew American soccer knew it. It was a mysterious travesty. Let's take a look at the original 10 MLS teams:

THE EASTERN CONFERENCE [1996]

Columbus Crew, D.C. United, New England Revolution, New York/New Jersey MetroStars, Tampa Bay Mutiny

THE WESTERN CONFERENCE [1996]

Colorado Rapids, Dallas Burn, Kansas City Wiz, Los Angeles Galaxy, San Jose Clash

There was no St. Louis. Here's why this was significant. For years, for generations in fact, St. Louis—the king of soccer—has led the soccer community in America. It's been the leader. No question.

Even folks from Chicago—which has a rich soccer tradition of its own—have admitted as much. If you know anything about the entrenched rivalry between St. Louis and Chicago, then you'd know this is saying something. There's the St. Louis Cardinals vs. Chicago Cubs; always draped in beer, it's a peaceful, yet overwhelmingly passionate affair. Then there's the St. Louis Blues vs. Chicago Blackhawks; always draped in beer, yet it's a tribal affair two steps away from a UFC cage fight. In the longstanding sports rivalries between St. Louis and Chicago it's difficult for people from Chicago to give St. Louis a compliment. End of story. It usually doesn't happen. If it happens at all, there better be a damned good reason. Take a brief example from back in 1992. (It may seem passingly trivial and innocuous, but it has a lot to do with the overall status of St. Louis in the grand landscape of American soccer.) I played high school soccer at Collinsville, Illinois, a St. Louis Metro East school second only to its neighbor, the colossal, legendary, mega-powerhouse jet engine that was Granite City High School which dominated the Illinois high school landscape in the name of St. Louis soccer for years. (Granite City has 10 state championships, in fact, still a record!) In 1992, my CHS team was about to win a fourth Illinois High School Association (IHSA) state championship, amid the final game against Evanston Township

High School. It was televised on SportsChannel[‡] and calling the game from Chicago were Mike Leiderman and Bob Dollaske. Speaking of the Metro East and St. Louis, Leiderman said: "For those who are not that familiar with high school soccer in general, the Illinois side though in particular, the downstate area really has an awful lot of competition with St. Louis schools. And St. Louis, of course, is the number one, the number one soccer area in the country." In turn, Dollaske added, "When we talk about downstate, it's really just the area, Belleville and Collinsville and Granite City, those that can go across the river and play in St. Louis where soccer is king."

For anyone from Chicago—or even standing on Chicago soil—to offer such a compliment to St. Louis is astoundingly significant. The announcers were echoing an 'ancient mantra' doused in fact that has lingered in America like a Greek myth. St. Louis: The King of Soccer.

Let's put it this way: In 1958, when the United States needed a club team to represent the US national team as proxy, did it call upon Seattle, Portland, San Francisco, Los Angeles, San Diego, Phoenix, Dallas, Houston, Kansas City, Chicago, Detroit, Cincinnati, Cleveland, Memphis, New York, New Jersey, Philadelphia, Pittsburgh, D.C., or Miami? No. The United States of America[§] asked St. Louis Kutis. When a nation calls upon one club team, from one city, to play as the national team, that's called being "the king of soccer."

Get used to it. That's how it always has been and it's how fans of St. Louis City SC intend for the future to be. These fans have been sitting back, astonished, since 1996 when St. Louis was left out of the initial MLS liftoff. Given the history of St. Louis soccer, it was bizarre.

[‡] Essentially, SportsChannel took off in 1976 with headquarters in New York City, and was owned by Cablevision (1979-98) and NBC (1988-98). It was superseded by Fox Sports Networks, Comcast SportsNet.

[§] Technically, the United States Soccer Federation. Grant it, there were a few guest players but this does not diminish the reality of Kutis playing as proxy for the US national team.

Imagine this sci-fi hypothetical: The United States shuts down for a month. It completely shuts down. Everything goes silent. All lights are turned off. Everyone hibernates. Then, all of a sudden, everyone wakes up and things start to operate again to full functioning capacity. Finally, everyone takes a sigh of relief. At this point, each city announces it will have an NFL team. In fact, everyone announces this accept for Dallas. That's right, Dallas. It turns out that Dallas is the only city with no NFL team. I know what you're thinking: *Well, this is kind of weird. Why wouldn't Dallas have a football team?* Then, lo and behold, the NFL community has to wait over 20 years for the Dallas Cowboys to become a team. What? How in the hell (pardon my French) is this possible? This is how insane it is that St. Louis—the king of soccer—took so long to have a Major League Soccer team. It just didn't make sense. So much so that when the league continued to expand, St. Louis was not included.

After the original 1996 MLS season, gradually the league grew successful. With this success came expansion. New teams were emerging onto the scene left and right it would seem. However, St. Louis was still not included. You might want to sit down for this: Salt Lake City, Utah, had a team and St. Louis didn't. Salt Lake City, that amazing beacon of soccer. It just didn't make sense. Wait, there's more. Orlando, Florida, had a team and St. Louis didn't. Don't get me wrong, Orlando is a great place, with a good soccer community. But anyone knows—especially people from Orlando, along with every other city in the United States—that St. Louis is the dominant soccer community between the two. It's a joke actually; it's not even worth a realistic conversation. That wasn't all. Let's not forget Montreal, Canada. When everyone thinks Major League Soccer, they automatically think Montreal, Canada. (Slight sarcasm.) Despite being an enthusiastic soccer city, Columbus, Ohio, had a team and St. Louis didn't. What a slap in the face. Columbus? Really? And not St. Louis? Okay, I guess. If you insist. (A little more sarcasm.) All in all, none of this made any sense.

Meanwhile, as St. Louis was living in an ongoing episode of *The Twilight Zone*, the years were piling up in Major League Soccer's gradual climb in popularity. After a while, more cities were joining the league: Portland, Seattle, Vancouver, Atlanta, yet no St. Louis. Then Minnesota got a team before St. Louis! What?! How was this possible? Well, it was. Who was next, Cincinnati? Yep. That actually happened. *That actually happened.* Cincinnati got an MLS team before St. Louis. Oy. I know. The weirdness kept piling up. If you're thinking, *What?* Trust me, you're not alone. Then again, you could be someone that looks at this whole situation and thinks it was completely normal. If you are, well, you're probably from Cincinnati. (Timeout. Before you think I'm having a go at Cincinnati or Ohio in general, I'm not. Soccer's no joke in Ohio, that's for sure. It's a state that's had multiple professional teams over the years. Youth soccer has been a big deal there as well. I remember at a U13 tournament in Germantown, Tennessee, I was playing as a mercenary on a very talented team from Cape Girardeau, Missouri—which, for a time, was number one in SLYSA, the top league in St. Louis—and we went up against Coke from Cincinnati in the championship game and they took it to us 4-1. In our defense, we were exhausted after a 1-0 revenge victory in the semi-finals over a team from Memphis that had defeated us 4-1 the night beforehand; it was a triumphant moment for us, and, indeed, our legs could barely move in the final. But the team from Cincinnati was good, not to mention it was sponsored by Coca-Cola (a major plus), and, just based on this one team, you could tell something was going on in Cincinnati. Add to this multiple pro teams over the years, along with the Akron Zips, and you can understand why Ohio is a legitimate soccer state.)

Whether we're talking about Cincinnati or Vancouver or a city with two names in Minnesota, the bottom line is this: It took a long time for St. Louis—the king of soccer—to get a Major League Soccer team. The struggle was real. Interestingly, St. Louis was even pleading to join MLS, with multiple well-intentioned attempts as Dale Schilly, a crucial figure in this process and a former coach of Saint Louis FC, can attest. These were attempts with a lot of momentum that unfortunately failed before crossing the proverbial finish line. Dale was part of two previous efforts, dating as far back as 2008. Lest anyone forget there was much underway before certain billionaire investors stepped in during the final push to victory.

It was a long process, there's no other way to put it. At one point, around 2015 or 2016 (I forget which exactly) I went down to an office—somewhere near downtown St. Louis—where efforts were being made to bring an MLS franchise to the Gateway City. I was given some information and that was about it. At the time, I was researching material for another book. But, the overall message I'm relaying to you is that an effort was indeed underway to bring Major League Soccer to St. Louis, which occurred in different phases, years before St. Louis City SC came to fruition.

The end result is a product—an MLS team—that will not only represent St. Louis proper but also the immediate area, and then some. Indeed, the introduction of any team has the potential to affect lives across the world. In some time, when MLS becomes the world's next super league (as I firmly believe it will), St. Louis could very well be the next Manchester United, Bayern Munich, Barcelona, or Juventus. The introduction of this jewel St. Louis City SC is, without a doubt, a historic event. A truly historic undertaking.

YOUR EFFERVESCENT GUIDE

The honor I have to bring you the history of the beautiful game in St. Louis is beyond compare. Through the lens of my experiences with St. Louis soccer I'm in a position to humbly reflect on St. Louis' vast history and put forth why this area is prepared to send forth a stellar MLS franchise in the form of St. Louis City SC.

From my travels throughout St. Louis soccer as a player I've realized that where there is amazing talent on the field the result is an aftermath of super-savvy aficionados of the game, which is what St. Louis City SC has inherited.

Just before 9th grade I moved to the St. Louis area by way of Collinsville, Illinois, in the Metro East. I'm originally from Carbondale, Illinois, which is about an hour and a half south of St. Louis, give or take. Essentially, for what it's worth, I was stuck in the wrong place to play soccer seriously. Carbondale was seen as the backwater of American soccer, the backwater of Illinois soccer, and the backwater of Southern Illinois soccer. That's a lot of backwater. Not good. It's the home of SIUC not SIUE, though both are related. When I was there it was a vibrant college town that focused on baseball, basketball, and football, with soccer as a fourth option. Though, from time to time, we did have some very good players, and we'd occasionally encounter teams from St. Louis in this tournament or that tournament.

Everyone knew that St. Louis was a soccer factory. Soccer was serious there. It was *the* place to be. If you encountered a team from St. Louis, you'd notice how the skill and intensity levels were higher across-the-board; the teams were confident and arrogant like nobody's business. Soccer was just plain better in St. Louis and it had been around a long time as well, there was a rich tradition going back generations.

Eventually, while living in Carbondale, I played in St. Louis when I was around 11-12 years old (we'll get to that in a second). Let's just say, I played on a lot of teams. When I say a lot of teams, I mean a lot of teams. To say I was a mercenary would be an insult to mercenaries everywhere, though, I would say I was essentially a player for hire.

As a result, I have many former teammates that helped shape my perspective on soccer, and like concentric circles forming in a lake from a rock hitting it, these players were part of an expanding circle that intersected with other circles in a vast array of connections over time. They are all interconnected; just as players such as Harry Keough, Carl Gentile, Pat McBride, Perry Van der Beck, Steve Pecher, Steve

16

Trittschuh, Mike Sorber, Steve Ralston, Tim Ream, and Josh Sargent have played a role in making those circular patterns, so too have a myriad of teammates and opposition around them along the way. Now, with various circles combining into one, St. Louis City SC has formed from a community—household names on ESPN right down to aficionadas that only dabbled in youth soccer—that has been invested in the game for generations.

The St. Louis soccer experience has touched the lives of many, and, long before St. Louis City SC, I was fortunate to be a part of it.

When I was around eight or nine, my earliest experience with St. Louis' famous Soccer Park* (that I can remember) came after a scrimmage game against Fenton.

Fenton was a team that would show up to the Cape Girardeau tournament in southeast Missouri and annihilate opponents. The All-Star team I was with from Carbondale—where I first began playing—made the trip up to Fenton and lost 3-1, in a game after one of their practices. This was just before the Fenton kids transitioned to teams like Busch and Johnny Mac; this Fenton side likely consisted of Tony Williams, Timmy Pratt, Tommy Rohr, and Jason Feeney. Our goal-scorer that day was Dylan Bates. Dylan—the former CEO of ATI Physical Therapy—was a gifted four-sport athlete—baseball, basketball, football, and soccer—that eventually played college basketball. As was the case with most kids in Carbondale, soccer was typically his last choice, though, oddly enough, it might have been his best sport—a natural. Defender Andy Vanawken, who later played soccer for Eastern Illinois University, and forward Gregory Gimenez, who eventually suited up for SIUE, were also on our side. It wasn't enough. A typical result. This was the fate many clubs from across the country endured when they went up against a St. Louis team. It was the culture, it was the tradition St. Louis had to its advantage (not to mention, a substantial population).

---

*   Soccer Park is thought of as a St. Louis gem, though it's technically located in the south suburb of Fenton, Missouri.

This Fenton team, by the way, wasn't just one group of guys operating in a vacuum. At this point in time, the early to mid-1980s, the St. Louis Steamers were roaring with insane attendance numbers, and players like the ones we had lost to were taking all that in, watching top-notch performers, while also receiving strong coaching that flourished in the area. This wasn't just one game as a model. This Fenton team and others nearby were indicative of a large culture of soccer. When you have players as good as they were, along with a pro team, the Steamers, you'll also have strong fanfare for the sport, which was the case. We had entered a section of the country where soccer was a cultural phenomenon. Today, when you visit a St. Louis City SC game, you'll probably come across middle-aged men walking to their seats with a beer in hand, many of whom might've put on a little extra weight and haven't done a sit-up in maybe 15 years, waddling around, and you'd never suspect that at one time they were youth soccer badasses. After talking with them for about 30 seconds, you'll come to realize their soccer IQs are off the chart.

Following the loss to Fenton, a few of us went to Soccer Park which was down the road a bit and sat in the bleachers that overlooked the whole thing—a pristine multi-field complex equipped with a concession area, deck, bleachers, night-lights, scoreboard, and parking lot. I imagined teams around my age, wearing Umbro and Patrick uniforms (which were popular in the 80s), playing on the two turf fields. It was an awe-inspiring sight. Then we trampled on one of the side grass-fields with a ball, feeling lucky to tread on such perfect grass. We had a field complex back home, but not quite like this. Ours was nice though (Parrish Fields). There were two fields on one side of the road, and about six on the other. There was a YMCA there. There was also a shed...for our basic communal uniforms—reversible jerseys with the colors of red on one side and gold on the other—along with flags and other such things that fields need. Soccer Park, on the other hand, was special. You could feel it.

I also played for the Cape Girardeau Cobras—my first mercenary gig—that competed in the late 1980s in SLYSA† and for a time we were

---

†   St. Louis Youth Soccer Association.

18

number one (how'd that happen?). A few players included Seth Benton, Derek Doyle, Ty Eggiman, Gregory Gimenez, Damon Harkins, Shannon Lee, Todd Nordman, Sean Pfeiffer, Craig Scheer, and Phil Tomlinson. This was a very competitive team whose dads were on a quest each game to prove they were former Civil War Generals. Armed with a fleet of minivans at their disposal, it was an era in American soccer that saw club competition soar, with St. Louis leading the nation. It would seem the sole intent of this team was to dismantle the mighty reputation of the Gateway City. In fact, within Missouri, Cape Girardeau might be considered the second St. Louis—it's a very talented soccer city.

Subsequently I played with a Carbondale club team, the Pharaohs, which competed in SISL.† Some players were Dylan Bates, Jason Clark, Gregory Gimenez, Matt Henry, Matt Lawrence, Leandro Sapiro, Andy Vanawken, Matt Wadiak, and Jason Wooley. Once upon a time, as underdogs, we beat Granite City 1-0, a great achievement.

Eventually, at the start of my freshman year in high school, to pursue soccer at a higher level, my mom got a job teaching in Jennings (just north of St. Louis), and I moved to Collinsville, Illinois, and let's just say, Carbondale was far enough away that when I arrived my new classmates got a kick out of my Southern accent.

Back to my travels as a mercenary. I played with the Granite City Elks, Troy Chargers, Busch Soccer Club (with whom I won a Missouri club state championship), a one-off Metro East team coached by Ed Gettemeier—a former goalie for the St. Louis Steamers—that won the Holland Cup, Edwardsville Soccer Club, Collinsville United, and Collinsville High School whereby I was part of two high school state championships, thank you very much. I wasn't kidding: That's a lot of teams in the St. Louis area! From these various squads, the amount of teammates was vast, yet a mere handful would include Rick Artime, Jamey Bridges, Marty Bub, Pauli Bucherich, Jason Feeney, Doug Hartmann, Jaron Hines, John Houska, Josh Jenkins, Casey Klipfel, Mike

---

†   Southern Illinois Soccer League. This was a Metro East league that mainly included Belleville, Collinsville, Edwardsville, Granite City, and Alton.

Masters, Timmy Pratt, Ryan Seim, and Steve VanDyke. Hold on, there's a bit more. Moving into my elder years, I played on an all-African team for a game or two, and, not to mention, while I was attending SIUC for graduate school, I reluctantly played for the Southern Illinois Blast, a team that competed in a Metro East indoor league. At the age of 32, I even had a brief stint in professional soccer with the St. Louis Illusion in which I would argue I made Bob Uecker look like Stan "The Man" Musial. All in all, I submit that I've lived St. Louis soccer like no one else. I also have over 30 trophies and awards to boot (35 to be exact, but who's counting?). Ahem. Not to mention, I gathered two consecutive MVP awards from Indiana Soccer Camp. Well that's just petty, come on Shane, get a grip. (Now I'm just shamelessly bragging; let me get it out of my system and we'll get back on track very soon, I promise!) Ahem-ahem!

Shameless and pathetic bragging aside, this next point is actually very apropos. Let's rewind for a second. When I was around 14, I was fortunate enough to stay in Porto Alegre, Brazil, and train with a farm team of Sport Club Internacional. Why do I point this out? Good question. Good answer, I hope. I realized that the best of Porto Alegre, Brazil, were no different than the best of St. Louis. This meant the top talent of SLYSA within my age group—Chris Klein, Craig Corbett, Kevin Kalish, Tony Williams, Kevin Quigley, Timmy Pratt, Casey Klipfel, Jason Feeney, Mike Moriarty, Pat Moriarty, and others—were among the best players in the world. This had been the case before my time, and, certainly, it will continue to be so.

The following year, when I was part of an undefeated team that won the U16 Holland Cup, with the brilliant Ed Gettemeier as our coach, the opposition consisted of teams from Netherlands, Denmark, Austria, and Italy. These were top teams and yet again I realized how they were tantamount to top SLYSA teams in my age group.

Well, you might be thinking, if that's the case, if St. Louis youth players were and are as good as others in leading nations around the world, then why hasn't the USMNT won the FIFA World Cup? Great question. Great answer, I hope. The question of why the USMNT has not won the World Cup is out of the scope of this book, yet, it raises a valid—and very tantalizing—point nonetheless. After all, when the USMNT inevitably loses in World Cup competition (an all too familiar outcome these days) it leaves US players and fans alike to commiserate over yet another mysterious hurdle left to climb within the lexicon of the dominant American sports landscape. Let's reiterate that last point as simply as possible: The United States has won every other title in sports except for men's soccer.[§] As it turns out, soccer is America's last athletic frontier. It's an interesting phenomenon.

The only thing standing in the way of complete American sports dominance comes in the form of the men's soccer Olympic gold medal and FIFA World Cup championship. That's it. (Go figure; yes, it's that simple.) Let's face it: Since 1990, the USMNT has never reached the semi-finals of a World Cup. So why hasn't the USMNT won a World Cup? The answer is multifaceted. Again, the reasons for this are not directly within the scope of this book. In brief, one important reason has to do with the following: There is an interesting disconnect with youth soccer in America (which is competitive worldwide) and the results of the USMNT in World Cups. While youth soccer players in America are as good as any players from around the world, something seems to click—in a negative way—when it comes to adult competition. Here's the thing, though. For US soccer fans there is hope; for international soccer fans there is reason for massive bouts of trepidation. The continued improvement of MLS will only help contribute talent (and invaluable high-level experience) to the US men's national team, which, in turn, will have better chances of eventually, potentially, winning a World Cup.

---

§   You may have guessed: The United States leads the world in Olympic gold medals.

This next point is perhaps most interesting of all. St. Louis is now directly back in the limelight and part of the equation (along with every other MLS franchise). It's all interconnected. St. Louis and fellow MLS franchises—acting as incubators for the USMNT—are right on the threshold of history. Hence, in this interconnected world, fans of St. Louis City SC—who, in all likelihood, are already aficionados of the game—essentially have a vested interest to be part of not only an MLS team's success but also that of the USMNT.

Given the vast and impressive pedigree of St. Louis soccer (tantamount to practically no equal in the continental United States), there has been speculation as to whether or not an "all St. Louis roster" should represent the USMNT similar to how Barcelona players were a salient factor in Spain's success during the Triple.* Pat McBride (a former SLU national champion, NCAA All-American, St. Louis Stars standout, USMNT midfielder, and St. Louis Steamers coach) told me, despite an overwhelming amount of past success, and considering how soccer has grown substantially around the nation, "it would be a tough sell." Unfortunately, for St. Louis soccer and USMNT fans, this is true. Despite the USMNT in the 1950 World Cup being comprised of five starters from St. Louis, a side that yielded a 1-0 victory over giant England, that was a long time ago, a different era. McBride—a St. Louis legend that gathered much of his keen insight from another St. Louis legend, Bob Guelker—also has a master's from SIUE in Physical Education and is no one to scoff at when it comes to such matters. Perhaps, deep down, he probably knows that a magical St. Louis roster in the modern era could make history; and, yes, without a doubt, such speculation might be more valuable than what an average soccer fan realizes.

Regardless, it's an exciting time. As a soccer fan in America, you really couldn't ask for more. In fact, it's not just an exciting time. It's a historically significant time. The addition of all these new teams to MLS,

---

* The Triple is in reference to when Spain won the 2008 UEFA Euro, 2010 FIFA World Cup, and 2012 UEFA Euro in a row. No other European nation has ever done this.

St. Louis included, is like a soccer fan's dream come true. It couldn't be a more exciting time for US soccer at large.

As I weaved in and out of research for this book, it became apparent how fortunate I've been to have played with and against many players that helped put St. Louis soccer on the map. Aside from a number of players in my immediate age group that were distinguished high-level talents (such as Chris Klein, who subsequently played for the USMNT and became President of LA Galaxy), as a 15-year-old center midfielder for Busch I was obliged—in scrimmages—to guard a very quick, fast, high-jumping, and highly skilled Tim Leonard (who eventually became a SLU standout, pro player, and interim coach of Saint Louis FC), who was on the Busch team a year ahead of me, no less...if that didn't make me a better player (and thinker of the game) I don't know what would! (It was never a walk in the park, by the way.) From the teams and players I've played with and against in the St. Louis area, I've gathered indispensable insight from it. Furthermore, in researching this book (what a great journey it was), I interviewed influential St. Louis soccer icons that not only represent soccer at the highest level but also provided invaluable information about the past, present, and future state of St. Louis soccer.

So to rewind for a second...what does all this personal experience have to do with the history of St. Louis City SC? As a kid, way back when, never in my wildest dreams did I think I'd be writing a book about a pro soccer team in St. Louis and the area I grew up playing soccer in! Never, not once! (To say it's an honor would be an insult to the word honor!) As such, without knowing it, I was consequently imparted with valuable wisdom I never went looking for in the form of the following three points.

I just covered it a tiny bit, but first off, to reiterate, having experienced St. Louis soccer as a player—with various teams—provided indispensable insight on the subject. This seems obvious yet it's worth pointing out all the same.

Secondly, from my travels throughout St. Louis soccer as a player I've realized that where you have an overwhelming number of players—at all levels that spans generations—you also get an aftermath of super-savvy fans of the game, which is what St. Louis City SC inherited.

And thirdly. Luckily (thank God), this isn't about me. You might be thinking otherwise at this point, but I assure you, to the best of my ability, it's not. Though, credentials-wise, it's worth pointing out I've had the "outsider looking in" and "insider looking out" experience in the world of St. Louis soccer, and I'd argue this is exactly what you need as a guide for a book like this. I'm no psychologist, just a 400-hundred-pound gorilla; yet, I would imagine if you were writing a book about New York City fashion, it would help if you've had some experience in the realm of New York fashion. You see, an outsider looking in has limited perspective. For that matter, an insider looking out also has limited perspective. Luckily I've played both roles. You're welcome.

Unlike many who carry the somewhat cumbersome responsibility of being attached to one club, high school, or college, for instance, I have a different perspective. Originally, before I had an insider's view of St. Louis soccer, as an outsider looking in, one that played with numerous clubs, I always had the luxury to empathize with many teams and see them all as distinctly great in their own way, like puzzle pieces with the ability to be combined into a greater purpose. While many players have enjoyed deep instilled rancor toward opposing jerseys, based on rivalries,† I've luckily had the freedom to appreciate any and every great team with unclouded judgment. For instance, my high school team—Collinsville High—traditionally played CBC early in the season to kick things off, so to speak. I'd like to sit back and enjoy animosity toward that program, but I can't; as a team led by future SLU players Mike and Pat Moriarty, they were just too damn good; and if a program is that good it earns my respect and it should earn anyone's respect. Certainly players from, say,

---

†   Such as the Northside-Southside clashes that go back generations, even, if you can believe it, before the 1960s.

Vianney, had dislike for CBC while still holding onto a healthy level of respect; though, I would imagine, a certain amount of animosity trickled over as well. This is where I feel lucky to have separated myself from the norm with the ability to roam free from judgment over any team based on a deep-rooted, passionate, rivalry.

There are generations of people in St. Louis that have been tied to a club, high school, college, and pro team in one way or another. Essentially, Scott Gallagher, CBC, Vianney, St. Thomas Aquinas-Mercy, St. Louis University, and others, serve as handy gateway tools to understanding how in-depth the St. Louis soccer love affair is. Of course, the clubs— such as Kutis, Busch, and Scott Gallagher—have all been interrelated with the local high schools, which have been interrelated with the local universities, which, in turn, have been interrelated with the pro teams (e.g., St. Louis Stars and St. Louis Steamers), Olympic teams, and national teams. In one way or another, it's an interconnected system. Where you have talent this good (CBC for example), there's a natural spillover effect into the immediate athletic community, and community at large. In aggregate, within the interrelated world of club, high school, college, pro, and national team soccer, you have generations of people that are highly knowledgeable of the game.

Not too long ago, I came across an old friend, a former teammate of mine in SLYSA. We reflected on the high-octane atmosphere of that league, and the prominence of St. Louis soccer nationwide. To have played in SLYSA was to play against the best in the country, hence the world. The teams we played against had such a strong sense of pride for the jersey they wore.

As Confucius said, "Hold faithfulness and sincerity as first principles." St. Louis has that and then some. People are not only loyal to their club but also to St. Louis soccer as a whole, all that it stands for, and all of its individual parts that have piled up trophies on top of trophies. Needless to say, but it should be said nonetheless, if people set aside past rivalries, every ounce of St. Louis soccer, regardless of who contributed, adds up to greatness. Setting aside past grievances is a small premium to pay yet the big picture is nothing less than all-encompassing St. Louis pride, kind of like a large museum everyone can walk though, appreciate, and say, "I added to a small part of this structure."

People now have a once-in-a-lifetime opportunity to pledge their allegiance to one pro MLS team, similar to how many players in the past attached themselves to a club or high school team, players I was envious of, to an extent, for their ability to 'be attached to one team as their own.' To the delight of many, all tradition now pours into one St. Louis MLS team at the very top of the soccer pyramid. Ultimately, if you didn't already know, now you do: St. Louis has been the king of soccer in America for as long as anyone can remember.

Now, St. Louis is finally joining the ranks of LAFC, LA Galaxy, Seattle Sounders, Sporting Kansas City, New England Revolution, Atlanta United FC, and the rest. Oy. It was a long, mysterious, wait. Former SLU All-American, St. Louis Stars standout, USMNT captain, and St. Louis Steamers skipper, Al Trost, said, "I'm going to be a season ticket holder for sure." Former NASL Rookie of the Year who became President of the St. Louis Soccer Hall of Fame, Jim Leeker, pointed out, "It's a very exciting time!" noting that aspects of the stadium are similar in style to that of LAFC, where St. Louis soccer legend Mike Sorber landed as director of soccer operations back in 2017. The stage is set. St. Louis is all in.

The fact that it took so long for Major League Soccer to come around to St. Louis is intriguing, and, as you'll see, it's a perfect place for a new MLS franchise. It may sound like I'm pitching the city for some tourism grant money from the US government. Well, I'm not (unless there's something in it for me). We can talk later. For now though, I'm just laying out the facts for you. This story of soccer in St. Louis and the rise of MLS in this amazing sports city is truly a great piece of

American sports history, and American history. Period. St. Louis—which has been home to the Cardinals, Blues, professional indoor and outdoor soccer, previously the Rams, and even a pro basketball team that Bob Costas started out with, the Spirits of St. Louis—is deserving of such an opportunity like no other city. (If it hasn't become somewhat clear to this point, well, frankly, I suspect you're from Cincinnati. There I go again, having a go at Cincinnati. It's too easy, I tell yah.) The process, in fact, like Brian Wilson finally dropping Pet Sounds, was an arduous struggle for St. Louis (collectively over the years) to put together a plan that would impress MLS executives enough to allow entry.

On this vast and exciting journey of St. Louis receiving an MLS team, we'll look at many things along the way to this pinnacle, including but not limited to the clubs that stood out, such as Kutis, Busch, Scott Gallagher; the high schools, all-mighty St. Thomas Aquinas-Mercy, big shot CBC, the great Vianney, De Smet, St. Mary's, Granite City; the colleges, the one and only SLU, SIUE, UMSL, Florissant Valley Community College; the pro teams, the legendary Stars, all-time classic Steamers, Storm, Ambush, Illusion, Illinois Piasa, AC St. Louis, Saint Louis FC; the coaches, Bob Guelker, Harry Keough, Bob Kehoe, Vince Drake, Gene Baker, Pete Sorber (just to name a few); the players, Harry Keough, Pat McBride, Jim Leeker, Ty Keough, Daryl Doran, Steve Trittschuh, Taylor Twellman, Brad Davis, Tim Ream, Josh Sargent (and so many others in-between); the ownership group; the magnificent stadium; and of course the new MLS team itself.

Ron Jacober—the iconic voice of the St. Louis Cardinals who also called games for the original St. Louis Steamers, St. Louis Storm, and original St. Louis Ambush—reminded me there are thousands upon thousands of players in St. Louis today. That fact (which is resonating throughout the nation) is a revealing representation of how the world's beautiful game landed in America generations ago, and time (interlaced with passion and effort) has brought MLS to St. Louis where soccer is greater than ever and it's about to launch into a new stratosphere. The story of Jack Maher—a Scott Gallagher product that, according to the *St. Louis Post-Dispatch*, "...spent two invaluable summers training with St. Louis FC of the United Soccer League"[5]—is just a sign of things to come. After a strong career at Indiana University—a goliath of a school that has acquired numerous St. Louis players over the years—Maher began plotting out a journey in MLS just as St. Louis was about to embark on its inaugural season. From this point forward, future players such as Maher, who grew up in the St. Louis area, will have a local team to lean on, to cheer forward, and to glean inspiration from.

Just as St. Louis City SC is inheriting super-savvy fans of the game from participants of all levels (that span generations), along with passionate, rowdy, dedicated, experienced, organized, steadfast, unwavering, and über-loud fans under the umbrella of the St. Louligans (founded 2010), it will undoubtedly pull in fans from around the world as well. After all, it's joined the international family of club soccer.

For some 10 years when I owned a restaurant in the wine country of San Francisco—in the historic downtown of Petaluma, right around the corner from the wine shop of soccer-enthusiast Jason Jenkins—plenty of people talked soccer. Some knew of St. Louis, some didn't; local soccer-guy Ron Masi, for instance, needed a little dropping of the science. Most knew something of St. Louis, though. They should've, after all. The legend of St. Louis soccer and all its glory has been lurking out there, in the ether of society, for a long time. Having said that, despite knowing about St. Louis soccer, many people didn't know the full gamut of the situation; when it's all said and done, it should go without saying, there are a myriad of details that go unnoticed unless brought to full clarity.

I'm glad you've joined. Sit back and enjoy the ride like a jazz odyssey from Vince Guaraldi (so we hope). I can't wait to get started. Well, technically we have. Here we go. (By the way, if I ever do live tours ((doubtful)) and talk like this, hopefully you'll leave a tip at the end. But seriously, more than a dollar—papa needs a new pair of shoes, Blues tickets are getting more expensive, and there's a jacket I've been eyeing down at Frontenac. Okay, let's move on!) I'm honored to bring home the full story of St. Louis soccer to you, in its entire splendor, and elucidate why it's in perfect harmony with Major League Soccer.

As you'll see, there's nothing quite like St. Louis soccer.

PART I
A HISTORY OF ST. LOUIS SOCCER

St. Louis has always had strategic geographic importance. It sits at the confluence of two huge rivers, the Mississippi River, which essentially points north to south, and the Missouri River, the longest river in North America that starts in Montana and weaves its way down—in a direction one could argue as east and south—where it eventually joins the Mississippi. Mayor Michelle Harris of Clayton, Missouri, points out, "We have this amazing confluence that people can go to and actually see the Missouri and the Mississippi come together." It's a unique feature that carries with it historic significance. In the early days around the St. Louis area there were a lot of French explorers, followed years later by German, English, Irish, and Italian immigrants, among others, of course. It was—and is—a well-positioned river town; after all, just about midway down the Mississippi River you'll find St. Louis. So, back in antiquity, when river trade was a thriving industry, St. Louis had value in its access to a plentitude of areas north of it (such as the area around Chicago), and the vast region south of St. Louis, by way of the Mississippi River, that eventually allows access to the Gulf of Mexico.

Part of the unique love of soccer in modern-day St. Louis is tied to an assortment of immigrants that eventually brought their way of life from Europe. However, before they arrived there was a previous civilization that had established a foothold in the area.

Long before St. Louis, as we know it today, there were the people of Cahokia. An article by Dr. Sarah E. Baires in *Smithsonian Magazine* explains: "Around 1100 or 1200 A.D., the largest city north of Mexico was Cahokia, sitting in what is now southern Illinois, across the Mississippi River from St. Louis. Built around 1050 A.D. and occupied through 1400 A.D., Cahokia had a peak population of between 25,000 and 50,000 people. Now a UNESCO World Heritage Site, Cahokia was composed of three boroughs (Cahokia, East St. Louis, and St. Louis) connected to each other via waterways and walking trails that extended across the Mississippi River floodplain for some 20 square km."[6] Monks Mound—the feature attraction—has steps that rise to the summit, a few stories above ground. I've run the steps more times than you can shake a stick at. Up top is an eye-opening view of downtown St. Louis to the west, the looming smokestacks of Granite City, South Roxana, and other industrial towns to the northwest and north, the Bluffs which include Edwardsville, Glen Carbon, Maryville, and Collinsville roughly to the east, and the area to the south which would be Washington Park, East St. Louis, Caseyville, and beyond. Eventually, you might come across Alorton, Briar Hill, Centreville, Sauget, Cahokia, Westview, Imbs, and Dupo...towns (or more accurately, dwellings) the Illinois Department of Tourism has long overlooked, but that's another story. Let's put it this way: People from Ladue, a luxurious suburb of St. Louis, likely have no idea Imbs exists. In fact, even close neighbors of Imbs don't know Imbs is a place. People from Imbs are probably surprised to learn Imbs is on the map, quite frankly. As it turns out, Collinsville—just a short drive north of Imbs—was the original location for a proposed MLS soccer stadium; we're jumping ahead though; we'll cover why this idea tragically failed in due time.

Cahokia Mounds Historic Site is a very fascinating place. There are many mounds—of different sizes—arranged across a large flatland area. Given the Mississippi River's geographic connection with the Gulf of Mexico, it could be speculated that Mayan and/or Aztec civilizations influenced the Cahokia Mounds in the distant past. (After all, the layout of Cahokia has similarities with the layout of many Mayan and Aztec architectural sites). There has always been a tantalizing possibility for an exotic connection with other cultures. From Baires' article in *Smithsonian Magazine* we find, "Early archaeologists working to answer the question of who built the mounds attributed them to the Toltecs,

Vikings, Welshmen, Hindus, and many others."[7] At the same time, there is a school of thought that believes the people of Cahokia built the mounds on their own, with no outside influence. The bottom line is the Mounds are mysterious, impressive, and thought-provoking. Today, equipped with a parking lot, walking trails, and an interesting museum, the Cahokia Mounds Historic Site offers tourists a lot of information, including a panoramic interactive map of the location which lights up points of interest with the press of a button.

There is still plenty of research that may or may not take place regarding the Mounds; the results might reveal a connection with distant cultures that theoretically could've taken place thousands of years ago.

Be that as it may, after the arrival of Columbus in 1492, Europeans gradually began to settle the New World. In the early days of European colonization, in the 1500s and 1600s, fur trading—with which the French were heavily involved—was a big commodity. Entry into the St. Louis region began to be felt around the late 1600s. According to *Wikipedia*, "European exploration of the area was first recorded in 1673, when French explorers Louis Jolliet and Jacques Marquette traveled through the Mississippi River valley. Five years later, La Salle claimed the region for France as part of *La Louisiane*."[8] Down the road, particularly in the 1700s and 1800s, fur trading was thriving as a big undertaking in the St. Louis region; a leader in this regard was the Missouri Fur Company—known in some circles as the St. Louis Missouri Fur Company—that lasted from 1809-1830 AD.

Timeout! We're not here to talk about the Cahokia Mounds—and possible ancient connections with far-reaching Central American civilizations that revered jaguars—or fur trading by a bunch of wild Frenchmen, living like swamp people, foraging through the untamed forestland of the great, unsettled, Midwest. No. We're here to talk about soccer in St. Louis! Indeed, we'll get there. There's a lot of soccer to talk about. In due time. First, as superfluous as it may seem, we have to discuss some of the wild, belligerent French traders, whose efforts, after many years, led to modern St. Louis whereby soccer has become a big deal.

So without further adieu, *veuillez vous asseoir et écouter,* let's give these wild, hard-living, heavy-drinking, rough and tumble, French fur traders their due. These were hard-living men that did everything Bear Grylls can do accept with a lot of tobacco and moonshine. It was a different time. These were men who likely consumed some form of tobacco for breakfast, with a side of raccoon, with a large helping of sugar, a little moonshine, then went about their way; raccoon for lunch, along with more tobacco products, followed by moonshine; raccoon leftovers for dinner, followed by more tobacco products and moonshine. It was a cyclical process that occurred day to day; they would gather as many pelts as they could or simply fall over. Thus, great American history was being made. Good old-fashioned frontier history. It was tough living. Explorers—who intermingled with Native American tribes—were living off the land in a way that's tantalizingly mythical. It was the Wild West before the Wild West.

St. Louis, 1764. The city is officially founded. Essentially, galvanized by fur trading, Gilbert Antoine de St. Maxent and Pierre Laclede started the search for a base in 1763; through the efforts of Laclede, with the help of his step-son, Auguste Chouteau, who was only 14 at the time, a site was found and in 1764 St. Louis began its meager and small existence on the western side of the Mississippi River.ꝉ Oddly enough, in the early years of its establishment, St. Louis turned out to be a bit of a rogue town as it was not overseen by any larger government force and things were pretty much left in Laclede's hands. Should a settler have wanted to own a lot in town, they'd go through Laclede. (Missouri was admitted into the Union in 1821.)

ꝉ   Today, Laclede's Landing—right near the Arch and the enchanting depravity of the Lumiere Place Casino & Hotel—is a quaint area with brick roads that make driving a cumbersome affair that consists of shops, restaurants, and bars (that once featured the now defunct Mississippi Nights, where bands like Red Hot Chili Peppers and Nirvana performed—the thunderous base reverberating throughout neighboring buildings). Chouteau Avenue is a well-known street in St. Louis as well.

Of all things, legend goes that Jean Lafitte (1780-1823), a French pirate that acquired large sums of wealth around the Gulf of Mexico, planned to send some of his loot to St. Louis for storage or tried to and got derailed.

At this point, soccer's not even a thing yet (unless you count rudimentary attempts in England which essentially amounted to village 'warfare').

Subsequently, French activity in the region led to the name of St. Louis, which was in honor of King Louis IX of France, who lived from 1214-1270 AD. (Incidentally, Louis IX was crowned at the age of 12. Let's fast forward into soccer land for a little bit; that is why we're here, after all. A few generations after Al Trost, Pat McBride, Ty Keough, Daryl Doran, and Steve Trittschuh, in my age group of 1976, around the age of 12, a crafty, creative, devastatingly skillful, arrogant, tenacious, talented player from the St. Louis area named Timmy Pratt was essentially crowned as the best among my peers, even in a field that included Chris Klein, and Pratt's own teammates, Kevin Quigley and Tony Williams, who would turn pro. Timmy, as a freshman in high school, went straight to Vianney's varsity squad during its glory days, practically unheard of. Similar to Louis IX, Timmy—who was kinglike in his ways—was known by many very early in life. Though, unlike Louis IX, who would live on in the pages of history, Pratt drifted into soccer obscurity, somewhat mysteriously. St. Louis, which has had so many talented players sprout up from its fields, is replete with situations like this. Moving on.)

As indicated previously, St. Louis was founded in 1764. Some years later, in 1822, it was incorporated. Who knew that big-time soccer was around the corner? (Relatively speaking, of course.) At that point, no one even knew what soccer was. It would be 128 years before the US team defeated England 1-0 in World Cup 1950 with five St. Louisans—Frank Borghi, Harry Keough, Charlie Colombo, Gino Pariani, and Frank Wallace—in the starting lineup. Certainly, the years 1764—when St. Louis was founded—and 1822—when St. Louis was incorporated—represented a time long before clubs like Kutis, Busch, and Scott

Gallagher, and the national success of St. Louis University, and the emergence of players like Billy Ponzalagin, Harry Keough, Bob Kehoe, Carl Gentile, Pat McBride, Jim Leeker, Al Trost, Mike Seerey, Dan Counce, Denny Vaninger, Tommy Howe, Ty Keough, Steve Pecher, Tim Walters, Greg Villa, Perry Van der Beck, Dan King, Mike Gauvain, Jim Kavanaugh, Daryl Doran, Mark Moser, Mark Santel, Steve Trittschuh, Joel Shanker, Ken Godat, Mike Sorber, Steve Ralston, Tim Leonard, Chris Klein, Taylor Twellman, Brad Davis, Pat Noonan, Will Bruin, Tim Ream, Josh Sargent, and Jack Maher.

IMMIGRANTS: ITALIAN, IRISH, GERMAN...THE INFLUENTIAL TRIUMVIRATE

By the 1840s, immigrants from Ireland and Germany rolled into St. Louis "...in significant numbers starting in the 1840s, and the population of St. Louis grew from less than 20,000 inhabitants in 1840, to 77,860 in 1850, to more than 160,000 by 1860."[9]

Generally speaking, we know a salient factor about immigration: Over a period of years—circa 1880-1930—some 28 million people arrived in the United States from Europe. This wave of immigration brought hoards of people from Italy, Ireland, and Germany (among other places) to St. Louis. Interestingly, in the era when Native American groups lived in Cahokia (just across the river from present-day St. Louis), it was a place where people converged. As Sarah Baires wrote in *Smithsonian Magazine*, "We know Cahokia's population was diverse, with people moving to this city from across the midcontinent, likely speaking different dialects and bringing with them some of their old ways of life."[10] In similar fashion, immigrant groups from Italy, Ireland, Germany, and elsewhere, brought their old ways of life to St. Louis; in turn, many people suspect that these groups were fans of soccer when they arrived, or, at the very least, familiar with the sport. After all, clubs had formed early in Europe: Liverpool (1892), Juventus (1897), the lessor known Irish side, Shamrock Rovers F.C. (1899) and Bayern Munich (1900); also FIFA, the organizing body of world soccer, was formed in 1904.

The general feeling is that descendants of these European immigrants—from circa 1880-1930—had a love for the sport and continued supporting soccer throughout the United States, and, particularly, in the St. Louis area even when it was not among the top sports in this country.

Before one gets into the vast impact German immigrants have had on St. Louis, it's sometimes easy to forget, to an extent, the strong presence of people with roots in Italy and Ireland that have played an important part in shaping what is present-day St. Louis. Italians—revered for passion, great cooking, engineering, technical ability, artistry, and an uncanny sense for fashion—etched out a prominent presence in St. Louis.

The Hill—a tad west of downtown St. Louis, resting in-between Forest Park and Tower Grove Park as Highway 44 passes through it—is especially well-regarded. Anglophilia it is not. It's an Italian-American neighborhood replete with brick houses, which, to this day, is a hub for elegant and family-oriented Italian restaurants. Brick houses in St. Louis? Get used to it. From a piece in *The New York Times*, Jane Smiley—who grew up in Webster Groves, Missouri—wrote: "Brick! If there is anything that screams 'St. Louis!' it is brick. And 199 types were made south of Forest Park, not far from the Cheshire Inn, in an area called Dogtown. In this rather small area (six-mile periphery), there were at least 14 brick factories."[11] Okay, that's a lot of brick factories St. Louis...seriously now.

The Hill—in all its classic splendor—also steps into the athletic realm—and lore—as it produced two well-known baseball players in their day, Yogi Berra and Joe Garagiola Sr. And, not to mention, even by way of *Wikipedia*, it is noted that a salient feature of this illustrious neighborhood includes a famed victory—heard around the world—in the history of American soccer: "...Four of the five St. Louisans on the US soccer team that defeated England in the 1950 FIFA World Cup came from The Hill."[12]

Across the river, a huge party rages on as Collinsville, Illinois, hosts an annual downtown celebration referred to as "Italian Fest." It typically fills the streets with people, vendors, and music.

Initially, one might overlook the influence of Italians in St. Louis compared to, for instance, the Italian influence in New York, but Italy has brought great history, tradition, and beauty to the River City. Around St. Louis, Irish immigrants—full of personality, passion, and pride— have made a big splash.

As with most cities, the St. Patrick's Day Parade is a big deal around St. Louis. The celebration dates back many, many generations, as does a little forgotten neighborhood, Kerry Patch. From a story that appeared in *St. Louis Magazine* in 2014, Stefene Russell wrote: "When the first St. Patrick's Day Parade wound through the city, in 1820, one-seventh of the city's 700 men were Irish. By 1851, when the U.S. census recorded a St. Louis population of 70,000, approximately 14 percent of those people were born in Ireland. Today, Dogtown is considered to be St. Louis' most Irish neighborhood. But between the mid-19th century and the early 20th century, no place in the city was more Irish than the Kerry Patch."[13]

The Kerry Patch neighborhood was, let's just say, an interesting place, a place where a book on the Do's and Don'ts of Royal Etiquette couldn't be found, to put it lightly. Regarding Kerry Patch, Russell reported, "Its origin dates back to 1842, when a group of Irish immigrants arrived here—apparently from County Kerry, hence the name. Being quite poor but not wanting to live in crowded, dank rooming houses, they settled on a stretch of open land north of downtown."[14]

In the beginning, crude homes—or dwellings—were built. Russell added: "The neighborhood's boundaries shifted over time—Irish families moved farther west, as German, Polish, and Eastern European immigrants settled around them after the Civil War. But during its heyday, the Patch was generally described as being between N. 15th Street and Hogan Street, Division Street and Cass Avenue. The heart of the neighborhood was squeezed into the tight rectangle between 16th and 18th streets, Cass Avenue and O'Fallon Street—a few blocks east of St. Stanislaus Kostka Church in near north St. Louis."[15]

The general state of poverty in Kerry Patch, which was very prevalent in the beginning, led to an assortment of inhabitants. "It was a place that produced crime bosses and pickpockets, but also judges and state senators. Silent-film star King Baggot grew up in the Patch. So did William Marion Reedy, editor of *Reedy's Mirror* and publisher of Tennessee Williams, T.S. Eliot, and Theodore Dreiser. The Patch even had a series of elected 'kings,' including Dennis Sheehan, James Cullinane, and eventually Dennis' son, Jack Sheehan, who was crowned in 1873, at the age of 21, at a huge party preceded by a neighborhood-wide torchlit procession. Sheehan, the last king of the Patch, paid rent for people who could not, helped mitigate legal disputes, and organized an annual Fourth of July fireworks show."[16]

This wasn't the only attraction of Kerry Patch. In addition to rudimentary dwellings that didn't pass muster and a line of kings that were most definitely not sanctioned by the government, there were gangs, "including the Biddle Gang, the Hogan Gang, and the Ashley Street Gang, which eventually turned into the crime syndicate Egan's Rats,"[17] brick fights, and, you guessed it, roosters that "fought to the death"[18] as gamblers watched on in the basement of a sketchy bar. "(Those laying bets, as well as those producing fighting birds, came from every corner of the city; the Humane Society of Missouri harangued them at every step.)"[19]

You get the sense there could've been a 'Leonardo DiCaprio and Daniel Day-Lewis meets Charlie Sheen and Tom Berenger moment' around every corner...anything and everything wrong seemed to be the norm in Kerry Patch. But at the same time, Patchers stuck together, and bread was shared from neighbor to neighbor. Go figure. Was this in proximity to the notorious Northside where so much soccer in St. Louis took flight? That would be correct.

Nearby—yet not part of the Kerry Patch "domain"—were the parishes of St. Matthew's (founded circa 1893), St. Engelbert (founded circa 1891) and St. Leo's (founded circa 1888), all of which were instrumental in the youth soccer scene—by way of the parish leagues—throughout the 20th century.

The mystic area of Kerry Patch is a short distance north of the new MLS stadium, just over a mile or so.

As with ancient civilizations that get lost in time, there are traces of old monuments that still peek out from the shadows of history with the helping hand of archaeologists that elucidate how elderly structures from a distant past can still peer out from underneath newer architecture built on top of them. An example would be in 1870 when Heinrich Schliemann excavated levels of Troy—a city thought to be founded circa 3500 BC and abandoned at the close of the Trojan War which lasted circa 1260-1180 BC, only to be repopulated by different groups thereafter. Gobekli Tepe—an ancient megalithic site dating to circa 9000 BC in present-day Turkey—was buried allegedly for thousands of years until unearthed once again. It's interesting how remnants of old structures pass through time. Kerry Patch—overrun with poverty, crime, gangs, gambling, alcoholism, illegitimate kings, and dilapidated housing—is nowhere near the level of intrigue that Troy and Gobekli Tepe are, but nonetheless it constitutes the same idea of old vestiges lingering around, among us. Russell pointed out that 'traces' of Kerry Patch remain to this day, but hastened to include the research of historian, Etan Diamond, and noted "...that by the end of World War I, [Diamond] 'the original Patch had all but disappeared. The once-concentrated Irish community had dispersed; many Patch children had grown up and moved elsewhere. The St. Louis suburbs, rapidly growing since the turn of the century, proved far more attractive to them than the crowded city neighborhoods.'"[20]

To this day, with or without the influence of Kerry Patch, there are a number of Irish-related bars around St. Louis, such as Tigin Irish Pub, Maggie O'Brien's, Irish Corner Pub, Flannery's Irish Pub, Seamus McDaniel's, The Pat Connolly Tavern, and The Dubliner in Maplewood—places that fans from a St. Louis City SC game might stumble upon. While Irish immigrants made a big impression, Germans also infiltrated the area around the same time. Let's take a closer look at German heritage in and around St. Louis. Will you find people walking around, mispronouncing *Ws*? Probably not. Yet the presence of a German influence is quite ubiquitous in last names, architecture, and, of course, beer.

It's interesting how Lemp Brewery and Anheuser-Busch have represented the German community of St. Louis and helped launch the city into virtual stardom. Lemp Brewery—founded in 1840 as Western Brewery by German immigrant and St. Louis grocer, Adam Lemp—made big news. It was a historic undertaking—one felt around the nation and world—that happened to grow out of St. Louis. Also, Anheuser-Busch—launched by German-born Eberhard Anheuser and Adolphus Busch—has thrust onto the national and international scene like few companies in the history of the world.

As it turns out, Anheuser-Busch has always been heavily involved with sports and has advertised its products in brochures, print ads, TV commercials, and ads on perimeter walls for soccer games—ranging from pro games to FIFA World Cup competition—for generations. It's interesting that Busch beer would eventually sponsor a major St. Louis youth and amateur soccer program, one of the best in North America, Busch Soccer Club. Yet, before this undertaking would occur (and gain many trophies), Lemp Brewery was setting the stage for beer production in St. Louis.

Lemp Brewery—former beer giant—is steeped in tantalizing mystery to this day as it is somewhat unknown to laypeople, though it has a peculiar underground following. An article at *Wikipedia* pointed out: "Adam Lemp's beer became very popular due to the increase of German population in the area. Lemp was one of the first in the country to produce German lager, which differed greatly from the English ale and porters. The business prospered, and when a large storage space became necessary, a cave in south St. Louis was used for this purpose as it provided natural refrigeration. The cave was below the current locations of the Lemp and Chatillon-DeMenil House and the Lemp Brewery."[21]

When Adam Lemp died, his son, William J. Lemp Sr., who attended St. Louis University, took over. "In 1864 he began building a larger brewery above the caves where Western had been storing its goods. Under William Lemp, the Western Brewery became the largest brewery in St. Louis, and then, the largest outside of New York with a single owner. William began to brew and bottle the beer in the same facility to meet growing demand, a practice that was rare at that time. Further demonstrating his innovation and business sense, in 1878 he installed the first refrigeration machine in an American brewery, and then extended the idea to refrigerated railway cars, in a successful attempt to be the first beer in the United States with a national reach. Soon, Lemp Beer was sold worldwide."[22]

The refrigerated railway cars used by Lemp likely would've gone through Union Station, basically right next door to the new St. Louis City SC stadium. It's amazing to think that beer being consumed at St. Louis City SC games has a lineage of sorts that reaches back in time to this forgotten St. Louis brewery. Yet in the vast sea of beer manufacturers, Lemp was an early American pioneer who put St. Louis on the map.

Eventually, "In 1892, the William J. Lemp Brewing Company was founded from the Western Brewery with William as President, his son William Jr. as Vice-President, and his son Louis as Superintendent."[23] The Lemp family—in its rise to beer stardom in the country—was no stranger to intrigue. William Lemp Sr.'s son, Frederick, died in 1901 and as things turned out, in 1904, Lemp Sr.'s friend, Frederick Pabst, passed away. In the same year, Lemp Sr. killed himself. Then, after a nasty divorce, Lemp Jr., known as Billy, had difficulties with the company. "The Lemp Brewery suffered in the early 1920s when Prohibition began. The brewery was shut down and the Falstaff trademark was sold to Lemp's friend, 'Papa Joe' Griesedieck. The brewery complex was sold at auction to International Shoe Company for $588,000. On December 29, 1922, Billy Lemp shot himself in his office—a room that today is the front left dining room."[24]

If you haven't guessed, Falstaff, a well-known beer in its time, came about from the days of Lemp. There's a big imposing Falstaff sign to this day in the area of the former Kerry Patch neighborhood, just a short drive north of the St. Louis City SC stadium.

The Lemp Mansion—which is said to be haunted—lives on to this day (tours are available). It's near the Lemp Brewery and Anheuser-Busch, a short drive south from downtown St. Louis. As the Lemp family carved out a prestigious name in beer, there was a union taking shape in the form of Anheuser-Busch.

Unlike Lemp Brewery, Anheuser-Busch—whose current mega, city-like structure of a brewery is just down the road from Lemp's impressive defunct facility—flourished throughout the 20th century and its success—on both domestic and international fronts—continues to this day. Prior to the purchase of the company in 2008 by InBev, Anheuser-Busch was operated by Busch family members.

Essentially, we have to step way back to 1852 whereby, according to a broad-stroke *Wikipedia* article, "German American brewer and saloon operator George Schneider opened the Bavarian Brewery on Carondelet Avenue (later known as South Broadway) between Dorcas and Lynch streets in South St. Louis."[25] This would be the beginning of something special. "In 1860, the brewery was purchased on the brink of bankruptcy by William D'Oench, a local pharmacist, and Eberhard Anheuser, a prosperous German-born soap manufacturer. D'Oench was the silent partner in the business until 1869, when he sold his half-interest in the company. From 1860 to 1875, the brewery was known as E. Anheuser & Co., and from 1875 to 1879 as the E. Anheuser Company's Brewing Association."[26] (This was back when soccer wasn't yet flourishing. This was long before Busch Memorial Stadium where the St. Louis Stars would play, and long before the Busch logo that eventually would adorn soccer jerseys over many decades for the club that bore its name and began in the 1970s.) "Adolphus Busch, a wholesaler who had immigrated to St. Louis from Germany in 1857, married Eberhard Anheuser's daughter, Lilly, in 1861. Following his service in the American Civil War,

Busch began working as a salesman for the Anheuser brewery. Busch purchased D'Oench's share of the company in 1869, and he assumed the role of company secretary from that time until the death of his father-in-law."[27] Eventually, "The company was renamed Anheuser-Busch Brewing Association in 1879; in 1880, Adolphus Busch became company president upon Anheuser's death. The Busch family fully controlled the company through the generations until Anheuser-Busch's sale to InBev in 2008."[28] August Busch IV—who graduated from St. Louis University with degrees in finance and business administration—was CEO when the sale went down. As *Forbes* put it: "The family passed down the company through the generations but ended up selling an estimated 25% of the business from 1989 to 2008, leaving them powerless to stop the $52 billion buyout bid."[29] Allegedly, during this process, August Busch IV was using his auxiliary office at Soccer Park—in Fenton, Missouri—as his war room. Soccer Park originally came about in 1982 thanks to Anheuser-Busch; this is where Busch Soccer Club teams would practice and host games, while it also was used by the USMNT for big games; it eventually was purchased and became known as World Wide Technology Soccer Park. From a *Wikipedia* article on World Wide Technology Soccer Park it says: "August Busch IV, the former CEO of Anheuser-Busch, who disliked going to Anheuser-Busch's headquarters, renovated a portion of the Soccer Park offices complete with his own luxurious and secluded office that includes a private bathroom (formerly soccer club coaches offices with a shower) and conference room. During Anheuser-Busch's takeover by Belgium beer maker InBev, the board and executives of Anheuser-Busch met in August's conference room at the Soccer Park. At one point during the takeover proceedings, August said 'My war room is the Soccer Park' describing the frantic effort of the executives to save Anheuser-Busch from being sold."[30] This was the same August Busch IV—Mr. rock and roll—who led police on a high-speed chase back in 1985. "Busch was arrested at the age of 20 in St. Louis after leading undercover police in an unmarked car on a chase with speeds reaching between 85 and 90 mph on Kingshighway Boulevard in the

Central West End of the city. He was returning from visiting PT's Sports Cabaret, a strip bar in Sauget, Illinois. The officers ended the chase by shooting out the rear tire of Busch's car. Busch claimed he thought they were attempting to kidnap him. The police accused him of trying to run over two officers with his Mercedes. Busch was acquitted of assault by a St. Louis jury."[31] Sauget, Illinois, by the way, is near Imbs—that long-forgotten place on the map. In desultory fashion, Busch's actions that night—which culminated near the location of St. Louis City SC's new stadium—were tantamount to something you might have seen from W. Bush in his pre-presidential romps. Neither here nor there, this was the 80s and the Busch family was riding high, a beer empire, top of the world.

Subsequently, since the 2008 takeover of Anheuser-Busch by InBev, the Busch family remained in the beer business. According to *Forbes*, "Billy Busch founded William K. Busch Brewing in 2011 with two lagers, Kraftig and Kraftig Light."[32] Though in 2019, *KSDK* reported, "The William K. Busch Brewing Company announced it is shutting down all operations of Kräftig and Kräftig Light beers due to market demand."[33] As of 2020, Billy Busch, and family, entered the reality TV business with *The Busch Family Brewed* on MTV.

From all this time in the beer business, surpassing a hundred years, *Forbes*—as of 2016—listed the Busch family wealth at approximately $13.4 billion.

Such a fortune is rooted in time and the caves, breweries, buildings, convenience stores, restaurants, bars, sporting events, and streets of St. Louis. Throughout this fascinating tale of American history, Anheuser-Busch—a reliable beer regaled by drinkers—was a unique bellwether of the German community in St. Louis in the late 1800s and early 1900s. As the 20th century progressed, Anheuser-Busch grew substantially greater (as if beguiling the nation toward its steady, mainstream brew), and, thus, along with other factors (such as the St. Louis Cardinals and music), St. Louis as a whole gained notoriety, through which sponsorship and general involvement in local sports flourished.

Anheuser-Busch didn't just sit back and produce beer. To the contrary, over many generations, Anheuser-Busch has been a strong supporter of St. Louis sports. An obvious example of involvement in the community would be Busch Memorial Stadium (later changed to Busch Stadium), which the St. Louis Cardinals have called home for years. Many generations ago, the Cardinals began racking up World Series championships, second only to the New York Yankees. Eventually, down the road, beginning in the late 1960s, the St. Louis Stars would play games in Busch Memorial Stadium as well. However, the Stars weren't quite as successful as the Cardinals. Though, for many pro soccer games, Busch Memorial Stadium was center stage and the mere fact that it was hosting a Stars game brought enormous prestige to the event.

The Anheuser-Busch arm reached further than just a downtown stadium. I sat down with Jim Leeker—a former NCAA national champion with SLU, and a prominent player with the St. Louis Stars—and Vince Drake—a former NCAA national champion with SLU, and legendary high school soccer coach at St. Thomas Aquinas-Mercy—back in February of 2020. We met at J Smugs—a bar with piano included—in St. Louis. (This was just before coronavirus—COVID-19—took hold in a big way.) The two savvy soccer legends began recalling old times over a wooden table near the bar. Each was casually dressed; you'd have no idea they were part of the soccer fabric whose accomplishments in the sport over the years have inadvertently contributed to the rise of an MLS team. They explained how Denny Long, who was President of Anheuser-Busch in the 1970s, set out to make Busch Gardens Soccer Club—later renamed Busch Soccer Club around 1980—the best it could be and hired the best coaches with the intent of attracting the best players possible. One such coach, among many, was Steve Pecher, a former captain of the St. Louis Steamers and USMNT whose career flourished in the 1970s and 80s; Pecher coached Busch teams for some 20 years. As a result of coaches like Pecher, along with top local talent, Busch—as it was commonly known—was a powerhouse. As one of the elite clubs in North America during its time, Busch attained a large number of youth national titles.

The prosperity of Anheuser-Busch spoke for the community, and the overall sports scene benefited from its association.

In fact, thanks to enthusiasm from influential people like Denny Long, the St. Louis Soccer Park—later renamed Anheuser-Busch Center, and currently known as World Wide Technology Soccer Park—was established in 1982 and served as a soccer flagship for St. Louis and the nation at large; it was a frequent location for US men's national team games in the 1980s. Whether they were qualification games for the Olympics, FIFA World Cup, or friendlies, from 1987 to 1990, the US played Canada, Trinidad and Tobago, Jamaica, Costa Rica, El Salvador, Iceland, and MISL Select XI at the coveted Soccer Park. (The location must have been a lucky charm for the US, by the way, as all the aforementioned games were wins outside of a tie with mighty El Salvador; you never know with those guys; they're tough, they're gritty.)

To think, from simply brewing beer from a colossal city-fortress brewery—with roads, intersections, horses, carriages, trees, gates, lamps, and statues—just south of downtown, Anheuser-Busch has put so much money into local St. Louis soccer efforts. Thanks to the efforts of Anheuser-Busch, Denny Long, and others, it could easily be argued that Busch ranks among the top club teams in the history of St. Louis soccer. In fact, such an argument is ridiculous. Busch does rank at the top of the list, alongside Kutis and Scott Gallagher. In addition, Busch was one of the great clubs nationwide.

The Busch family contributed so much. There was Busch Memorial Stadium where the Stars played, Busch Soccer Club, St. Louis Soccer Park, and the heavy sponsorship of professional and international soccer games for ages.

Another obvious argument could be made on behalf of Scott Gallagher Soccer Club—established circa 1976—for bringing a great deal of attention, along with success, to St. Louis soccer. Busch Soccer Club—once a major rival to Scott Gallagher—plays into this scenario in more ways than one. In 2004, Busch Soccer Club became St. Louis Soccer Club and around 2007 it merged with Scott Gallagher and Metro

United Soccer Club to become one Scott Gallagher mega club. Scott Gallagher now operates World Wide Technology Soccer Park (formerly operated by Busch Soccer Club). In fact, although Lemp Brewery made an initial big splash, followed by a tumble into obscurity, Anheuser-Busch managed to stay afloat. Much of the same occurred with Busch Soccer Club, which also made an initial big splash, then disappeared, but was followed by Scott Gallagher managing to stay afloat.

In the grand scheme of things, Busch and Scott Gallagher arrived many years after a slew of teams that had already laid out the proverbial tablecloth. Despite Busch and Gallagher dating back to the 1970s, long before most Gallagher players gallivanting around today were even born, these are recent St. Louis club teams. Of course, St. Louis, like other locations around the nation, has been a landing place by inhabitants from various backgrounds. As things stand today, there's a strong Bosnian presence in the Gateway City, for sure.

Yet, dating back to the early days of St. Louis soccer, it could be argued that the main driving force behind the passion for soccer was pushed along by people of Italian, Irish, and German backgrounds. As a result, soccer in St. Louis has been a real presence, with roots from immigrants past.

Everything, like the accelerating universe, transforms and turns into new things. Prior to the implementation of Busch's strong resources to provide elite teams starting in the 1970s, the stage was being set decades before by other club teams. Long, long ago, St. Leo's would emerge in the early 1900s as a team competing in St. Louis. From these efforts, new teams would blossom into powerhouses.

ST. LOUIS CLUBS

ST. LEO'S
St. Leo's. A club team and pro team going deep into history...

Soccer in St. Louis dates to 1875. In the early 1900s, there was a groundbreaking team, St. Leo's. We should step back for a moment, though. By today's standards, set by MLS for instance, St. Leo's likely was not a typical pro team. Let's be realistic here. By no fault of its own, it was simply a different era with a sport that was essentially new to the world at large. Be that as it may, St. Leo's is truly a historical team within the lore of St. Louis soccer.

Early in the 20th century, St. Leo's put itself on the soccer map as one of the first professional teams in the US. According to *Wikipedia*: "Nicknamed the Blue and White, St. Leo's was founded by William Klosterman in 1902 as a recreational team for the St. Leo's Sodality, a Catholic men's organization. It competed in the Junior League, winning the league title. In 1903, St. Leo's moved up to the Amateur League which competed at Christian Brother's College where they again won the league title. During the 1904-05 season, they competed in a league at Forest Park. In 1905, they entered the St. Louis Association Foot Ball League where they won three consecutive league titles. Following its 1908 championship, the AFL merged with the St. Louis Soccer League which had been established the year before. St. Leo's quickly asserted its dominance as the only fully professional team in the new league."[34]

By 1918, St. Leo's had become known as the St. Louis Screws.

So it was...St. Leo's was a club and professional team based in St. Louis in the early days of soccer. Grant it, St. Leo's put forth a lessor known effort at pro soccer in the US when such a thing was not a massive force. Yet, something was going on; something, for lack of a better term, was brewing. The pot of soccer had been stirring worldwide from the late 1800s-1930.

As soccer was substantially growing around the world, there was major interest in South America and Europe, particularly with clubs like River Plate, Liverpool, Manchester United, Bayern Munich, Real Madrid, Juventus, A.C. Milan and Inter Milan. Inter Milan, for example, had gained its first Serie A title in 1909-10.

Meanwhile, the U.S. Open Cup—originally named the National Challenge Cup in 1913-14—was a tournament that featured the best teams in the United States. To this day, the tournament is open to men's teams and the spectrum ranges from amateur sides all the way up to MLS franchises.

While baseball was popular in the United States around the introduction of the U.S. Open Cup, soccer had its place, albeit a few notches below baseball and a few above whitewater rafting. The U.S. Open Cup—which, by the way, has also been known as the Lamar Hunt U.S. Open Cup—was initially a remarkable tournament for soccer in the States. Representing the East Coast, Brooklyn Field Club was the first winner in 1913-14. Ben Millers—a St. Louis team that received sponsorship from the Ben W. Miller Hat Company—won the title in 1920; this would be the first for a St. Louis team. Many more would follow. The list includes Ben Millers (1920), St. Louis Scullin Steel F.C. (1922), Stix, Baer and Fuller F.C. (1933), Stix, Baer and Fuller F.C. (1934), St. Louis Central Breweries (1935), St. Louis Simpkins-Ford (1948), St. Louis Simpkins-Ford (1950), St. Louis Kutis S.C. (1957), St. Louis Kutis S.C. (1986), and St. Louis Busch Seniors (1988).

As most know, since the introduction of MLS in 1996, the U.S. Open Cup has largely been dominated by MLS teams. But, what's important to take away here are the amazing results St. Louis teams have achieved throughout the ages.

In and around the time of St. Louis teams doing so well in the U.S. Open Cup, the FIFA World Cup began in 1930. The inaugural tournament was hosted by Uruguay. The US, by the way, placed third in this tournament, go figure. It was certainly a different time for soccer, but the US was as active then as it is today (relatively speaking, of course).

Prior to MLS coming to fruition in 1996, the USMNT played in only four World Cups: 1930, 1950, 1990, and 1994. A few St. Louis players represented those World Cup teams. In 1930 you had Raphael "Ralph" Tracey, and Frank Vaughn; in 1950 you had Frank Borghi, Harry

Keough, Charlie Colombo, Gino Pariani, and Frank Wallace; by 1990 there was Steve Trittschuh; and in 1994 Mike Sorber took center stage.[§]

That aside, prior to 1996 during the pre-MLS years, the US didn't have a consistent, bellwether, pro outdoor soccer league. The NASL (1968-84) was a good attempt, but it unfortunately folded. Also, during the pre-MLS years, US players, largely speaking, were not welcome in foreign pro leagues. A big reason was that foreign coaches knew the US didn't have a sustainable pro league which made the players look, for lack of a better word, untrustworthy; coaches assumed they lacked vital experience. Some of these coaches also knew that soccer was low on the totem pole in the US which made them look at US players with suspicion. Subsequently, with few US players signing pro contracts abroad, you had thousands upon thousands of players stuck in the US, competing with one another domestically.

Interestingly, this made club, high school, and college soccer in the States all the more competitive. By this avenue, club teams in St. Louis were gaining a strong, even mythic, reputation throughout the country by way of capturing so many U.S. Open Cups. The success of St. Louis teams in the U.S. Open Cup had a lot to do with the coveted church leagues which allowed youth players to discover the game, build their skills, compete, and graduate to higher levels. In fact, prior to the club soccer scene that dominates the St. Louis landscape today, many up-and-coming players competed in the St. Louis church leagues.

Long before the mythical soccer-boom of the 1970s and 80s, and before Busch, Scott Gallagher, and Lou Fusz marched onto the scene, parishes played against one another, heated rivalries ensued, thus setting a path for club soccer and traveling teams down the road. A few teams that stood out from the illustrious parish days include St. Matthews, St. Rosary (Holy Rosary), St. Engelbert, and St. Philip Di Neri. According to Gene Baker, a former SLU NCAA Division I national soccer champion and legendary high school coach at Granite City, back in the 1930s and 40s, St. Matthews was an early soccer hotbed.

---

§   Down the road, Brad Davis was on the USMNT during the 2014 World Cup.

From the Northside church leagues, two exemplary players stand out.

Pat McBride was a product of Holy Rosary who graduated to SLU, the St. Louis Stars, and USMNT. And Al Trost came up through Holy Rosary, St. Engelbert's, and St. Philip Di Neri before he became a standout for SLU, the St. Louis Stars, and captain of the USMNT. Each player, like so many others, gained early experience in the church league system in St. Louis.

The famous CYC—Catholic Youth Council—exists to this day. It officially launched athletic leagues back in 1941.

As things turned out, soccer became somewhat of a calling card for the CYC. In the 1950s, the CYC All-Star squads played host to various visiting teams, including some international travelers from Europe and South America. From the 1960s and 70s, Father Louis F. Meyer, with help from Bob Guelker (who served for a time as CYC Sports Director), pushed soccer in new directions with some sponsorship by Pepsi Cola Bottlers in St. Louis, which helped promote the Junior District soccer leagues. In 1965 the Gold and Silver Boots came to fruition as awards that honored those involved in CYC soccer and the sport in general; Frank Borghi, Ebbie Dunn, Bob Kehoe, Harry Keough, Pat McBride, Dent McSkimming, Gino Pariani, Syl Raftery, and Al Trost were a few distinguished names. Following Bob Guelker, Joe Carenza—who previously was active with the Khoury League—helped guide CYC sports and soccer with much aplomb. In the early 1970s, even Pele stopped by the CYC, a big event. By that time, Pele had won the FIFA World Cup multiple times and was considered the best player in the world.

For a myriad of kids, the CYC was an introduction to the sport. In the course of many decades, from the work of many people involved in youth soccer, the CYC and parish teams began laying the groundwork for the increased popularity of the sport in greater St. Louis. By the 1970s, and particularly so in the 80s, soccer was climbing to new heights.

ST. LOUIS CLUBS ARE THRIVING

Once you work your way into the mid-1950s, and then into the beginning of the modern era in St. Louis soccer, which, arguably would be the

1970s, you realize how much of a true impact St. Louis was leaving on the sport nationwide. Actually, during the 1900s, it was becoming very clear just how athletically unique St. Louis was.

One way to explain how club, high school, collegiate, and pro soccer have been so good in St. Louis might, in fact, have something to do with the success of the St. Louis Cardinals. If you can believe it, the Cardinals date back to 1882 and since then have spread athletic know-how over the area.

It's been said by practically anyone and everyone that St. Louis Cardinals fans are the most knowledgeable baseball fans in the country. Who said this? Do I need to find a source? Frankly, that's a silly—no, ludicrous—suggestion. Let's put it this way: If you're from the United States and you haven't heard this before, I don't know where you've been living. But it's fair to assume that many smart people, who, granted, are not baseball fans, might have overlooked this little tidbit over time. It's very possible.

Generally speaking, a Cardinals fan knows the minutest inner-workings of the sport of baseball to the point that it's somewhat bizarre. This is a fan that is dead set on understanding fastidious details, no matter how trite and superfluous it might seem at first glance. To a Cardinals fan: no detail is too trivial. Every nuance counts for something, with the idea that talking about it casually—yet passionately, somewhat incessantly, with a touch of arrogance—will reveal its inner beauty. A few domestic beers don't hurt, either. Nonetheless, it has become, for lack of a better word, the "job" of a Cardinals fan to understand such things as foot placement in the batter's box, or a subtle shift of said stance mid-season at the behest of a team therapist, or perhaps the position of a batter's hips at the moment of a swing, or perhaps the placement of one's hands on a bat (which can go in endless directions by way of speculation and analysis).

Chicago Cubs fans are a little different whereby they definitely understand the game, three strikes you're out and what not, but they show up to the stadium more so to have a good time followed by fun in the streets with Wrigleyville as their oyster wherein they can make plenty of bad decisions. And make bad decisions they will. Kansas City Royals fans are a little more like Cardinals fans without all the championships. We're getting off track. The point is: Whether we're talking about fans of the Cubs, Royals, Orioles, Twins, Tigers, Astros, or Dodgers, it's widely accepted that followers of the Cardinals are certainly the smartest around.

How did the Cardinals fans get so knowledgeable? Where did this come from? Typically, if the local team is overwhelmingly successful there will be spillover into the immediate community. Since the Cardinals are second only to the New York Yankees in World Series championships, spillover would be a natural expectation. What is spillover exactly? Spillover comes in the form of knowledge, appreciation, know-how, and attention to detail when it comes to recognizing, interpreting, and understanding high level athletics; eventually coaches absorb these finer points as well; then players learn and eventually pass on their knowledge, and the process repeats itself ostensibly forever. (However, if the Cardinals were to revert into a horrible team it would be an interesting development to see if the opposite would occur in the community over time. Good luck waiting for that to happen!)

Therefore, over the years, all the knowledge from past teams, players, coaches, and staff resonated with locals and you were left with a community of brilliant baseball fans. Natural spillover.

It can be deduced that this baseball spillover made its way to soccer in the form of "athletic know-how," patent pending.

In fact, despite soccer and baseball being two distinct sports, you can apply "athletic know-how" from one to the other. For instance... Fans, observers, if you will, know something good when they see it. Stan Musial, Ozzie Smith, Andy Van Slyke, Jim Edmonds, Albert Pujols. When you're around a winning culture, like that of the St. Louis Cardinals, with elite talent that transcends the sport, you get used to knowing when something's good or not. Hence, if you transition from baseball to soccer, from one sport to another, you can apply what's good and what's not despite the sports being different in terms of the rules of each game. "Good technique" and "good plays" can be defined as universal appreciations. Lo and behold, it's not surprising that a brilliant baseball community endowed with one of the most successful franchises in the history of the sport is also very keen when it comes to soccer. Add to this the historical passion for soccer in the area, which was carried over largely from Italian, Irish, and German immigrants (circa 1880-1930). When the worlds of baseball and soccer overlapped there was athletic prowess.

This would explain, in part, why St. Louis has (for so long) been extraordinary in the worlds of club, high school, college, and pro soccer. St. Louis became famous for soccer in so many ways. Yet, everything starts with youth soccer. And in St. Louis, club teams reign supreme. Throughout the nation, virtually everyone has figured out as much. Any tournament that top St. Louis teams venture to is going to be an eye-opening experience for competitors. This has been the case for generations. It all starts with youth club soccer. And look no further, St. Louis has been home to the best clubs in American soccer history.

THE 1950 FIFA WORLD CUP & ST. LOUIS CLUB SOCCER INTERMINGLE

Keep in mind, the first FIFA World Cup was in 1930, hosted by Uruguay. Oddly enough, the USMNT placed third, if you can believe it. It was a different time, but a great accomplishment nonetheless. Members of that team with a St. Louis connection included Raphael "Ralph" Tracey (who played for St. Louis Vesper Buick, and Ben Millers), and Frank Vaughn* (who played for Ben Millers)—both are in the St. Louis Soccer Hall of Fame and the National Soccer Hall of Fame. Way back in the day, the momentum that St. Louis soccer was riding funneled its way into the 1950 FIFA World Cup. There was one game in particular that made

---

*   Interestingly, Frank Vaughn did not see playing time in the 1930 FIFA World Cup. He played in exhibition matches for the USMNT against non-national teams so he never received credit for an actual international game, i.e. country against country.

headlines during that World Cup, and it remains well known to this day. That headline would read: 'The United States upsets England 1-0!'

As it turns out, the St. Louis contingent for this colossal game in US soccer history was quite significant. First off, to give credit where credit is due, the goal-scorer was Joe Gaetjens, who was originally from Haiti. Though, as many people know, five players in the starting 11 were from St. Louis. (That's a lot!) Here they are.

In goal, solidifying everything in front of the net, you had Frank Borghi. Jim Leeker—who, at the time I spoke with him, was President of the St. Louis Soccer Hall of Fame—told me that during a 2013 friendly at Busch Stadium between Manchester City and Chelsea, Mike Summerbee, a former pro player from England, told him Borghi had legendary status in England thanks to his 1950 World Cup performance that defeated the Three Lions. Aside from this well-known game, Borghi represented the USMNT from 1949-53. In the US, he played for St. Louis Simpkins-Ford, a very successful team in its day.

Harry Keough, a key defender for the US, played for the US national team from 1949-57. Outside of the USMNT, he also played for St. Louis Kutis, St. Louis Raiders, St. Louis McMahon, Paul Schulte Motors, and the San Francisco Barbarians.

The *Wikipedia* article for Harry points out that: "Keough was born to Patrick John and Elizabeth (née Costley) Keough, and grew up in St. Louis, Missouri, attending Cleveland High School. As a youth he played several sports, including track, swimming, and fast-pitch softball, particularly excelling at soccer. His soccer career began in 1945 as a member of the 'St. Louis Schumachers', who won the 1946 National Junior Challenge Cup. In 1946, he joined the U.S. Navy. He was assigned to a naval base in San Francisco, California where he played for the 'San Francisco Barbarians', which had dominated west coast soccer in the first half of the 20th century."[35] Keough made his way back to St. Louis after completing his military service. "In 1948, he played for Paul Schulte Motors. The next year the team came under the sponsorship of McMahon Pontiac and played in the lower division St. Louis Municipal

League. He was with McMahon when selected for the U.S. national team as it entered qualification for the 1950 World Cup. When he returned home from the cup, Keough rejoined his team, now known as the St. Louis Raiders of the first division St. Louis Major League. The Raiders won both the league and National Amateur Cup championships in 1952, giving Keough his first 'double'. Following the 1952 season, Tom Kutis took over sponsorship of the team, renaming it St. Louis Kutis S.C. The team continued its winning ways under its new name, winning the 1953 and 1954 league titles, and went to the 1954 National Challenge Cup final where it fell to New York Americans of the American Soccer League. The St. Louis Major League had folded in 1954 and Kutis continued to play both as an independent team and as a member of various lower division city leagues over the next decade. Despite this turbulence, it continued to dominate both the city and national soccer scene. Kutis would win the National Amateur Cup each year from 1956 to 1961. In 1957, it won the National Challenge Cup, giving Keough another double."[36] Keough, of course, went on to coach St. Louis University to five legendary national championships thus solidifying his place as one of St. Louis' most renowned soccer figures of all time.

Charlie Colombo—a center midfielder that played for the US national team from 1948 to 1952—was a member of St. Louis Simpkins-Ford in his day.

Gino Pariani played for the USMNT from 1948 through 1950; he also had experience playing for St. Louis Simpkins-Ford, along with a few others.

Frank Wallace—who played with the USMNT from 1949-50—was a forward that also played for St. Louis Simpkins-Ford, and a few others. Along with manager, William Jeffrey, and the remainder of the lineup, the 1950 World Cup side managed to hold on tight as the English surged forward, throwing everything into its attack. With hard work, a little luck, and, not to mention, St. Louis ingenuity, the team held on to a 1-0 victory, thus creating a place for itself in World Cup history.

This was a flamboyant, peacock-like, feather in the hat for St. Louis soccer at large. Clearly, around 1950, or as one could quantify it, "the pre-NASL and St. Louis Stars era," the idea of a solid professional outdoor league was ephemeral, at best. It was the club team experience that benefitted the five St. Louis players in so far as it helped push their talents to such a place that enabled them to compete so well in World Cup competition.

It's fascinating to note that during the 1930, 1950, and even the 1990 FIFA World Cups, it was a time in which soccer was largely an afterthought to the American public. Of course, there were aficionados that relished anything and everything soccer-related, but, by and large, many Americans were iffy toward the sport, if not outright against it.

Within this national atmosphere, St. Louis largely embraced the sport and St. Louis club soccer was highly competitive.

THE WORLD OF CLUB SOCCER IN ST. LOUIS CONTINUES TO AMAZE

St. Louis Simpkins-Ford, which won the U.S. Open Cup in 1948 and 1950, stands out as a great St. Louis team from days past. In doing so, it thereby pushed the conversation in favor of St. Louis soccer dominance even further.

Then there's Kutis. St. Louis Kutis S.C.—the pride of St. Louis club soccer during its time—won some big tournaments in its day. Yet, it could be argued, there were none bigger than the 1957 U.S. Open Cup and the 1986 U.S. Open Cup.

Following the success of St. Louis teams in the U.S. Open Cup during the 1920s, 30s, and 40s, Kutis was reigning supreme among the pack, especially in the 1950s. First, aside from local St. Louis success, gathering the 1957 U.S. Open Cup was a huge score for the club. While there were plenty of top-notch teams outside of Kutis, it can't be stressed enough that when organizers of United States soccer called upon Kutis in 1958 to play as proxy for the US national team, it distinguished the club from all others. For perspective, 1958 was the same year that Pele, Garrincha, and Brazil won the FIFA World Cup in Sweden. Kutis, lost in the shadow of such a feat, was riding its own wave in the world of US soccer, whereby, within this realm, Kutis was, and is, legendary. Certainly, as the years go on, as US soccer continues to grow in terms of success from MLS and the USMNT, Kutis should have a place in history within conversations of international circles as a team that mattered. As is the case with so many legendary teams, one reason Kutis found success was simple, actually. Former Kutis forward, Jim Leeker, recalled that Harry Keough and Val Pelizzaro would referee games in the St. Louis area and recruit players for Kutis. This, in part, helped make the club stronger. As it turns out, the late 1950s marked the beginning of St. Louis University's amazing 10 title run in the NCAA tournament (head coach Bob Guelker started the push, then Harry Keough and assistant coach, Val Pelizzaro, led the second charge). A lot of that success was intertwined with the soccer culture that had built up in St. Louis, thanks to the U.S. Open Cup titles from various teams in the 1920s, 30s, 40s, and 50s.

The 1950s, 60s, and 70s were special times for St. Louis soccer. The landscape was sprinkled with brilliant teachers of the game.

The one and only, Bob Guelker—who played basketball and not soccer—turned into one of the brilliant coaches of his time. There's a bit of mystery surrounding the legendary Guelker. It seems that he never played soccer, but found a knack for it as a coach. Likely he had touched a soccer ball at some point in his youth (just as practically everyone has), though, as many people pointed out, he did not come from a soccer background (as most coaches are former players). As an adult, he was the Sports Director for CYC and played an important role in the development of youth athletes around St. Louis. As head soccer coach, he would eventually lead SLU to multiple NCAA Division I national championships (five in total from the late 1950s into the 60s); these were the first in the school's illustrious soccer history. Then he moved onto SIUE—which was just across the river—and led the Cougars to an NCAA Division I title in 1979. He also coached the US Olympic team. Players that were coached by Guelker—Pat McBride, Tom Howe, and

Ed Gettemeier—all shared a similar sentiment about 'Guelks': He had an innate ability to understand the game, players, and how to piece it all together in order to get the best out of players, and to win. In doing so, Guelker paid close attention to outside coaching techniques from soccer and other sports—anything to improve his knowledge of the game.

The legend, Harry Keough—a player for Kutis, a brilliant defender with experience on the USMNT that competed valiantly in the 1950 FIFA World Cup—eventually took over as the coach of SLU whereby he won five national titles, just as his predecessor, Guelker, had done. Alongside Keough was assistant coach and fitness guru, Val Pelizzaro. It was a different era as both coaches had a side job as postal carriers. In terms of setting St. Louis apart from other US cities, Harry and Val did so with a high soccer IQ and national titles that reverberate to this day.

The great Bob Kehoe—a captain of the USMNT in 1965, later its coach in 1972—was instrumental in passing on valuable information and know-how about the game. During his time, Kehoe was a valuable member of Kutis. Around the time Kehoe was captain and later coach of the USMNT, he played on the St. Louis Stars in 1968, coached the team from 1969-70, and later coached Granite City North High School from 1973-83.

By the 1960s, St. Louis soccer was feeling the influence of instrumental figures, Dave Berwin and George Mihaljevic.

Dave Berwin began playing in the schoolyards at Saint Engelbert's parish. He would play for Saint Engelbert's youth and senior teams. Right out of high school, circa 1958, Dave got his first coaching gig with a 5th grade team out of his parish. He was part of a family coaching lineage. His uncle, Marty Clarke, coached Bob Kehoe and Bill Lubi, two exceptional players, in the 1940s at St. Philip Neri.† Dave's uncle, Marty, coincidentally, is the father of Joe Clarke; that would make Dave and Joe first cousins. Joe starred at St. Louis University in the 1970s, played

---

†   Berwin pointed out that St. Philip Neri would be the same as St. Philip Di Neri.

professionally, and eventually coached the Billikens before leading Washington University from the sidelines.

More interesting connections continue to pile up as Dave reflected on a time back in the day when a young Pat McBride was making his way from the north of St. Louis, literally hitchhiking for a ride, to a CYC All-Star game down in Forest Park. Dave, who was woven into the soccer fabric of the area, noticed McBride amidst a neighborhood commonly adorned with brick and gave him a lift. Moreover, he chuckled about McBride's simplistic approach to arrive at a game 50-odd years later.

As Dave explained it, around 1964-65, CYC formed the "Pepsi league" which was a district league that was still the CYC, as sponsored by Pepsi. Dave coached St. Philip Neri during the 60s, with such players as St. Louis soccer heavyweights Al Trost, Buzz Demling, Joe Hamm, Mike Seerey, and Pat Leahy (who eventually was a placekicker in the NFL, with the Jets). In 1968 and 1969, St. Philip Neri won two back-to-back National Junior Cups, or, as it's known, the U19 McGuire Cup. Dave was right in the middle of the storm. As he said, in 1967-68, the team had to go through Lindbergh Cadillac of St. Louis, on route to the Missouri title. From there it was a road game against a Chicago team in the windy city, then back in St. Louis against a team from Louisiana. Finally, in the championship held in St. Louis, St. Philip Neri took down a team from the East Coast.

In 1969, Dave transitioned to coaching senior ball with St. Philip Neri, during which he acquired four Missouri titles.

This led to Berwin's leadership as coach of 7UP. Also, Berwin coached Big Four Chevrolet around 1971-72, which lasted until 1978. Big Four Chevrolet was a big-time team, with such players as Ty Keough, Greg Makowski, and Pete Collico, all of whom eventually played pro. When asked about Ty Keough—a diamond fixture of St. Louis soccer royalty by way of being the son of Harry, a star with St. Louis University, the St. Louis Steamers, the USMNT, and iconic TV soccer commentator for years—Berwin said, jokingly, "He was all right." He pointed out that Ty was a great talent, a hard worker that could play anywhere on the field, along with being a very intelligent player.

Shortly after Big Four Chevrolet, Berwin stepped back to coach his kids at St. Jerome's parish. Then, Tom Matteau—who worked at Busch brewery—reached out to Dave, and as a result, Busch Soccer Club came calling under the leadership of Denny Long, who was heavily involved in the soccer program on behalf of the beer giant. Berwin subsequently coached there from 1980-83. He guided mainly 16- to 18-year-olds, some of which included Paul Bilickie and Dave Gauvain (cousin of longtime Chaminade College Preparatory School coach, Mike Gauvain).

All in all, much of Berwin's success came from things he gleaned from George Mihaljevic. According to Berwin, Mihaljevic changed the game in St. Louis and deserves a lot more credit than he ever got.

As it turns out, George Mihaljevic defected from Yugoslavia and eventually landed in St. Louis, because, according to Jim Leeker, he wanted to go where the best soccer was. Leeker was quick to point out St. Louis soccer benefitted from Mihaljevic's arrival, noting he was a very skillful player and coach. In addition, Berwin pointed out that when it came to Mihaljevic's approach, skill work and passing the ball were paramount, with a lot of short passing, using the wings a lot, and, "everybody touched the ball." The latter quote may sound like a no-brainer, yet many coaches during this era were okay with not utilizing fullbacks in passing schemes whereas Mihaljevic intentionally used fullbacks by way of having players pass back to them, to regroup in possession. His ability to showcase skill for players to observe and copy was a valuable asset. Likewise, his passion for getting players to use skill in passing combinations reverberated wherever he went, thus adding yet another layer of quality to the overall St. Louis soccer scene. During his time in St. Louis, Mihaljevic created the club White Star (which featured players such as Pat McBride and Carl Gentile), and also put his coaching talents to work with the St. Louis Stars in the 1967 campaign.

Interestingly, with great coaches and personalities such as Bob Guelker, Harry Keough, Val Pelizzaro, Bob Kehoe, Dave Berwin, and

George Mihaljevic in and around the game, soccer was thriving in St. Louis in the 1950s and 60s.

In particular, things were roaring with Kutis.

Under the influence of Harry Keough, Kutis, of course, won the 1957 U.S. Open Cup, a great achievement, and in 1958 Kutis competed on behalf of the USMNT for a few World Cup qualifiers.

In 1963, Chris Werstein joined Kutis and flourished for seven years as a tough defender and midfielder. He had previously played for Schumacher, where he was part of a National Junior Cup championship in 1962. Werstein was the St. Louis League MVP in 1968-69 and eventually played for the St. Louis Stars in the NASL during 1969-71.

With Werstein and other greats, the club was a brilliant 'hand-picked from above' kind of club that served as an ambassador for St. Louis and American soccer.

Incidentally, after Kutis won the 1957 U.S. Open Cup there was a time lapse until 1986, when, you guessed it, Kutis won the title a second time. Members in 1986 included Steve Hunsicker, Lance Polette, Terry Brown, Albert Adade, Paul Dueker, Don Huber, Dave Bozdeck, Bob Matteson, Ted Hantak, Steve Maurer, Ken McDonald, Joe Clarke, Joe Eppy, Denny Vaninger, and Denny Bozesky, with coaches Jim Henson, Jim Bokern (who also played), and manager, Bill Hense.

Then in 1988, Busch Seniors—which included Steve Trittschuh—won the coveted U.S. Open Cup national championship for St. Louis again. Busch, of course, had its beginnings back in the 1970s.

As it turns out, the 70s were an interesting time for soccer in St. Louis, and America. True to form, FIFA World Cup excitement spread throughout nations around the world. The World Cups of 1970 (won by Brazil), 1974 (won by W. Germany), and 1978 (won by Argentina), were reaching wider audiences worldwide as TV sets were becoming more common, and, very importantly, color TV sets were capturing the action which added a whole new element to anyone's game-watching experience. With full color people could see the yellow, blue, and white uniforms of Brazil as Pele climbed above the blue and white kits of

Italy to score a head-ball; the white and black uniforms of W. Germany clashing with the majestic orange and white kits of Holland; the confetti adorning the Argentinian field as the home side, wearing white and baby blue stripes, captured first place. This added value of color TV brought the excitement of the world's most popular sport into households like never before; American viewers had a new opportunity to see the game of soccer from a new angle. The NASL—which definitely benefitted from FIFA World Cup excitement—was in full swing. Youth, high school, and collegiate soccer in America were making big strides in the 70s; the sport was getting more and more popular. A large part of this had to do with FIFA World Cups, TV sets becoming more widespread, the availability of color TV, and the NASL.

Indeed, while many parts of the United States were becoming acquainted with soccer for the first time, St. Louis was far ahead, producing top-level players like Ty Keough, Greg Villa, Steve Pecher, and Greg Makowski (each of which played for the USMNT).

Perry Van der Beck, a true legend, one of the area's most accomplished players, represented the USMNT from 1979-85. In 1985 he was named U.S. Soccer Player of the Year; this honor is given to one player a year and other recipients have included Christian Pulisic, Michael Bradley, Clint Dempsey, Landon Donovan, and Tab Ramos, to name a few. Originally from Florissant, Missouri, Van der Beck was treading his own path to greatness in the 1970s. He gained inspiration and knowledge of the game from watching Dave Berwin, Pat Leahy, Bob O'Leary, Al Trost, and Pat McBride. Van der Beck made a name for himself in 1978 as the first player drafted straight from high school into the NASL, whereby he joined the Tampa Bay Rowdies. Such a player as Van der Beck was bringing ever more attention to the illustrious soccer scene in St. Louis. The soccer city was something like an automobile plant, and, it would seem, year after year, the cars kept getting better and better.

Around this time, the grand decade of the 1970s, the CYC—Catholic Youth Council—got a little competition, as did the Khoury League. (The Khoury League, which was big into baseball, also hosted soccer leagues around St. Louis and on the Illinois side of the river sporadically from the 1950s to approximately 2015, as Khoury League CEO, Joe Calcaterra, explained over the phone on July 29, 2020). It came in the form of an elite club soccer league.

SLYSA—St. Louis Youth Soccer Association—emerged in 1975 as St. Louis' "premiere league," which (as of July 2020) is how SLYSA described it on the official SLYSA web page. The web page also read, "COMPETE AGAINST THE BEST." Same thing every time. In other words, if you were to drop by a SLYSA game in 1980 or 2030, you'd come across the best talent in the area, hence, talent that's as good as anyone from around the world.

Moreover, it was the 1970s during which Busch Gardens Soccer Club and Scott Gallagher had set flight. From there on, the club soccer scene in St. Louis would never be the same.

THE ELITE FORCE OF BUSCH

Busch Gardens Soccer Club was formed in the 1970s by Denny Long, the President of Anheuser-Busch at the time. According to Jim Leeker and Vince Drake, Denny was a very friendly guy that wanted to hire the best coaches and players he could find. This was the goal, and, subsequently, Busch turned out to be a powerhouse. A number of coaches were part of the program including but not limited to USMNT captain Steve Pecher, Frans van Balkom from the Netherlands, who was the national team coach of Hong Kong and Indonesia for a time, and St. Louis Steamers defender and Canadian Olympian Carl Rose. Some players that wore the uniform over the years included Ed Gettemeier (St. Louis Steamers), Steve Trittschuh (USMNT), Tim Leonard (St. Louis Ambush), Casey Klipfel (Nashville Metros), Vedad Alagic (St. Louis Illusion), D.J. Newsom (St. Louis Steamers), and many others.

By 1980, the team was known simply as Busch Soccer Club.

In 1982, St. Louis Soccer Park—known today as World Wide Technology Soccer Park—was erected in Fenton, Missouri (just a bit south of St. Louis proper). Anheuser-Busch was behind the construction of the site. This is where Busch teams practiced and hosted home games. Soccer Park, as it was colloquially known, featured an impressive display of next-level athletic prowess. (Soccer Park was eventually acquired by Scott-Gallagher, Busch's former rival—sometimes all good things come to an end. To this day, the complex is essentially the same.) You'll find a driveway leading into a parking lot that immediately features two pristine turf fields, large bleachers included. Overlooking these fields is a terrace connected to the concession area, which, in turn, is connected to meeting rooms. Next to the turf fields and below the building structure is the main grass field where only a few select games are played, including but not limited to that of SLU (in the past) and the USMNT. Around the main field are a few other practice pitches that see games every now and then. Throughout the complex are stadium-like lights for night play.

With Soccer Park in place, along with top coaching and elite players, Busch dominated SLYSA, local tournaments, and, as you might have guessed, Busch had great success nationally. In fact, Busch won the U16 national championship in 1978, 1980, 1988, and 1989.

Additionally, on the adult side, a huge victory came in 1988 when St. Louis Busch Seniors won the prestigious U.S. Open Cup championship (just two years after fellow St. Louis club, Kutis, won the title in 1986). As the 1990s turned into the 2000s, things got interesting. From Scott Gallagher's official website, we find that Busch Soccer Club assumed a new identity: "In 2004, the evolution continued, as the club changed its name to St. Louis Soccer Club to better represent and support the mission of the club and its community. The club had been consistently ranked among the top 20 girls programs by Soccer America, and in the 30+ years of existence, the boys and girls teams of St. Louis Soccer Club / Busch Soccer Club have claimed 15 National Championships in addition to winning more State Championships and advancing more teams to Regional Championships than any other club in the country."[37]

So it was, Busch came to an end. In 2004, Busch Soccer Club became St. Louis Soccer Club. This didn't last long. By 2007-08, St. Louis

Soccer Club, Metro United, and Scott Gallagher merged into one mega Scott Gallagher club. It should be pointed out, if nothing else than for the sake of argument, that despite the recent ubiquitous soccer takeover by Scott Gallagher, most prominent of all in the lore of St. Louis soccer has arguably been the involvement of Anheuser-Busch (with Busch Memorial Stadium where the Stars played, Busch Soccer Club, St. Louis Soccer Park, and the heavy sponsorship of international soccer games for ages). With Busch Soccer Club gone, there's a touch of sadness as one of the area's most renowned landmarks—Anheuser-Busch Beer—does not have its hands on the lever of one of the most prestigious clubs to ever come out of St. Louis and America. In its place, Scott Gallagher has risen higher than anyone originally thought possible.

THE SUPER CLUB OF SCOTT GALLAGHER

Shortly after Busch, back in the grand decade of the 70s, Scott Gallagher arrived on the scene.

The elite.

When you look at mighty Scott Gallagher today, you see the following: In each age group, there are a number of Gallagher teams. Each team is placed into a category, such as a superior Gallagher side, a somewhat less superior side, and so on down the list. Though, considering that Gallagher attracts the best talent in the area, it is sometimes difficult to discern which Gallagher team is the best. So, a fight for the title of "best team in a certain age group" essentially comes down to one Gallagher side against another. Every once in a while, a rival club—like Lou Fusz—will plant its flag in the ground and defeat a Gallagher side. Though, most often, Gallagher rules the landscape. As the top club in St. Louis to date, it has left the public in somewhat of an obsequious position to its haughty detachment over its cohorts. While many other clubs flourish in St. Louis, Gallagher is the heavyweight champ. From humble beginnings, Gallagher has turned into a goliath of a club, known nationwide.

The large corporate structure that Gallagher embodies today is a far cry from its inception. From its own website we find that: "The Scott

Gallagher Soccer Club traces its roots back to 1976, when St. Louisan Jim Scott—the owner of a sheet-metal company called Scott-Gallagher, Inc.—began lending sponsorship assistance to a small soccer club from north St. Louis County called Ruiz S.C. One year later, Mr. Scott assumed the sponsor role of the club, and after a two-year transition period, the club officially began playing as Scott Gallagher Soccer Club in 1979. At that time, the club consisted of only four select boy's teams. Just two years later, the Scott Gallagher U19 boys team went on to win the club's first national Championship in the 1981 McGuire Cup. In 1983, the club received wide recognition for its unprecedented achievement of winning four Regional Championships in the same year. In 1984, Scott Gallagher S.C. notched its second McGuire Cup National Championship. Regularly ranked among Soccer America's list of the top 20 boy's soccer clubs, through 2008 Scott Gallagher S.C. has amassed 11 National Championship titles and countless Regional and State championships."[38]

On its website, Gallagher mentions 11 national championships as of 2008, and that number is sure to increase in the future. Scott Gallagher won the coveted U19 national championship (McGuire Cup) in 1981, 1984, and 1996. The last U19 national title was a stacked team (as usual), coached by Mike Gauvain and Tom Howe.

In order to attain so much success, there must be talented coaching. Indeed, there have been countless influential figures inside the halls of Gallagher. Some of whom would include Gauvain, Howe, Tim Rooney, Dan Gaffney, Rick Benben, Mike Collom, Patrick Barry, Steve Pecher, Dale Schilly, Kip Thompson, Scott McDoniel, Tim Kelly, Sterling Wescott, Ken Godat, Pete Collico, and so on.

The highly structured conglomerate that Gallagher is today, with World Wide Technology Soccer Park as its base, does not necessarily reflect the original optics of the organization. In fact, back in the late 70s, there wasn't a headquarters per say, and coaches might gather at this or that bar for a meeting. As the 80s and 90s passed, the club kept growing.

Around 2007, the colossal merger of three club teams was an interesting turn of events that remapped St. Louis club soccer forever.

From Gallagher's website: "In early 2007, St. Louis Soccer Club [formerly Busch Soccer Club], Scott Gallagher Soccer Club, and Metro United Soccer Club, explored the possibility of bringing the three groups together to better serve the soccer community of the Greater St. Louis Metropolitan Area. By combining the talent and efforts of three of the area's leading clubs, St. Louis would boast a unique, vertically integrated soccer organization of the highest quality—from entry level all the way through the professional ranks. A vision was developed that would allow St. Louis to remain competitive nationally as the game of soccer was growing and developing at a record pace.

Since the merging of the area's three leading youth soccer clubs in 2008, St. Louis Scott Gallagher has emerged as a national leader in youth soccer."[39]

Interestingly, SLSG (St. Louis Scott Gallagher) was paving a new path in St. Louis soccer as it set out to intertwine club and pro ranks. According to Gallagher's website: "In 2014, SLSG announced the acquisition of Saint Louis FC, a professional men's soccer team to compete in the United Soccer League (Professional Division II). Beginning with its first season in 2015, Saint Louis FC quickly became a best in class organization in professional soccer in the United States."[40]

Before Gallagher morphed into its current form, which is comprised of kids from all over the St. Louis metro area, Tom Howe explained that in the beginning it was more or less composed of players from the Northside while Busch largely pulled in players from the Southside. When asked about his early days coaching Gallagher, back around 1978, Howe, one of many legendary Gallagher coaches, said, "Gallagher was a club that was like a family." Coaches had history together and it grew from there. Over the years, Howe has been involved with many successful teams. "Yeah, there were about seven or eight teams that won a national," Howe told me, bluntly, without too many words. I was told he wasn't a chatterbox, that's an understatement. Of Gallagher's total national titles, Howe—a former CBC standout that Bob Guelker recruited for his first year at SIUE and who eventually played for the St. Louis

Stars—had coached so many that the number and years have blurred into one; the brilliant soccer mind suffered from too much success. This was the same crafty and speedy midfielder that had a classic, calm 'I don't give a damn' look from the 70s, fully equipped with mustache and long hair—the one who's top of the list for 'coolest guy of the decade' award. Nowadays, the mustache might be gone, replaced with glasses, while the soccer IQ is still intact, perhaps more fine-tuned than ever. When I tried to narrow down the year for one such title, that included Brandon Barklage, Tim Walters (the son of Tim Walters), and Pat Brazill, he guessed a year. "Something like that," he added. Bottom line: Too much success. (Vince Drake had a similar response when I asked of his most memorable championship runs with St. Thomas Aquinas-Mercy; there were so many it was kind of a blur.) Essentially, it was around 2004-05 when Howe coached Gallagher to a well-deserved U17 national championship. Kevin Robson—who won two high school state championships with Chaminade and two national championships with Indiana University—was coached by Howe on a Gallagher team; he had been around the 2004-05 U17 national championship squad and was impressed with them. According to Robson "...that was a pretty special national championship for the city of St. Louis and Tommy Howe in particular." Robson added, "That was kind of an underdog team that won one for Tommy Howe." It was a solid team that bought into Howe's approach, and outplayed opponents that brought a more physical, direct style. "That team really epitomized his style," Robson commented, in that it was similar to teams Howe likes such as Brazil and Ajax—playing the ball on the ground, and playing in tight spaces. Howe's approach to the game has revolved around dominating tight spaces on the field with smart passing, a possession-oriented approach. Gallagher teams, as Howe said, are always good passing teams.

When you combine a "vertically integrated soccer organization of the highest quality—from entry level all the way through the professional ranks" and Howe's vision of smart passing teams, along with the virtuous advantage of hiring coaches that typically are former pro players or collegiate players (or in some way bring a high level of soccer IQ), the end result is nothing less than a refracting image of La Masia, the youth training system of FC Barcelona. (La Masia, a youth academy, is an incubator for Barcelona, and, ipso facto, the Spanish national team, as so many players have gone through La Masia's doors and walked out as stars of Barcelona's first team and Spain's national team...thus, exuding the system of thought that La Masia emphasizes, which, in summary, is a highly-structured approach to possession-oriented passing, by way of short passes coupled with a high-degree of technical ability. The La Masia academy and Barcelona have roots in the knowledge passed down from one of its former players and coaches, Dutch superstar, Johan Cruyff, who was educated in the Ajax system of passing which is interrelated. It could be argued that the end result is most players emerge from La Masia with a "Ph.D. in possession soccer.") Since the late 70s, the result of Gallagher's efforts has been a myriad talented players—ranging from Tim Strange, Mark Santel, Chris Klein, Jeff DiMaria, Taylor Twellman, Brad Davis, Brandon Barklage, Tim Ream, Josh Sargent, Jack Maher, and the list goes on—that exude the highest quality possible.

As the new decade of 2020 kicked off, history was lingering in the air like never before. COVID-19 caused havoc around the world, as social unrest hit the United States like a tidal wave slamming into a seaside village. Meanwhile, as time was treading ever so close to the new MLS team in St. Louis, Scott Gallagher still had ties with the pro outdoor team, Saint Louis FC, whereby an academy relationship between the two echoed similarities with that of La Masia to Barcelona. Furthermore, "graduates of Scott Gallagher"—such as Tim Ream and Josh Sargent in recent days—have gone on to represent the USMNT, just as players that walked through the halls of La Masia and Barcelona have "graduated" to the Spanish national team. Ostensibly, in the years ahead, it seems highly likely that a similar interrelated system will flourish between Gallagher and St. Louis City SC.

Some may argue Gallagher is the only show in town and if players don't make it there they won't make it anywhere, and equally talented kids that play for Lou Fusz—or elsewhere—don't get a fair shot at the highest levels of soccer outside of high school (going so far as the national team). This is an interesting argument. It essentially asserts that "quality players on less prestigious teams" won't get a fair shot at the top colleges or perhaps even the national team, by way of connections with the top-level Gallagher coaches. This argument, at its core, has a place, however, when it comes down to it, an academy for the local pro team—a "La Masia serving the interests of Barcelona," which Gallagher is morphing into— has to have a headquarters, a ground zero. As it turns out, that's the case with Gallagher. In today's soccer landscape, Gallagher has branched out to include all of St. Louis, including clubs for the Missouri side of St. Louis and the Illinois Metro East side of the city. While players from smaller clubs with less prestigious reputations may suffer, unfortunately that's just the nature of things.

There is an upside for Gallagher being the main show in town that streamlines a path for players to potentially compete in college, at the pro level, and possibly with the national team. The experienced coaches within Gallagher, trusted coaches by and large, have the foresight to notice talented players *within a group of talented players* and push them through with proper training and insight to make them even better. After all, despite politics and such things that go hand-in-hand with any sport, Gallagher offers a training platform for elite talent, and such a place provides an atmosphere of competition which enhances players for the next levels (which, again, would potentially be college, pro, and the national team). As is the case with La Masia, certain players, who are very talented, don't make it through to the next level; there are only so many positions available on a roster, that's how it goes; some Barcelona stars have felt guilty, seeing former teammates from youth, with plenty of talent, be let go. The same will go with the inevitable relationship between Gallagher and St. Louis City SC; hearts will be broken along the way as some talented kids won't get quite as far as others...meanwhile, fans watching the games will only see the product on the field without fully knowing the lifetime of training behind the curtains.

So the theory goes, however you look at the competitive structure of professional sports, this is a near perfect atmosphere to select the next leaders of the game—the best players that have potential to become household names.

An example of a talented player being discovered early on would be former St. Louis University standout and USMNT member, Brad Davis. Even at the age of 10, Howe and other Gallagher coaches spotted his talent. "We knew then that he was a special player," as Howe said. "He had unbelievable skills. His soccer IQ was, you know, he played like a professional when he was 10 years old, as far as decision-making and stuff like that." Furthermore, "He had an incredible left foot. Unbelievable touch." Howe coached Davis during his time at the club, from the age of 10 through U19. (A few Gallagher teammates of Davis were Kevin Thibodeau, Danny Hilson, and Kevin Hudson.)

Davis, lo and behold, has returned to Gallagher's organization after a lengthy career in MLS, along with the USMNT. As Tom Timmermann of the *St. Louis Post-Dispatch* reported in May of 2020, "The last time Brad Davis lived in St. Louis, he was in a dormitory at St. Louis University.

It was 2002, and the Chaminade grad was a sophomore at SLU. After that season, he turned pro, being taken third in MLS draft and embarking on a career that took him across America, as well as the world in his time with the U.S. national team.

Eighteen years later, he's finally coming home, though presumably to some place larger than that dorm room, considering he now has a wife and three kids."[41]

Timmermann added, "Davis was announced last week as the new club director of the Missouri boys division of the St. Louis Scott Gallagher soccer club, the group he played for growing up. He'll be working with all levels of boys programs, up to the club's academy team, overseeing all aspects of their operation."[42]

Aficionados may be interested to know that, as of 2021, the top five all-time assist leaders in MLS history are (from first to fifth) Landon

Donovan, Steve Ralston, Brad Davis, Carlos Valderrama, and Preki. Ralston and Davis, of course, are Gallagher products.

Unlike Davis, who landed with the stellar St. Louis University Billikens out of high school, Ralston had a less prestigious climb to the top. Back in 1994, a story by Joe Lyons appeared in the *St. Louis Post-Dispatch*. It pointed out that "Ralston, 5 feet 9 and 150 pounds, got only minor recruiting interest before deciding on Forest Park Community College. He earned All-American honors there, with 17 goals and seven assists."[43] He went from an inauspicious starting line of junior college to Florida International University. Eventually, after playing briefly with the St. Louis Ambush during the 1995-96 season, he suited up with Tampa Bay Mutiny and New England Revolution and raised his game to such a level that he sits second only to Landon Donovan on the MLS all-time assist list. Not bad. Moreover, he was a frequent member of the USMNT for around 10 years from 1997 onward with 36 caps.

Oddly enough, Preki—the only two-time MLS MVP to date, who is originally from Yugoslavia—landed with the St. Louis Storm in the early 1990s (just before signing with Everton), where he was a handful for goalies. He eventually coached Saint Louis FC—a branch of Scott Gallagher—in 2017.

The association of Gallagher with Davis, Ralston, and Preki is certainly a feather in the hat.

The addition of Davis to Gallagher's staff is a tremendous move for the club. It indicates a common trend in soccer whereby a player can go out, become a great success, and return from whence he originated to teach the game. As Davis said, "'This is kind of the ability to close that circle of being born and raised in St. Louis.'"[44] Davis, a six-time MLS All-Star, won the MLS Cup on two occasions, and he also played in the 2014 FIFA World Cup. He joins the list of many noteworthy figures on Scott Gallagher's roster of leadership, such as Steve Pecher, a former captain of the USMNT. Amazingly, it's a club that continues to set trends for soccer not only in St. Louis, but also nationwide.

BEST OF THE REST

Despite Gallagher currently fielding multiple teams in each age group, there are a handful of clubs offering a healthy dose of resistance that comes in the form of Ajax, Gateway Rush, Oakville United, Sporting STL, St. Louis Steamers SC (founded in 2015 and overseen in part by Jim Thebeau, who was born in 1975, a former center midfielder for Busch Soccer Club), Juventus Academy Saint Louis, Kixx United FC, Glen Ed United, JB Marine, Pumas Futbol Club (which travels from Paducah, Kentucky), Missouri Rush, Lou Fusz, and so on.

The modern enthusiasm of clubs in St. Louis providing *la résistance* harkens back to the days when Gallagher hadn't yet gobbled up so much real estate and the field of clubs seemed to go on forever. Roughly from 1976 (the inception of Gallagher) to 2007-08 (the merger of Gallagher, St. Louis Soccer Club—FKA Busch Soccer Club—and Metro United), the field of clubs was vast, including but not limited to Pepsi, Norco, Coke, Busch, River City Kickers, Johnny Mac, Gundaker, White Star, Liebe, and others that—by way of a charitable description—were less prestigious.

While the 1970s were certainly a step up from the 1960s, it was the 1980s where club soccer exploded. Back in the 80s, whether it was a SLYSA league game or a local tournament, there was a buzz on the grounds; each field was littered with players, teams, parents, flags, banners, lawn chairs, tents, coolers, beers (for the parents), and mini-vans. It was a sea of excitement that told a story: soccer is here. Back then, there didn't need to be a pro outdoor team for people to know that something was brewing. The magical 80s and part of the exciting 90s shared a commonality: There was no viable pro outdoor team in St. Louis. However, for those in the game, soccer felt like a serious endeavor.

JOHNNY MAC VS. RIVER CITY KICKERS: THE ST. LOUIS INVITATIONAL TOURNAMENT, 1989

Whether watching pro or World Cup competition on TV, nothing has quite captured my imagination like three games I've seen in person. And despite being games on a lower amateur level, I'm tossing these three games in with the likes of France vs. Brazil in the 1986 FIFA World Cup quarterfinals (a great, epic showdown for the ages), and France vs. West Germany in the 1982 FIFA World Cup semifinals (another great, epic game).

Call me a mad man, but the three games I'm referring to, which I was fortunate enough to see in person, are all St. Louis-related. Believe you me, with experience playing in Brazil, Holland, and SLYSA (the latter of which might be the most impressive), I'd like to think, maybe, just maybe, I know what I'm talking about. (I already bragged in the intro so let's not relive that.)

The three games I was lucky to see include St. Louis University vs. Indiana University in 1990 (featuring Brian McBride, Mark Santel, Juergen Sommer, Chad Deering, John van Buskirk, Kenny Godat, and Kenny Snow); Granite City High vs. Collinsville High in the Illinois State Sectional of 1991 (featuring Tim Henson, Brent Dipple, Steve VanDyke, Mike Verning, and Matt Chandler); and, last but not least, Johnny Mac vs. River City Kickers in the U14 division of the St. Louis Invitational Tournament circa 1989 (featuring Timmy Pratt, Tony Williams, and, likely, Kevin Quigley).

These are the types of games that represent ages of great soccer in St. Louis thick as a forest in southern Germany. I'm certain that before these three games there were others like them, from a time when magical moments were occurring all around the greater St. Louis area, when players and teams were carving out a mythical presence for the sport, thus laying down a pathway for generations to follow. Back in the day, because of guys like Bob Kehoe, Pat McBride, Jim Leeker, John Pisani, Gary Rensing, Al Trost, Ty Keough, Pete Collico, Perry Van der Beck, Don Ebert, Jeff Cacciatore, Joe Clarke, Larry Hulcer, Daryl Doran, Dan King, Mike Gauvain, and so many others, the game progressed forward. Thanks to these guys—playing in the rain, on muddy fields, with cleats yielding the grass and mud, jerseys dirty from slide tackles, aspirations momentarily quenched from a good battle—the three phenomenal matches I saw were made possible. A few players that inherited this wave of club greatness—drenched in quality and intensity—were Mark Santel, Steve Ralston, Matt McKeon, Tim Leonard, Chris Klein, Taylor Twellman, Pat Noonan, Tim Ream, Will Bruin, Josh Sargent, and so many more.

You see, as coach of the St. Louis Steamers back in 1981-82, Al Trost, a former captain of the USMNT, wrote something very wise, and it went like this: "The development of the St. Louis indoor soccer player will make great strides with the advent of year-round indoor soccer facilities in this area. Many cities will, again, follow our course. This growth will lead to a more knowledgeable and experienced soccer player. I only hope to nurture this development by bringing out the full potential of each individual player and providing an opportunity for him to demonstrate his talent."[45] The words Trost spoke were evident in the three games I saw that impressed me so much. The majority of players in these three games had more than likely watched St. Louis Steamers soccer and participated in indoor facilities around St. Louis.‡ As a result, these players gained insight and valuable experience from being around pro players and having the ability to fine-tune skills in an indoor setting (in which you get more touches on the ball). It's akin to that of, for example, Rivaldo, Ronaldo, and Ronaldinho taking in the game from players with ties to Pele, Jairzinho, Zico, and a multitude of Brazilian greats along with the added luxury of futsal being available to Brazilian players.

The St. Louis University vs. Indiana University game in 1990 (which fielded a ton of St. Louis talent) featured skill at the highest level and it was nonstop.

The Granite City High vs. Collinsville High showdown in 1991 also had skill at the highest level, the intensity was relentless, and there was the added passion of a playoff game between two bitter rivals with everything on the line—two Metro East teams battling for a chance to represent greater St. Louis at the Illinois state high school tournament in

---

‡   Obviously, some of the players from the St. Louis University vs. Indiana University game in 1990 were not from the St. Louis area.

Chicago...both of which had honed their talents from experience against St. Louis teams throughout their entire lives.

Let's just say, the Johnny Mac and River City Kickers game I saw was special, almost floating on a cloud all its own though still resonating every epic game before it by local adult legends—that had trampled on the same ground—when they were also 13 years old. (After all, 13 is that magical age in soccer—and other sports—whereby players typically achieve a high level of skill and tactical awareness that often is lacking at younger ages. At that age, I certainly recall a revelation, so to speak, in terms of combining skill with tactical awareness, and I sensed the same from my teammates. It's a great time for soccer players. Within the confines of their age bracket, despite being only 13, players have the potential to play at a "World Cup level," utilizing skill, tactics, passion, and athleticism.)

On another note, one might think that Scott Gallagher vs. Busch would be more of a classic game. Indeed, of the ones I saw, there were some gems. However, it happened to come down to Johnny Mac and River City Kickers, both of whom were in my age group. Certainly, among my peers, there were about four to six teams fighting for first place in SLYSA—that's how extremely amazing the talent was across-the-board. Those teams included Scott Gallagher, Busch, Pepsi-Norco, Coke, Cape Girardeau Cobras, Johnny Mac, and River City Kickers. What's more, from the greater St. Louis-area population of around 1.5 to 2 million people, these teams had cornered the elite talent. After years of domination by Kutis, St. Philip Di Neri, Seco, 7UP, Imo's Pizza, Big Four Chevrolet, Florissant Celtics, and Florissant Cougars, this was how SLYSA had taken shape in the late 1980s.

Coming from Carbondale, Illinois, originally, and playing for Cape Girardeau, Missouri, as a mercenary, I had played in SLYSA for two seasons, and for a time we were number one, having battled it out with all the aforementioned teams. Later, as an adult, I could see time blurring together; I could see how my previous experience with the SLYSA teams was a moment in time that was interdependent on the brilliant club teams before it, accentuated by smart people like Al Trost who saw how spillover from the popular Steamers—along with "the advent of year-round indoor soccer facilities in this area"—would affect the local soccer scene in a profound way.

The Steamers started up in 1979. By 1989, players on Johnny Mac and River City Kickers—who were predominately born in 1976—had taken in the amazing play from the Steamers while also benefitting from multiple indoor soccer facilities in the area.

Johnny Mac—which had sparkling white and red uniforms—had always been the fiercest competitor among its peers. (Just barely.) It was a group of guys that were obnoxious, loud, temperamental, and arrogant; they were the most skillful, the quickest, the most ruthless SOB-St. Louis-elitist-preppy-jerks you could possibly come across. And they knew it, they didn't care, and they didn't back down. On top of this, their coach and parents were right there supporting it! Perhaps their attitude and bravado was not what Al Trost—a pious individual— had envisioned for St. Louis soccer a few years earlier; yet, the skill on the field was certainly there. (By the way, I always thought most of that Johnny Mac description applied to me until I came across these guys and met my match. Believe you me, I was an arrogant SOB and was told as much by virtually everyone I met, yet, somehow the guys of Johnny Mac escalated their arrogance to levels on par with John McEnroe meets an outraged Argentinian national team on steroids; and once the game started, it intensified and intensified and intensified. In fact, anyone of this ilk met their match with Johnny Mac. I was always a little jealous that somehow they had captured this mysterious formula of arrogance with a consistency that was, well, a thing of beauty.)

By the time I saw this game, I hadn't yet moved to Collinsville where I eventually played for Busch. Though, given the experience I had had against the best teams of St. Louis, I realistically always thought Johnny Mac was the best of the best, just by a little bit. To bolster this claim, Johnny Mac had recently won the Missouri state championship and the Midwest regional championship. (Allegedly, in the Midwest tournament, they clobbered opponents.)

When I saw that Johnny Mac was up against rival River City Kickers I thought: *Well that's gonna be good.* I was enlisted as a guest-player for the Granite City Elks and stuck around to watch, as I knew both teams very well. Johnny Mac was like must-see TV. (Additionally, there was a rumor that Johnny Mac had traveled to a tournament in Mexico and lost all their luggage. I'm guessing they did well in the tournament and flipped off the whole nation every chance they got, thus ensuring retribution.)

Wherever St. Louis teams went, there was a certain arrogance associated to them. This game was on home turf, in St. Louis—Fenton, technically—and egos were on the line.

Keep in mind, these weren't just normal kids "playing a fun game of soccer"—eager to frolic around with orange slices at halftime. These were trained winners—who were focused and colossally ambitious—competing to the death. Each one certainly believed they were ready for a D1 college scholarship. There was attitude and swagger; it was as though they understood the game on a Ph.D. level. They were like miniature versions of Javier Mascherano and Hernan Crespo with a touch of Bobby Hurley, Tony Hawk, actors James Spader, Lochlyn Munro, William McNamara, Adam Scott, and, while we're at it, the blonde gymnast from *American Anthem*—all at their best, and in really foul moods. To my experience, that was St. Louis soccer. Sure, Scott Gallagher—within my age group—were stewards of sportsmanship, though fierce competitors. Yet, lurking around most corners were ruthlessly competitive guys that wanted to win and expected to win at all costs.

This Johnny Mac and River City Kickers showdown was similar to how Dan King described the North-South rivalry games back in the 1970s and before. Teams like the "Florissant Celtics, up north here," along with the Florissant Cougars, and "then you had the South County Dutch...the Missouri Mules were down south, Imo's" along with Busch Soccer Club in the south. As King put it, "The Northside against the Southside: It was a legitimate rivalry." He added, "It was like a gang thing but it wasn't like, you know, hurtful." Since the days of Kerry

Patch (St. Louis' rough, defunct, Northside neighborhood that followed the motto of 'anything goes'), the civilized world had prevailed. Despite not being a brick fight, soccer rivalries were taken very seriously, as in "be on time and be ready to go" as everyone practically lived for such a thing. King added that the passionate North-South rivalry had been fueled by guys before him. "That just got passed down," he pointed out. "My generation didn't start it. It was the generation before me in the 70s that cranked it up."

As best I can recall, Johnny Mac consisted of players from the Southside while River City represented the Northside.

From the first whistle it was a battle like I'd never seen before. To call it intense would be an insult to the word intense; as Nigel from Spinal Tap might say, "This was at 11." The referee was not loose at all; he could sense the tension and was "in a zone" of his own. There are certain games whereby each moment is magical—throughout the entire match—and this phenomenon doesn't happen very often. In this case, the battle never stopped, the skill was of the highest order, the focus was nonstop, the intensity was nonstop, and every possible scenario happened in terms of perfect passes, wall passes, artistic dribbling, hard tackles, slide tackles, quality shots on goal, great saves, and drama...which all occurred at a continuous high frequency that never let up. Could you imagine the game ended 0-0? Well, somehow, someway, it did. But it felt like 3-3.

Based on this game, at that age, these two spectacular teams could've gone across the globe and played any team from any country, against a hypothetical Messi or Beckham or Beckenbauer, and won. Johnny Mac and the best U14 side from Munich—you wouldn't have seen the difference. As we get into older age levels, in the adult world of international soccer, this changes. Or, anyway, it has always changed in regards to "American soccer" (which is improving year by year). But at U14, these two teams, among others from St. Louis, could've taken anyone in the world. I saw this firsthand, when, at around this very age, I lived in Brazil for a time and played with top players from Porto Alegre. I realized their best were the same as SLYSA.

There was a time when a multitude of St. Louis players, all products of the St. Louis youth soccer landscape, played for the USMNT. In fact, the USMNT has been riddled with St. Louis talent over the years. There was the USMNT in the 1950 World Cup that started five St. Louis players against England, one of which was Harry Keough. Bob Kehoe served as captain (1965) and later as coach of the USMNT (1972). Additionally, there was Pat McBride, Al Trost (who was captain of the USMNT), and Dennis Vaninger—three players that represented the national team in the 1970s. In the late 1970s, the tradition continued as Greg Villa, Ty Keough, Tony Bellinger, Perry Van der Beck, Steve Pecher (who was captain of the USMNT), and Greg Makowski were on the USMNT together. As you may have guessed, each in the latter group had a St. Louis background. (Despite a championship disparity, this, in effect, was very similar to how Spain fielded a national team with a large number of Barcelona players circa 2008-12.)

These were the types of players that influenced the generation of kids in the Johnny Mac vs. River City Kickers game I was lucky to see. In fact, a special game like that arguably might be impossible without such influential players before them—to lay down groundwork, a foundation, a paradigm.

As mentioned earlier, Scott Gallagher—with its previous connection to Saint Louis FC and its likely connection in the future to St. Louis City SC—essentially functions as a "La Masia" get-up.

Minus a grand entrance announcing such a thing, St. Louis—as a whole, before Scott Gallagher's functioning role—had actually served as an unofficial La Masia of sorts. This had been so based on generation after generation of former players having passed their knowledge of the game on within the confines of an organized, and passionate, club soccer scene.

Of course, at La Masia—the youth academy for FC Barcelona in Spain—a certain style is emphasized and the players live and breathe soccer. They get used to being around strong competition, elite coaches, elite star players, and the atmosphere of a real, live, professional game that takes place in a classic stadium (Camp Nou). As they get older, a few here and there make the top team of Barcelona. As a result, some of these players will represent the Spanish national team. When they eventually take center stage, they're ready. La Masia is crucial for the development of Barcelona's talent, and, hence, for that of Spain's national team. Such a system in place would only benefit the USMNT. As such, efforts *are in place* as we speak, across the United States, as each MLS franchise is more or less trying to emulate such a thing.

To reiterate, St. Louis, in its own unofficial way, has been doing this for generations; currently, the obvious future relationship between St. Louis City SC and Scott Gallagher is essentially a formula for a ground zero headquarters for a "La Masia" in St. Louis. Such a relationship can trace its roots back to a much earlier time—like an ancient Mayan calendar, with high points and kings that ruled—in the grand existence of St. Louis soccer. All the knowledge and wisdom from the days of Bob Guelker, Harry Keough, Bob Kehoe, and others, spilled over to the next generation of players. As Pat McBride, Jim Leeker, John Pisani, Gary Rensing, and others, took their talents to the St. Louis Stars, there was a younger generation present, taking it all in, such as Dan King, a former ball-boy for the Stars, who eventually played for a youth US national team, won two national championships with Indiana University, played some pro, and eventually coached the men's program at UMSL where he's passed on his knowledge of the game to the next generation of players.

The inevitable relationship between Scott Gallagher and St. Louis City SC is one that will benefit youth soccer in St. Louis and the product on the field for St. Louis City SC. As a result, if cards are played correctly, this connection should also benefit that of the USMNT—hence, US soccer fans around the nation.

It's interesting how the top brass of Barcelona has influenced its youth players, just as the leaders of St. Louis City SC will influence youth players in and around St. Louis...just as the top players from yesterday influenced the great St. Louis club teams of the past, ranging from

Simpkins-Ford to Kutis to Busch, as well as the fantastic play on the field exhibited by Johnny Mac and River City Kickers in 1989 at the St. Louis Invitational Tournament. From club, high school, college, to pro, we now have the ultimate prize: St. Louis City SC. Each step along the way has played a pivotal role in bringing an MLS franchise to the River City. Each, which should come as no surprise, is interrelated.

Following club soccer, the next step, quite obviously, is high school. While high school players still remain on club teams during 9th through 12th grades, high school competition acts as the next level in which school pride is on the line, as are potential college scholarships for individual players. As such, within the corridors of high school soccer, St. Louis has reigned supreme.

ST. LOUIS HIGH SCHOOLS

In our modern era, 1968-69 was the first Missouri state championship for high schools. First place went to the mighty and powerful, CBC.

On the Illinois side of the river, the St. Louis Metro East, the first state championship for high schools was in 1972-73 and first place went to legendary, Granite City. Among the great St. Louis high school powers, St. Thomas Aquinas-Mercy, CBC, Whitfield, and Vianney stand out above the rest of the class that includes De Smet, St. Mary's, and Chaminade, to name a few.

We'll save the best for last. Let's first take a look at the Metro East.

The coach that led Granite City to legendary status was Gene Baker, the great Gene Baker, who, coincidentally, attended CBC in his time. After he had collegiate success—as an outside back, Baker reached the top of the mountain by winning a national NCAA Division I title with SLU—he eventually moved onto Granite City High School where he coached the team to nine of its 10 state titles (1972, 1976, 1977, 1978, 1979, 1980, 1982, 1987, 1989, 1990). That is still the number one record for a soccer coach in Illinois high school history. In the most complimentary way possible, it's an ostentatious collection of trophies. St. Louis native and former USMNT captain, Al Trost, said, "What he did with Granite City was great." In harmony with the overwhelming amount of success, in 1989, Baker won The Jimmy Dunn "Coach of the Year" award (a distinguished honor for coaches in the area), and in 1997 he was inducted into the St. Louis Soccer Hall of Fame (another distinguished honor specific to St. Louis talent). Baker was a powerhouse coach, leading a powerhouse program. As he said, "I was lucky to have a lot of talented teams." He was also fortunate to have been coached at SLU by Bob Guelker (the SLU, SIUE, and US Olympic soccer team coach), and Baker took what he learned to Granite City with astounding results.

At the 2020 St. Louis Sports Hall of Fame Induction of Southern Illinois Sports Legends—held in the grand auditorium of the Gateway Classic Cars dealership in O'Fallon, Illinois, not too far from where Yadier Molina lived for a time while catching for the Cardinals—I saw the crowd roar for Gene Baker from my seat next to the gracious Jamie and Ellen Auffenberg (of the renowned Auffenberg Dealer Group), who were co-sponsors of the event that was put together by experienced organizers, Greg Marecek and Tim Moore. The crowd's response to Baker was like revisiting an epic era—an almost mystical time lost in the decades—when Gene and Granite City reigned supreme throughout the St. Louis area and all of Illinois.

The Illinois schools of the Metro East—a close geographical component of St. Louis—had to travel north to Chicago, where a tough soccer tradition awaited. Despite the level of the opposition, Granite City continually proved it was special.

Granite City's presence throughout Illinois proved to be an ambassadorship of sorts that reminded those in Chicago—who had often mistakenly assumed dominance over St. Louis-land—that Granite City, ipso facto St. Louis, might, in fact, be the king of soccer.

It can be said that Granite City wasn't the only show across the river. Although throughout Illinois, from the 70s through the 90s, it certainly was the undisputed king. As such it had many challengers, though its biggest threat wouldn't come from Chicago schools, but rather a Metro East neighbor.

Herb Roach—the Mayor of O'Fallon, Illinois, a lifelong sports fan—commented, "Collinsville has produced some very good soccer teams, and so has Granite City!" He added, "You talk about two hotbeds for soccer in high school, those two were very-very good!"

Granite City's biggest rival, Collinsville High School, would be like a worthy challenger with four state titles (1981, 1986, 1991, 1992), and less powerful schools subsequently followed. Indeed, in order to graduate to the state tournament, Granite City had other foes to contend with, such as Alton, Edwardsville, Troy, and Belleville, but Collinsville was the epitome of a rival, with sold-out crowds—laden with longstanding bitter respect for one another—for each encounter.

Granite City and Collinsville produced high school legends—Dave Fernandez, Craig Stahl, Joe Reiniger, John van Buskirk, Steve VanDyke, along with 'demi-gods' like Jeff Stephens and Shawn Petroski—that arguably were as good or better than any St. Louis-side player. Joe Reiniger, incidentally, went on to join the greatest all-time scorers in pro indoor history with over 600 goals. In addition, Reiniger was a key member of the St. Louis Ambush team that won the NPSL championship in 1995, which happens to be St. Louis' only pro soccer league title (to date). Furthermore, one surely not to be left out from mention would be Steve Trittschuh (a former USMNT defender that suited up in World Cup 1990 and coached Saint Louis FC), who went to Granite City North—when the schools were split up—at a time when Granite City South was the dominant side.

Part of the allure of Granite City and Collinsville is that the titles were achieved during a time when there was only one state champion.

Since the Illinois state tournament separated into a class system based on school size (which began in 1997-98), other state champions from the Metro East include Edwardsville High School (2000, 2013), whose coach was Mark Heiderscheid; Alton Marquette (2012, 2017); Waterloo Gibault Catholic (2005, 2006, 2007, 2013); and Waterloo H.S. (2015).

Make no mistake, the Metro East has produced prominent and supremely talented schools for many years, talented enough to set records in Illinois. Still to this day, Gene Baker and Granite City have the most state championships in Illinois' history—but the big show resides in St. Louis. Who has been the best in Missouri high school soccer? Within the realm of Missouri high schools, where the top schools of the nation have resided for generations, it basically has been a battle within the St. Louis metropolitan area. "Basically" is code for it starts and ends in St. Louis. Some resistance has arisen in past years from Kansas City, mainly in the form of Rockhurst, and, to some extent, Cape Girardeau, but, by and large, it has always been a showdown between the best of St. Louis.

From 1968 through 1984, Missouri had one high school soccer champion. Then, in the 1985 season, Missouri switched to Class 1A-3A (small schools), and 4A (big schools). In the 2002 season, Missouri switched to Class 1, 2, and 3 ("3" being the biggest schools). As of 2014, Missouri tumbled into Class 1, 2, 3, and 4 ("4" being the biggest schools).

The hierarchy of Missouri state high school champions from St. Louis would go as follows: St. Thomas Aquinas-Mercy (11),§ CBC (10), Whitfield (8), Vianney (7), De Smet (6), St. Mary's (6), Rosary (5), St. Dominic (5), John Burroughs (4), Chaminade (3), Priory (3), and St. Louis University High School (3). Outside of these leaders, there are a number of schools with one or two championships.

St. Thomas Aquinas-Mercy and Rosary have since merged into Trinity Catholic High School. Both St. Thomas Aquinas-Mercy and Rosary were located a short drive north of downtown St. Louis—huddled under the Missouri River to the north, bordered by the Mississippi River to the east—and both were top powers.

---

§ Two titles were under St. Thomas Aquinas.

In the case of St. Thomas Aquinas-Mercy, it was, and still is, the best of the best with a record 11 state titles (1975, 1977, 1985, 1988, 1989, 1990, 1992, 1993, 1996, 1997, 1998). It was a school that sat atop the throne of greatness—with top level players coming in and out of its doors such as Steve Sullivan, Bob Bozada, Perry Van der Beck, Dan King, and Mike Sorber—that was largely overseen by the mastermind, a coach of extraordinary talents, Vince Drake.

A list of the players he coached is a testament to Drake's greatness. Perry Van der Beck jumped right from high school to the NASL and eventually was named U.S. Soccer Player of the Year in 1985. Following in Drake's footsteps, Greg Koeller, a former player, has taken what he learned from Drake and turned it into a phenomenal coaching career at St. Dominic High School; Koeller has earned five state championships coaching the boys and certainly might get more. Dan King won two national NCAA Division I championships with Indiana as a defender and eventually became head coach at UMSL. Mike Sorber, who won two state titles with Drake—in 1985 and 1988—went onto represent the USMNT as a midfielder in the 1994 FIFA World Cup (where he became known as the MVP of the team) and eventually joined the coaching staff as an assistant alongside Bob Bradley on the sideline during the 2010 FIFA World Cup.

Drake—who was an outside defender for St. Louis University—won The Jimmy Dunn "Coach of the Year" award in 1990 and was inducted into the St. Louis Soccer Hall of Fame in 2014. Drake has touched so many lives as coach that one would need an abacus to keep an accurate count. As he told me, there were a lot of talented players that won all those state titles. From exposure to Bob Guelker, Drake was endowed with perfect qualities for a coach: he's smart, calm in nature, open-minded, interested in new ideas, perspicacious to detail, topped off with an approach that favors skill and intelligent passing. All of which was a formula for long-term success, which set St. Thomas Aquinas-Mercy apart as the all-time leader in Missouri high school state championships...to date.

The next greatest high school program following closely behind St. Thomas Aquinas-Mercy is the illustrious Christian Brothers College, or simply, CBC. (And not "Cannon Ball Cleaners" as some rivals may lead you to think.) With St. Thomas Aquinas-Mercy out of the way, CBC is unequivocally *the* school for soccer. "Men for tomorrow. Brothers for life." This is the motto of CBC, a private all-boys school founded in 1850. Adorning purple, gold, and white as school colors, the powerhouse soccer school resides due west of downtown St. Louis, about 20 minutes without traffic, near the Saint Louis Galleria mall. (Once upon a time, CBC was located just east of the Galleria. Somewhat recently it relocated, placing it a bit west of the Galleria.)

It was CBC that kicked things off back in 1968-69, when it won the first Missouri high school state championship as recognized by the Missouri State High School Activities Association (MSHSAA). All in all, CBC has acquired 10 state titles (1968, 1983, 1984, 1988, 2004, 2005, 2009, 2012, 2016, 2018), just one shy of St. Thomas Aquinas-Mercy.

After perusing the archives of history that is CBC, it's easy to recognize a salient feature. With great players heretofore like Harry Ratican, Jimmy Dunn, Jimmy Roe, Carl Gentile, Tommy Howe, Don Droege, Jeff Sendobry, Mike Freitag, Daryl Doran, Mark and Chris Santel, Jeff DiMaria, Brandon Barklage, Zach Bauer, and Tom Heinemann, CBC has set the standard for high-quality high school soccer. Often defenders don't get as much recognition as they should. However, one-time member of the Houston Dynamo, and well-traveled defender, A.J. Cochran, may change your mind as he earned a state championship with CBC, All-American honors and received the Missouri Gatorade Soccer Player of the Year award in 2011. (Keep in mind, with defenders over the years like A.J. Cochran and Jeff Sendobry, and all-around talents like Daryl Doran, most CBC Varsity squads could trounce a number of college teams.)

Similar to how Brazil enters a World Cup as a team loaded with talent, the team to watch, with expectations to win the whole thing, CBC has a similar drumbeat following its every move and is expected to win the Missouri state championship year after year. In doing so, it's not just the players on the field that matter. The coach is quite often a driving force behind continual success.

The Jimmy Dunn "Coach of the Year" in 1991 went to Terry Michler. Subsequently, in 2008, he was inducted into the St. Louis Soccer Hall of Fame. Michler—a legendary coach, with praise showered on him for generations—is found at the top of the list for all-time winning high school coaches nationwide. In addition, he was responsible for eight of CBC's historic titles. Now that St. Thomas Aquinas-Mercy is no longer a program, the door is wide open for CBC to take the lead.

In the 2002 season, Whitfield—a smaller private school founded in 1952 and wearing green and white—jumped out to gain its first state title for soccer, which, frankly, was something to which Whitfield had not been accustomed. In doing so, Whitfield dominated its class and has gathered eight state championships (2002, 2003, 2004, 2006, 2007, 2009, 2010, 2021). Its coach for seven of those trophies, Bill Daues, a student of the game, joined an elite class in 2008 as he was inducted into the St. Louis Soccer Hall of Fame, and thereafter received The Jimmy Dunn "Coach of the Year" award in 2011.

Throughout his reign, Daues had some help from heavy talent, such as Todd Wallace, Jay Alberts (who eventually went to Yale before playing professionally), Joe Klosterman, and Trevor House, among others. Indeed, very few players can claim a 'Pele moment' by scoring a bicycle-kick, much less to win a game and a championship. Somehow, Doug Londoff pulled all that off in the 2004 Missouri high school state championship game with a bicycle-kick to win it all, in the second overtime, no less...a legendary individual moment for a program—at that point in time—earning its place in the record books.

Outside of the actual state championships, of which there have been many, a significant milestone occurred in a game back in 2004-05, under the sideline leadership of Head Coach Daues, and Assistant Coach Michael Quantes, in which Whitfield managed to upset perennial powerhouse CBC by a score of 1-0.

The overall inference one gathers from Whitfield is that, despite enrollment size, it is a school no longer ensconced only in the world of academic achievement, but one that is ready for the best of the best on the soccer pitch.

Located in the southwestern section of St. Louis, where you find Kirkwood and Fenton, Vianney High School—which is very close to the Fenton location of World Wide Technology Soccer Park—is the next big gun that has won a walloping seven Missouri high school state championships (1978, 1980, 1981, 1982, 1987, 1991, 1992). Founded in 1960, the black and gold of Vianney—the Golden Griffins—has echoed quality—of the highest order—throughout the ages. Coach Mike Villa led the way for six of those state championships. Villa was awarded The Jimmy Dunn "Coach of the Year" in 1988; in 1999 Villa was inducted into the St. Louis Soccer Hall of Fame.

During the early 80s, Jeff Jacober—the son of legendary St. Louis Cardinals voice, Ron Jacober—was a defender for Vianney that was part of state championship glory. As the early 90s came around, Tony Williams and Casey Klipfel, two standout players, helped lead the team. Despite a three-peat (1980, 1981, 1982) and back-to-back championships (1991, 1992), there has been a long absence of titles, which eventually surpassed 25 years. However, given the rich tradition of soccer at Vianney, it wouldn't be surprising to see a comeback down the road.

In the hunt for seven state titles, and close behind the front of the pack, is none other than De Smet. The highly reputable private school founded in 1967 has attained six championships to date (1991, 1993, 1995, 1997, 2011, 2019). The maroon and white school colors of De Smet are on display in its location out west of St. Louis where you find Creve Coeur and Frontenac. Nearby are school neighbors, John Burroughs, Chaminade, CBC, Priory, and Whitfield.

Led in large part by standout coach, Greg Vitello, De Smet has cemented a case for being one of the best in a region of the country that exudes soccer royalty. Vitello won The Jimmy Dunn "Coach of the Year" award in 1992, and was inducted into the St. Louis Soccer Hall of Fame in 2016—a well-deserved collection of honors for the top-level, distinguished coach, one of the finest in the area.

For all intents and purposes, De Smet, a true power in the Valley of the Kings of St. Louis high school programs, has produced a number of top-level players over the years, some of whom would include the likes of Sam Bick (a defender who subsequently played for the hometown St. Louis Steamers along with the USMNT), Eric Delabar (an All-American goalie at De Smet that also was a member of the St. Louis Steamers), Matt McKeon (a midfielder that was an All-American at De Smet before he played in MLS and for the USMNT), Chris Klein (a Scott Gallagher standout who played in MLS, for the USMNT, and became President of the LA Galaxy), Craig Corbett (somewhat of a legend in Scott Gallagher that all but disappeared from the soccer scene; like his cohorts, he was a super-talent, one of the best you'd come across who played for SLU and the Lafayette Swampcats), Pat Noonan (a top-level talent who played for a handful of MLS teams and the USMNT), and Will Bruin (a forward who won the Missouri Gatorade Player of the Year before moving on to Indiana University, MLS, and the USMNT). The list goes on, and great players at De Smet could likely fill up two or three books. The high-quality of De Smet is a testament to the overall caliber of St. Louis high school programs across-the-board. Out west you'll find De Smet resting in wait, as the green and white colors of St. Mary's represent the south. With roots dating back to the 1930s, St. Mary's High became known as such in 1947.

One could easily point to St. Thomas Aquinas-Mercy, CBC, and Vianney as the top programs, and leave the conversation there. However, as most in St. Louis know already, if a person were to espouse such a belief there are many blanks yet to be filled in and such a biased, one-sided, opinion of powerhouse programs in St. Louis would be unjust, to put it lightly. If by chance a scientist—embedded within the walls of an MIT laboratory—wanted to explore the matter at length, he or she might want to finesse over a theory. If, indeed, a scientist espoused a theory that multiple powerhouse programs sprinkle the greater St.

Louis landscape with brilliance—like a ten dollar pumpkin latte with a perfect amount of cinnamon resting atop the foam on a brisk October morning—it would certainly include De Smet, and, without a doubt, the supreme St. Mary's High School. When it comes to the Southside, St. Mary's—situated exceedingly close to the Mississippi River, resting in the neighborhood of Dutchtown that holds a connection to the German heritage, a short jaunt from the Anheuser-Busch Brewery—has a very proud history. It is top of the list with St. Louis soccer programs. Its share of accomplishments dates back to 1969, when St. Mary's earned the first of six state championships (1969, 1995, 1999, 2000, 2001, 2010).

Rosary High is a little-known jewel from yesteryear. Back before Trinity Catholic High School, there was St. Thomas Aquinas-Mercy and Rosary High—soccer royalty, perched in the north of St. Louis—resting in wait. Both were east of Florissant; northeast of Ferguson; just northwest of Granite City and separated by the Mississippi River—like castles in 14th century Europe, looking down on the south and west portions of the metropolitan area with pity. Eventually the schools merged into what is currently Trinity Catholic High School. While St. Thomas Aquinas-Mercy was ruthlessly marching through opposition, Rosary, the smaller of the two, was making a name for itself in similar fashion as it managed to rise above the competition with stellar teams. In fact, for the first Missouri state championship back in 1968, Rosary finished second to CBC. In 1969, Rosary took second place yet again, losing to St. Mary's. One may view 'second-place finishes' as *de minimis* but they are telling. Then in 1970, Rosary acquired its first of five state titles (1970, 1979, 1985, 1987, 1991).

As someone that played against these high schools, knowing the history as I do (which means blabbering about these things from time to time in a manner that might, to a passerby or skeptical viewer, seem superfluous), I can assure you of the importance of such schools—Rosary and St. Thomas Aquinas-Mercy, for instance—that are rooted deep in the heart of the nervous system of St. Louis soccer. Without these schools (and the success they generated for St. Louis at large), and the efforts of club, college and pro soccer, there might not be impetus for an MLS team, after all! These schools—their soccer programs—are part of the bedrock of St. Louis soccer; as such, high school soccer is but a piece of the ever-fascinating puzzle that gradually delineates the whole picture. Rosary—a powerhouse obscured by the daunting shadow of St. Thomas Aquinas-Mercy—contributed to this overall picture of St. Louis soccer with such greats as Don Ebert, who eventually played for SIUE and the St. Louis Steamers, Greg Makowski, who played for SIUE, the St. Louis Steamers, and the USMNT, and none other than former pro player and co-owner of St. Louis City SC, Jim Kavanaugh.

Rosary might be a program from antiquity—a program no more, save for Trinity Catholic High School—though it lives on in the memory bank of St. Louis soccer. As Rosary and its neighbor St. Thomas Aquinas-Mercy are out of the picture—again, save for Trinity Catholic High—the door has opened up for new powers to emerge.

And how about Trinity Catholic High School? Whether or not it can garner a state soccer title is yet to be seen. Indeed Don Schmidt—its talented head coach in recent years who previously served as an assistant to Vince Drake—has his work cut out for him. About midway between the Mississippi and Missouri Rivers, where the rivers appear to bend away from one another on a map, you'll find the blue and white colors of St. Dominic High School.* Nonetheless, St. Dominic—which is located way out in O'Fallon, Missouri, northwest of St. Louis, just a bit west of

---

*   Geographically speaking, in this region the Mississippi River—on its north to south route—takes a curvy detour around the northern boundary of St. Louis; the Missouri River—which happens to be the longest river in North America that starts out in Montana and eventually meets here with the Mississippi—branches out to the southwest as it eventually forms a clumsy connection westward to Kansas City. Coincidentally, the confluence of the two rivers is actually near the— it's a terribly long title—Edward "Ted" and Pat Jones-Confluence Point State Park, on the Missouri side a short drive north of downtown St. Louis; and, on the Illinois side, you'll find the Lewis and Clark State Memorial Park, which is bordered by Hartford, Illinois, a village in Madison County most people tend to avoid, and the northern part of Granite City, another area scarcely visited.

St. Charles and St. Peters—is an unlikely candidate to be such a power-player in the greater St. Louis soccer community. Yet, St. Dominic's success speaks to the talent from St. Charles, St. Peters, and O'Fallon.

One such player, Tim Ream, subsequently played with Bolton Wanderers, Fulham, and the USMNT (whereby he's been a captain). Still though, St. Dominic—a private school that opened its doors back in 1962—is a relative newcomer to the world of Missouri state titles, with five to date (2004, 2008, 2009, 2012, 2013), and those trophies were overseen by Coach Greg Koeller, winner of The Jimmy Dunn "Coach of the Year" award in 2010.

Following close behind St. Dominic would be the blue and gold of John Burroughs, a small private school founded in 1923 that is situated on the western front of St. Louis (technically Ladue), which is surrounded by Richmond Heights, Clayton, University City, Olivette, Creve Coeur, Frontenac, Huntleigh, Rock Hill, and Brentwood—each is within driving proximity to the Central West End, the Galleria, and Frontenac shopping destinations. In similar fashion to St. Dominic, John Burroughs jumped into the game of amassing state titles relatively recently (in the grand scheme of things). Coach Alan Trzecki had a lot to do with opulent hardware rolling into the halls of John Burroughs whose program has four championships to date (2008, 2013, 2016, 2018).

Chaminade College Preparatory School—a private school west of downtown St. Louis resting between Creve Coeur and Frontenac—might not have quite the cachet that CBC has, but don't be fooled so quickly. Certainly Chaminade—whose top alum includes Brad Davis (formerly of the USMNT)—is a highly regarded school. Granted, it has some catching up to do in terms of state titles yet it's a school with a strong soccer program that warrants a tremendous amount of respect. Founded in 1910, the cardinal and white colors of Chaminade took flight in a big way back in the 1990s and specifically the early-to-mid 2000s when it won three state titles (2001, 2002, 2006). Who'd have thought that with only three state titles (so far) Chaminade could arguably have fielded perhaps the best high school team in Missouri's history? Such conversations, debates—or arguments—come down to opinion. Be that as it may, some circles have concluded the 2001 side could be one of the best, if not the best, in state history.

There was progress leading up to this legendary title run. Brad Davis and company had strong performances in the 90s. In fact, in 1998, Coach Mike Gauvain—an imposing former forward who is an avid sports fan—won The Jimmy Dunn "Coach of the Year" award. Things were rolling in a good direction.

Under the auspices of Coach Gauvain (a former US youth national team member alongside Dan King), Chaminade finally earned its first soccer championship in school history during the 2001 campaign. Kevin Robson played an integral role for Chaminade in the 2001 and 2002 championships. In point of fact, with a touch of Midwest sincerity and confidence, Robson told me: "Not to brag but we were very, very good. I mean we would just throttle teams. Our entire starting 11 went to Division 1, and that doesn't happen anywhere." He added: "We won the state final 4-0 and the semifinal 4-0." Humble, astute, and veracious, a true Midwest virtue; Robson was correct; it was a team for the ages. The 2001 group, which was inducted into Chaminade's Hall of Fame, attacked opponents with an assortment of weapons. There's fast, then there's the guy that's a little faster than the fast guys, which would be midfielder Danny Wynn, who, subsequently, played with the New England Revolution. Tim Collico, a forward that was "Named St. Louis Post-Dispatch Player of the Year,"[46] scored six game-winning goals in six playoff games. As Robson said, "That's unheard of."

While the 2001 team was special, Chaminade has continually kept up with the standard of excellence that is St. Louis high school soccer, fielding great teams and players. The Missouri Gatorade Soccer Player of the Year award has landed with four Chaminade talents: Brad Davis, Tim Collico, Mike Roach, and the most recent, Tommy Barlow, in 2013.

Lost in the forest of soccer giants, just a short drive west of Chaminade, would be the private school of Priory (St. Louis Priory School). Gallantly parading around as a smaller-medium-sized school, Priory has won the

Missouri state championship three times to this point (2005, 2011, 2017). Founded back in 1956, the red and blue colors of Priory fly high with the hopes of yet another title.

While SLUH—St. Louis University High School—has always had a very strong reputation for quality soccer, to the present time it has acquired three championships somewhat surreptitiously over three different decades (1972, 1990, 2003). If you can believe it, SLUH dates back to 1818. The private all-boys school owes its three championships to coaches Charles Martel (1), and Ebbie Dunn (2).

As is the case with rival schools, so many top-level players have graced the halls of SLUH.

John DiRaimondo—a midfielder that played for Colorado Rapids and D.C. United—took a somewhat different path to the high school experience as *Wikipedia* mentions part of that journey in that "DiRaimondo went through an accelerated high school program at St. Louis University High that allowed him to graduate a year early alongside fellow soccer player and childhood friend Brian Grazier. While on the team, DiRaimondo lived in Florida and was roommates with Grazier. In 2003, he was named as a Parade Magazine All-American and competed in the McDonald's All-American game. DiRaimondo received Student-Athlete of the Year in 2001 and completed high school being on the honor roll all four years."[47]

Prior to DiRaimondo, and plenty of others in the past few years even, there are a couple names that stand out significantly as well.

Few in St. Louis, or around the country, can lay claim to such an impressive list of achievements as Bob Kehoe. Back in 1943, he was on SLUH's original soccer team. Following his high school graduation in 1947, Kehoe, a multi-talented athlete, actually found himself in the farm system of the Philadelphia Phillies for a time, although, he preferred soccer, and baseball wasn't meant to be. As a defender, Kehoe not only found success with Kutis, he also played for the St. Louis Stars, coached the Stars, was captain for the USMNT, and later coached the USMNT.

Just before attending St. Louis University (where he received collegiate All-American honors), Pat McBride attended SLUH where his teams placed second in the district during his junior and senior years. This was an interesting time that was slightly before the 1968-69 introduction of the state tournament for Missouri high schools. While McBride might not have been part of the Missouri high school state tournament, his colossal list of accomplishments, well-known to many, goes on like an impressive ancient Egyptian scroll describing the conquests of a lauded king. Anyone that manages to win a NCAA Division I national championship at St. Louis University, then lead the St. Louis Stars and USMNT from midfield, and coach the original St. Louis Steamers is worthy of a king's mention.

Before becoming a NCAA Division I soccer champion with St. Louis University and later the CEO and Secretary General of the U.S. Soccer Federation, where he organized soccer for the entire United States for over a decade, the great Dan Flynn was enrolled at SLUH.

Tim Twellman went to SLUH before attending SIUE and then moving on to a pro career that began with the Minnesota Kicks and ended with the Kansas City Comets. Along the way, Tim suited up for a game with the USMNT in 1982. In 2020, he was appointed to the role of sporting community relations consultant with St. Louis City SC.

Ty Keough is one of the biggest names in St. Louis soccer history and was a midfielder at SLUH just prior to his All-American honors at St. Louis University. He had an illustrious pro career that included many years with the Steamers and time with the USMNT. Eventually Keough joined the field of broadcasting that saw him call international and World Cup games for ABC, ESPN, and TNT.

Great players exist in abundance in St. Louis; in fact, it would be hard *not* to find one. SLUH was lucky to have Kehoe, McBride, Flynn, Twellman, Keough, and things kept going in a positive direction with Jeff Cacciatore.

Jeff Cacciatore—a quick and elusive forward that stood around 5'2"—suited up for SLUH and electrified the field. His superb abilities were recruited by Bob Guelker at SIUE and the two teamed up with other greats to earn the NCAA Division I national championship in 1979. Thereafter, Cacciatore was well-known during the early days of the St. Louis Steamers—in its entire white, blue, and green splendor—which happened to be the golden era of indoor soccer where he scored 70 goals from 1981-87.

As time progressed, a future SLUH standout—much younger than Cacciatore and his contemporaries—would rise to eclipse Cacciatore's forward-playing lore, and represent not just SLUH but all of St. Louis for generations to follow.

Taylor Twellman was just an ordinary high schooler. Think again. Inside St. Louis University High School there might as well be a special wall entitled: "The Best Athlete in St. Louis University High School History: Taylor Twellman." As *Wikipedia* pointed out: "Taylor was raised in St. Louis, Missouri, and attended Saint Louis University High School (SLUH), where he was an all-star athlete in American football, basketball, soccer, and baseball, in which he was offered a contract by the Kansas City Royals. After graduating from SLUH in 1998, Twellman rejected the offer, electing to play soccer at Maryland on an athletic scholarship."[48] Twellman subsequently played for the New England Revolution, won the 2005 MLS MVP, represented the USMNT as a forward, and then transitioned to the microphone for various pro and international games as a TV broadcaster.

All in all, the St. Louis high school soccer landscape has been—and will continue to be—nothing less than first-class—the envy of the nation.

ST. LOUIS COLLEGES: THE EARLY DAYS

ST. LOUIS UNIVERSITY: THE MYTH, THE LEGEND!

To this day, St. Louis University stands at the helm of college soccer royalty with a record 10 NCAA Division I championships (1959, 1960, 1962, 1963, 1965, 1967, 1969, 1970, 1972, 1973).[†]

It should be noted that prior to 1959, in which the NCAA Division I tournament first launched, there were numerous champions from 1905-58. These years are said to be unofficial. These previous champions fell under the umbrella of the ISFL (Intercollegiate Soccer Football League), the ISFA (Intercollegiate Soccer Football Association), and something called the Soccer Bowl, which—appropriately—didn't last long. Without a law degree, one could still verifiably argue in court that from 1905-58 a rather unreliable way of attaining a champion was sought through different avenues.

Outside the possibility of some obscure book from 1950, entitled something like "A Chronology, East Coast Collegiate Soccer Men: Champions, Gentlemen, Owners of Yachts, Poets, Sturdy Statesmen,"[‡] it's difficult to find a history on pre-1959 college soccer champions. Let's just say, resting quietly, dormant in the archives of *Wikipedia*, you'll find that from 1926-35, champions were "Determined by the Intercollegiate Soccer Football Association"[49] or, for example, from 1936-40, without a selection from the ISFA, the champions consisted of "...outstanding teams that claim a share of the championship."[50] Claim a share? That's what happened.

This 1905-58 timespan should be thought of as the pre-college soccer era (even though it was *college soccer*), a time in which the game was growing and the national championship wasn't quite as we

---

[†]   Some say nine championships because of the 1967 co-championship St. Louis University shared with Michigan State due to weather. However, most would agree that SLU and Michigan State were co-champions in 1967 thus garnering the Billikens with 10 titles.

[‡]   Such a book is meant for Bob Bradley's basement shelf (with a plethora of bookmarks and previous notations).

know it today (i.e., from 1959 onward). Essentially, from an era where teams were probably delivering goal kicks with a toe-ball, we have an unofficial extended list of champions. When teams "claim a share of the championship" it thus leaves the idea of what a champion should be in disarray. For example, in 1926, evidently there were *three* champions (Penn State, Princeton, and Harvard). Okay. In 1935, there was *one* champion (Yale). That's more like it. Hold on though. In 1936, evidently there were *four* champions (Penn State, Princeton, West Chester, and Syracuse), which makes no sense whatsoever. It's kind of like how an octopus has three hearts and nine brains—it's unclear why, but it is *what it is*. When it comes down to it, we have what appears to be quasi-champions. Therefore, these champions have a well-deserved footnote following them wherever they go. In a weird way, it's a bit like someone getting an obsolete degree from Harvard.

This is not to say these pre-1959 schools are completely illegitimate. To the contrary. We're just having a little fun with the different approaches to crowning a champion or in some cases, champions. In fact, many Ivy League schools, and other East Coast colleges, helped push soccer to where we have it today. And many great players came out of that environment.[§] Ivy League schools, and other East Coast programs, such as Penn State, Haverford, and Springfield College, are very much a part of American soccer history. And they should be applauded. But, in terms of true champions, it was a different time.

Lo and behold, with the advent of the NCAA Division I Men's Soccer Tournament in 1959, the waters of uncertainty were calmed.

Enter St. Louis University, the king of college soccer. Founded in 1818, a long time ago, SLU is a private university located a bit due west of downtown St. Louis—in the active neighborhood of Midtown, just off of I-64. The new MLS stadium, which took so long to come to fruition,

---

[§]   Down the road a bit, in the post-1959 era, Bob Bradley played at Princeton (in the 1970s) and later coached there as well. In addition, Bruce Arena and Dave Sarachan played for Cornell (in the 1970s).

rests in the neighborhood of Downtown West, which is just "east" of SLU a tiny bit. Let's step back a little bit (going east to west), there's downtown St. Louis, followed by Downtown West, Midtown, Central West End, and Forest Park (along with a bunch of other auxiliary neighborhoods nearby like The Tiffany, but who's counting that?). Essentially, between the neighborhoods of Downtown West and Central West End you'll find SLU. Or, quite simply, in laymen's terms, between downtown St. Louis and Forest Park—there's SLU. Wew. (Who thought geography could be so much fun?!) It's an area that Mike and Frank from *American Pickers* would probably love to visit. Then again, they'd probably go to Soulard, an artsy-industrial area south of downtown where city-folks wear overalls and your breakfast order might take anywhere from two to three hours. Then you have the famous Soulard Farmers Market; not to mention, older roads that will depreciate the value of your car by a decade. The price to pay for a classic St. Louis neighborhood.

Midtown, on the other hand, has a very convenient yet not-so-cozy entrance to the SLU campus by way of I-64 and an off-ramp—within a maze of off-ramps—that mysteriously blends in with an adjoined Starbucks and Chipotle—fully equipped with an aberrant flying saucer-like roof. Just a short walk over, the college hustle and bustle increases; the blue and white land of Billikens; there is even the glow of royal-blue streetlights at night. Hidden within its campus are majestic looking buildings—such as Queen's Daughters Hall—that offer a reminder of Western European castles 500 years distant.

With 10 titles, SLU is currently the leader of all NCAA Division I schools. In second place, Indiana University has eight, then Virginia has seven, and down the list it goes. This is truly astounding to think about. For years college soccer has been like a pro league in the United States, in lieu of an actual viable pro outdoor league, that is. For generations this was very much the case, especially regarding NCAA Division I schools before 1996 (when MLS kicked off). Even during the NASL days—essentially the late 1960s through the early 80s—there were only so many positions available for each team, therefore college soccer acted like a lower professional league. Then you get into the matter of athletic scholarships and realistically speaking, those players with scholarships were (and are) like pro athletes as tuition and living arrangements are being paid for (which isn't cheap). Wherein American players were seldom sought after for pro contracts in Europe and elsewhere, NCAA Division I competition was *the* place to be for American talent, and it was very competitive (as it is today). And to think, SLU—to this day—has come out on top as *the* all-time leader is something else special... especially but not only when you're talking about the same class as Indiana, Virginia, Maryland, UCLA, San Francisco, Stanford, North Carolina, Connecticut, Clemson, and Michigan State, all powerhouses.

Each year in college soccer, only one player can win the Hermann Trophy award for the best collegiate player in the country. (Incidentally, the Hermann Trophy resides in St. Louis, and it was created in honor of St. Louis-native Bob Hermann, who was very instrumental in the world of soccer and owned the St. Louis Stars.) From 1969-73, three St. Louis University players won this prestigious award. Midfielder Al Trost earned it in 1969 and 1970; forward Mike Seerey took it home in 1971 and 1972; and forward Dan Counce rounded things off in 1973.

Over the years, in addition to the aforementioned Hermann Trophy winners, so many talented players sported the SLU uniform, including but not limited to Gene Baker, Don Ceresia, Pat McBride, Carl Gentile, Bill McDermott, Gary Rensing, John Pisani, Vince Drake, Jim Leeker, Steve Frank, Gene Geimer, Jim Bokern, Joe Clarke, Dan Flynn, Don Droege, Ty Keough, Pete Collico, Larry Hulcer, Steve Sullivan, John Hayes, Daryl Doran, Jim Kavanaugh, Mark Santel, Steve Kuntz, Mike Sorber, Brian McBride, Shane Battelle, Matt McKeon, Tim Leonard, Casey Klipfel, Craig Corbett, Kevin Quigley, Kevin Kalish, Mike and Pat Moriarty, Mark Filla, Jeff DiMaria, Jack Jewsbury, Brad Davis, Danny Wynn, John DiRaimondo, Tim Ream, Brandon Barklage, Mike Roach, and Robert Kristo.*

---

* For an extended list of players, which is lengthy, see the SLU section in the Golden Vault.

From the viewpoint of possessing a sophisticated awareness of the game, which SLU obviously has nurtured, many former players have graduated to the coaching ranks where they have passed on their intimate knowledge of the game. As a testament to the greatness of SLU's program, Vince Drake, once a Billiken outside defender, went on to become the all-time leading high school coach for state championships in Missouri, arguably the most competitive high school soccer state in the nation.[†] He also established himself as a leader nationwide with total wins, in league with Terry Michler of Christian Brothers College, Miller Bugliari of Pingry School in New Jersey, Gene Chyzowych of Columbia High School in New Jersey, and Greg Vitello of De Smet. I got a sense of just why he reached that plateau in my interviews with him. As I talked with many people, he stood out a bit—during our approximate three-hour conversation, largely on tactics—given his amazing attitude. As you could imagine, I was curious as to what made him tick, what set him apart. So I delved into as much theory and tactical stuff that he'd allow, which, as it turns out, was quite a bit. (As brilliant as many people were, not every person I talked to was eager to get into tactics.) I listened to his open-minded approach to the game, which had much respect for skill and creativity, and, lo and behold, any idea I put forth (being the interviewer, I tried to hold back) he made it seem like a great idea. He was positive—he'd bounce ideas off this or that. In a subtle way, he made me feel like a genius. (I liked that.) Without a doubt, I wanted to learn from him, and that I did. His upbeat and insightful attitude toward fastidious nuances of the game spoke volumes, resonated. In short order, I immediately thought: *Why couldn't I have played for this guy*?! I could easily see how his clear-thinking approach—with a positive, inquisitive vibe—got so much out of players.

To reiterate, he's but one former player who has passed his incredible wealth of knowledge to the next generation of players.

[†]   Other states worth mentioning that are high school soccer powers include New York, New Jersey, Pennsylvania, North Carolina, Georgia, Ohio, Michigan, Illinois, Washington, California, and Texas.

Vince Drake, long before his coaching days, was part of SLU's soccer machine in the 1960s where he was participating and learning about the game at a high level. Like many other players from that special era, he helped pave a way for success that few other colleges have gotten close to.

SLU's dominance is pretty much a cornerstone of American soccer today, notwithstanding St. Louis soccer as a whole, with its collective modular parts. Based on this achievement—10, count them, 10 college titles—it's hard to argue that St. Louis is not the mecca of college soccer. This combined with club, high school, and pro success, as well as USMNT representation, are reasons why St. Louis has been out in front for so long as the leader of soccer in the United States. SLU, by and large, was pivotal in this regard.

The 10 NCAA Division I championships were divvied up equally—five each—by two men.

Enter coaches Bob Guelker and later Harry Keough.

Many universities around the nation favored international talent. SLU, on the other hand, recruited heavily from the St. Louis area.

Under the leadership of head coach, and soccer visionary, Bob Guelker, St. Louis University got off to a historical start by earning its first national championship in 1959 by taking down the University of Bridgeport—a private school from Connecticut—by the score of 5-2 in the championship game.

Coincidentally, following the inaugural year for the NCAA Division I soccer tournament as it stands today, a storm of college soccer passion, money, programs, scholarships, training, resources, attention, and careers have flourished since.

For its follow up show, SLU took down Maryland 3-2 in the 1960 championship held in Brooklyn, New York, at Brooklyn College Field.

SLU couldn't win every year and in 1961 the Billikens lost in the final to West Chester.

In 1962, SLU got its third title against Maryland, a rematch from 1960, with an exciting 4-3 victory.

As for 1963, the very following year, SLU was back in form for its fourth title with a 3-0 walloping over a befuddled Navy—the final match was held at Rutgers Stadium in New Jersey.

With top players and local sensations like midfielder Don Ceresia, forward Carl Gentile, and midfielder Pat McBride (who was all over the field, an all-time great), the Billikens were too much for opposition forces. The talent was so rich that down the road Ceresia, Gentile, McBride, and many other Billikens, suited up professionally for the St. Louis Stars. SLU was a launching pad and much of the lineup included local players. As McBride said: "We were very proud of the fact that when we played some of the other universities, we played Maryland or Michigan State or whoever, I mean, a lot of their teams were foreign, and I think that's one thing that...that would bring us together, as a group, as a team, you know, that, 'hey we're playing for St. Louis,' you know, that type of thing." In fact, many players on the St. Louis Stars were former Billikens that transitioned from a SLU roster that was predominately local in nature to a pro roster that despite having foreign talent and players from here or there was very much a St. Louis University product down the line. It seemed that SLU's ace of hearts was the ostensibly unlimited pool of local talent to choose from. As a result, the ride of a lifetime was underway.

In 1965, SLU attained its fifth title with a 1-0 win over Michigan State in the final game held at Francis Field in St. Louis, Missouri.

Bob Guelker—who didn't have a soccer-playing background—coached the team to amazing results from 1959-66. It was an amazing five-title run. He then transitioned across the Mississippi River to SIUE.

In his place came the great Harry Keough of the famed USMNT from the 1950 FIFA World Cup; he subsequently coached SLU from 1967-82. For much of the time, Coach Keough was aided by Assistant Coach Val Pelizzaro. "And really, it wasn't a full time job for them. They were both mailmen, postal workers," Al Trost said. Trost—whose voice resonates honesty and leadership, like a clear glass of water—pointed out how they were a great team together: "They were just really prepared."

Val was known as a "fitness guru"—a common sentiment from Trost, Leeker, and others as well. The admiration and affection for the two coaches was unbounded.

One such virtue carried by Coach Keough was a keen ability to notice little things in a game to help sway a victory. Trost recalled that, "Harry had a really good knack of knowing and communicating with his players." It was certainly an added benefit that Keough had FIFA World Cup experience as a player. In addition, Harry and Val were involved with Kutis soccer club, the renowned team that represented the US for World Cup qualifiers in 1958. Both were adept players. They were right at the forefront of this mysterious Midwest gem of soccer, and they were putting all their energy into dominating NCAA Division I soccer, which they did with aplomb. St. Louis University was the leader, a special place. According to Trost, "There's a tradition there that you're going to do everything you can to uphold the soccer tradition at St. Louis U."

In 1967, Keough and company wasted no time. Due to weather, SLU were co-champions with Michigan State. Rules were rules then. Co-champions or not, this brought the worthy Billikens to six titles altogether.

There were plenty of salient talents at Keough's disposal, some of which included super-forward Gene Geimer, exemplary midfielders John Pisani and Steve Frank, along with defender-extraordinaire Gary Rensing. Bill McDermott, one of SLU's most well-known alums, was an important figure on the 1967 and 1969 history-making squads. With these players it was hard to miss. In fact, Geimer, Frank, and Rensing eventually represented the USMNT.

In the 1968 NCAA Division I tournament, during Al Trost's sophomore year, SLU lost out to Maryland. "That was a tough loss," Al said, chuckling. "We had a real good team." He pointed out, "That was a tough one, that was a game we should've won, but I think Maryland had a good team." Following that experience, Al said, "For the next two years we didn't lose a game." After perhaps one tie to Quincy, that was it for the 1969 and 1970 seasons—the team went on a winning rampage.

During the 1969 championship run, Jim Leeker, a 6'2" power forward who could finish with a canon-like strike and distribute, recalled playing Harvard in the semi-finals, which took place in San Jose, California. "Harvard was a technical team, very East Coast in their approach, a tough team," said Leeker. Despite Harvard's resistance, SLU yet again found its way into the final match. During this competition, Leeker—who was sporting adidas cleats—helped SLU earn the championship trophy against the University of San Francisco in the final. In fact, SLU administered a decimating 4-0 defeat to San Francisco in Spartan Stadium for the school's seventh championship. Goals in the final came from Al Trost, Jim Leeker, John Pisani, and Gary Rensing.

Interestingly enough, around this time in SLU's history, Harry Keough had family down in Mexico and upon visits he would order the team's uniforms from a distributor down there. Maybe it was a good luck charm, because, in those days, SLU was on a mission to win titles. And win titles it did.

Championship number eight arrived the very next year in 1970 as SLU defeated West Coast power UCLA 1-0 in the final game hosted by SIUE.

With midfield maestro Al Trost, and dynamic forwards Mike Seerey, Dan Counce, and Jim Bokern, the sky's the limit. Trost—who lived at home while at SLU and commuted the 30-minute or so drive to campus—eventually captained the USMNT; Counce suited up for the USMNT in a handful of games himself. These players were an extension of previous SLU greats to represent the USMNT. Take Carl Gentile and Pat McBride for example. As a matter of fact, around this time in history, St. Louis was like a laboratory for the national team (SLU's close rival, SIUE, also contributed players). SLU was acting as a platform for that transformation. College soccer and in many ways the USMNT were being defined from the perspective of St. Louis University, headed at this point by Harry Keough (with obvious influences from his predecessor, Coach Guelker) and his band of talent that was largely regional in its origin. Players overlapped over the years, as is the case in college soccer, and despite the transient nature of things the product remained at an optimal level.

At this point it didn't matter where the opponents were from; SLU had bested any and all challengers in the final from coast to coast, including the Midwest.

In 1971, SLU earned second-place in Miami, Florida, after suffering an unfortunate 3-2 defeat to Howard, a team stacked with international talent.

Then SLU earned its unprecedented ninth title the following year in 1972 with a 4-2 win over UCLA in the final, which was hosted by Miami, Florida, again.

As for 1973,[†] it was the magical 10th title in which SLU had a rematch with UCLA in the final, which coincidentally was held in Miami, Florida, yet again. *The New York Times* reported the story: "MIAMI, Jan. 4—Dan Counce scored two goals tonight, the second one in the sudden death overtime, in leading St. Louis University to its 10th National Collegiate Athletic Association soccer championship. The Billikens defeated the University of California, Los Angeles, 2-1."[51] This thriller placed SLU on a throne over all colleges as soccer king.

As for the following season in 1974, SLU had a good chance to take down Howard in St. Louis, at Busch Memorial Stadium. Pete Collico— who eventually played for the St. Louis Steamers, and, once upon a time, scored a hat-trick against the New York Arrows—recalled Howard as a tough opponent with players from West African and Caribbean nations. As it played out, the internationally stacked Howard managed to get a close 2-1 championship victory that fell into overtime. Instead of an 11th title, SLU walked away with second place.

The versatile Ty Keough joined SLU from 1975-78 with stellar performances.

[†]   Incidentally, this championship match for 1973 took place on January 4, 1974.

The 1976 SLU roster, for example, was loaded with talent with Ty Keough and teammates (including but not limited to) Dave Brcic, Gary Brcic, Pete Collico, Don Doran, Don Droege, Dan Flynn, Kevin Handlan, Don Huber, and Larry Hulcer.

A rush of standout players continued to flow in, such as the skillful, strong, and tough Daryl Doran, the quick and shifty Mark Santel, the midfield maestro Mike Sorber, complimented by the aerial prowess of Brian McBride, the midfield dominance of Matt McKeon, the crafty midfield play of Tim Leonard, the skill, precision, and organizational passing of Jeff DiMaria, and the skill and field awareness of John DiRaimondo. The list goes on.

Another salient feature of SLU's soccer program is that of a former player turned soccer-broadcaster. Bill McDermott—a talented member of the 1967 and 1969 SLU conquests, a former player for St. Philip Neri— graduated from NCAA national champion on the field to legendary soccer-broadcasting pioneer. From the Billikens official website, Josh Sellmeyer wrote: "The Saint Louis University men's soccer team has played approximately 400 home games since the start of the 1972 season. Bill McDermott estimates he's missed no more than 15 of them since he became the Billikens' first—and to this day, only—full-time public address announcer that year."[52] As Sellmeyer pointed out, this "means McDermott—a 1970 SLU alumnus who helped lead the men's soccer team to national championships in 1967 and '69—has attended and announced better than 95 percent of the Billikens' home contests the past 42 years."[53] In addition, in 1972 McDermott "called a North American Soccer League contest between the St. Louis Stars and Dallas Tornado, which aired on KPLR Channel 11 in St. Louis."[54] Amazingly, McDermott has established himself as a soccer-announcing legend. "One of McDermott's career highlights was providing color commentary for the first soccer game televised on ESPN—a 1979 tilt between Saint Louis and UCLA—alongside play-by-play broadcaster Kevin Slaten."[55] And it doesn't stop there. "McDermott was part of another first when he served as the sideline reporter for ABC's broadcast of the inaugural

Major League Soccer game in 1996."[56] His accomplishments in the field of soccer have been astounding. "More than 40 years after his first broadcast, McDermott holds the title of being America's longest-serving soccer broadcaster. It's no wonder McDermott's longtime friend, Bob Costas, calls him 'Mr. Soccer,' a nickname that's stuck through the years."[57] Bill is thrilled to have been a part of soccer-announcing history and he still loves Billiken soccer. "'I still get excited when I do it. I love watching these players,' McDermott said. 'I don't know if I'm going to be around, but one of my fondest aspirations or desires is to see Saint Louis U. get an 11th star on their shirt. I'd sure as heck like to see it happen.'"[58]

Championship number 11 is certainly within reach.

Though, interestingly, from 1973 onward, as things currently stand, SLU has been absent from the first-place podium. At the time, circa the mid-1970s, it would've been tricky for one to portend such a turn of events. Essentially the 1980s witnessed an explosion in soccer's popularity around the nation, particularly in the collegiate ranks. A dynasty that existed in the 1960s and 70s would be hard to duplicate today. In fact, to be a dynasty in perpetuity is just unrealistic. Much of the same occurred with UCLA's basketball program—led by John Wooden—that happened to be surging as a colossal force around the same time that SLU was racking up soccer championships.§ What were the common denominators? Elite talent, for sure, and the Pythagorean theorem effect: Bob Guelker equals Harry Keough equals John Wooden—each coach was brilliant. Each coach knew talent and how to guide it the right way. Each coach and school reached legendary status, though, it didn't last forever. Eventually UCLA, like SLU, found itself drifting away from being the perennial number one. Still, in lieu of a first-place NCAA Division I trophy, SLU has certainly remained an elite

---

§   John Wooden's UCLA won NCAA Division I basketball titles in 1964, 1965, 1967, 1968, 1969, 1970, 1971, 1972, 1973, 1975, and Coach Jim Harrick got one years later in 1995.

soccer-playing university and a top destination for blue chip student-athletes to eventually land and call home.

Having said that, since the golden age of relentless titles, SLU has had good runs in the NCAA Division I tournament and in the 1990s it reached the semi-finals in 1991 and 1997.

In 1991, the team was loaded. Bill McDermott pointed out the "1991 team is considered by many to be the best SLU team not to win a championship." Joe Clarke, a former defender for SLU (1972-75), the St. Louis Stars, California Surf, St. Louis Steamers, and Kutis, returned as head coach for the Billikens from 1983-96. He led the show in '91 with the on-field magic of Mike Sorber, Brian McBride, Shane Battelle, Steve Kuntz, Scott McDoniel, and Chris Santel. It was a team for the ages but as things can go in soccer, it wasn't meant to be.

For the 1997 team, McDermott added it was "Bob Warming's first year" as coach and there was "Dan Donigan, Bob Warming's assistant for the 1997 team (and later the head coach at SLU)." The team was full of mega-talent, including Tim Leonard, Brian Benton, Casey Klipfel, the Moriarty twins (Pat and Mike), Kevin Kalish, and Kevin Quigley...top-notch across-the-board.

Talented midfielder and CBC product Jeff DiMaria—who helped push SLU to great heights in the late 90s—missed the '97 run as this was around the time of his return from UConn while recovering from a knee injury.

Subsequently, Jack Jewsbury, Brad Davis, Danny Wynn, John DiRaimondo, Tim Ream, Brandon Barklage, Mike Roach, and Robert Kristo continued the tradition of high-quality play that has continued to unfold to this day.

As great players have come and gone, SLU has set a precedent for tournament prowess that may be a thing of the past for some yet it holds up to time, and the record books don't lie.

Outside of the NCAA national tournament, SLU has made history with a local rival, SIUE. Dating back to the 1970s, the Bronze Boot game—which took a break due to intercollegiate differences but has recently been rekindled—has been overwhelmingly popular with extremely large crowds for the annual event. The matchup in 1980 drew the biggest regular season NCAA crowd of all with a little over 22,500 people in attendance at Busch Memorial Stadium. (That's for a college game, if you can believe it!) The outpouring of fan support has been a testament as to how popular soccer is in St. Louis and to how talented SLU and SIUE have been.

The ever-popular Bronze Boot rivalry—steeped in history—might just be the spark needed to rejuvenate a rally come tournament time for SLU. Perhaps a perfect location for it would be at St. Louis City SC's stadium. Such a setting and possibly a shared ticket with a St. Louis City SC game would only serve to honor the tradition of St. Louis soccer.

As for SLU's prospects in the near future, St. Louis continues to produce top-level talent at club and high school levels, a gold mine for recruiting. And each year brings with it the hope of a new dawn, a new chance to revisit the storied past.

Currently, former SLU player and head coach of SIUE, Kevin Kalish, is a Billiken yet again. He has the coaching position and for soccer aficionados, given its history, SLU has an auspicious road ahead, albeit a challenging one.

SIUE: 1979 REIGNS SUPREME!

SIUE—Southern Illinois University Edwardsville, founded in 1957—hopped onto the national stage with the help of savvy veteran coach, Bob Guelker, who led the Cougars from 1967-85. After his remarkable results at SLU, Guelker created a soccer oasis right across the river—a short drive from SLU's campus—in the hilly Edwardsville, Illinois, landscape that's covered by a symphony of trees that crowd the bluff for miles on end—so much so that squirrels could likely visit cousin squirrels three-to-four towns over, leaping from tree to tree without touching ground. The actual playing fields—which includes the main field for college games, currently referred to as Ralph Korte Stadium (Bob Guelker Field), along with nearby practice and game pitches for youth teams—are in a flat area at the base of the bluff, next to some farmland. A hill close to the practice grounds has been utilized from time to time for stern fitness; up the hills just a short drive is the main campus where most of the players attend class and reside. Centered on St. Louis St., Vandalia St., and Main St., Edwardsville's downtown—which is surrounded by older houses with a late 19th-century feel—is a small distance northeast of campus. It's not huge, but boasts quaint stores comingled with a few bars and some local restaurants. In general, Edwardsville is a wooded community, sometimes littered with tree leaves, acorns, squirrels, and the occasional deer. On a walk or drive through town one is likely to encounter dogs on leashes, students, local workers, commuters, and families. Simple, laid back, very middle class, it is a far cry from the old days of Kerry Patch in north St. Louis.

The forest of the Metro East became Guelker's new stomping ground. He made quick work.

SIUE's inaugural season with Guelker was a winning one at that. "We had a good team," Tom Howe said. Howe, a man of few words, had just graduated from CBC and was recruited by Guelker. "He pretty much was responsible for college soccer back in the day," said Howe who subsequently played midfield in the NASL for the St. Louis Stars (1973-74).

By responsible for college soccer, Howe was referring to college soccer nationwide. Guelker coached not only SLU and SIUE, where he set trends, but also US Olympic squads. His influence throughout the nation was widespread from his headquarters in St. Louis. This involved the finer points of the game in reference to player development and tactics. He also had a wide vision of the sport; he knew the potential soccer had in America. Guelker's dominant success early on with SLU, and his later achievements with SIUE, created a model for others to emulate. In a broader sense, in fact, during Guelker's time at the helm of SLU, he'd sporadically tell the guys at halftime to back off a bit on the score against inferior opponents so as to keep the opposing team extant for the following season; he didn't want SLU, for example, to throttle every team and discourage fledgling programs from continuing; let's face it, if you were a school with little experience in the 1960s and Goliath SLU clobbered you 18-0 you might throw in the towel which wouldn't have been good for American soccer in the larger scheme of things; Guelker realized this and he wanted to encourage the growth of soccer as much as he could.

What made Guelker so successful? Many people I asked said it was a good question and didn't have an exact answer, and, from my point of view, it was basically a mystery. This might be what happens when someone is naturally brilliant, like Guelker. Though, a common consensus was that he had a keen eye for talent (much the same thing I heard regarding Harry Keough). Along with being interested in new trends in the game, Guelker recruited well and had a knack for getting the most out of players.

He also wisely called on north St. Louis native Pat McBride—of the St. Louis Stars and USMNT—to assist him from 1968-75. McBride—who was coached by Guelker at SLU—got a master's from SIUE around this time. Regarding Guelker, McBride—an all-around class act who sounds a tiny bit like he grew up in Cleveland and recently vacationed in Wisconsin—truly had an insider's view and said: "More than anything else, he was just a great example. He was a tireless worker; he wore so many different hats. He was the head soccer coach, he was the athletic director, he was President of the United States Soccer Federation," he said chuckling in admiration. "He had all these titles. He was the Olympic coach—the United States Olympic coach." He added: "I think, more than anything, everything with him was team oriented, and everything I've read about John Wooden, alright, as a man and as the coach, I would, Bob Guelker is John Wooden, I mean, in terms of, hey, they, the same principles, the same idea...he had a list of nine intangibles that he would make the players learn and the first one is you have to have the ability to adjust." McBride didn't lay out the other eight intangibles but his point was that Guelker had a plan with the best intentions in mind for his players. Interestingly, as McBride pointed out, "He never had a soccer background but he would stay up with whatever was going on, you know, with the game, and anything new and that type of thing—he would be relentless." And as McBride noted, Guelker would watch and gather information from other coaches as well. Certainly, based on a working relationship and the ability to coach, McBride held Guelker in the highest regard.

If there were a movie script for the SIUE journey in Guelker's life, it would likely (hopefully) depict a legendary coach experimenting with a new school, coupled with a legendary player, with success lingering in the air given that Bob Guelker and Pat McBride were both former national champions from their time at SLU, and both were representatives of American soccer by way of the US Olympic and national teams. Guelker—the pioneer genius-coach with virtually no soccer background—was at the forefront of American soccer, the leader. In a way, Guelker's aberrant path to soccer stardom has similarities with a modern-day coach that never played professionally, Maurizio Sarri, the Italian banker that coached his way up with small teams you probably never heard of to the ranks of Napoli, a major club in Serie A, and then to Chelsea in the EPL, and Juventus, Italy's top club—absolutely unheard of. Guelker, in his own way, was implementing his brilliant athletic mind onto the American landscape of soccer. The bottom line: A storm was raging for any team that got in the way of SIUE.

In 1972, SIUE was classified as an NCAA Division II program. In the first year of the Division II tournament, SIUE came out on top as national champions. This was Guelker's first major triumph with the Cougars.

Guelker had an eye for talent and a lot of special players came his way.

John Stremlau—a St. Louis-born forward and midfielder—made a few appearances for SIUE from 1972-75; then he moved onto play professionally for the Dallas Tornado, St. Louis Stars, Houston Hurricane, Houston Summit, St. Louis Steamers, and Kansas City Comets.

From 1974-77, Greg Makowski—who was born in St. Louis and had experience with Scott Gallagher and Rosary High—stepped in as a leader of the team. After leaving the Cougars, Makowski, a defender, had a lengthy pro career with a handful of teams—including the Atlanta Chiefs, St. Louis Steamers, Kansas City Comets, among others—and also played for the USMNT.

From 1975-76, Greg Villa—who was born in St. Louis and played with Busch Soccer Club—joined the Cougars as a forward. Villa subsequently played pro and appeared with the Fort Lauderdale Strikers, St. Louis Steamers, Kansas City Comets, and others. Like Makowski, Villa also represented the USMNT.

As the 1979 season came around, SIUE, sporting red and white uniforms, had since transitioned to NCAA Division I status. In 1979, it was becoming clear that Guelker had a team stacked with talent. With players like Bob Bozada, Jeff Cacciatore, and Don Ebert, how could you go wrong? The goalkeeper at the time, Ed Gettemeier, explained that Guelker "believed in a strength of schedule." He would organize games outside of SIUE's conference with elite programs to prepare his guys for any challenge. In those days, it was less about the conference and more about playing the best teams you could find. At the beginning of the 1979 season, Guelker loaded up the schedule with some West Coast powers: Seattle Pacific in Washington, Santa Clara, UCLA, and University of San Francisco. On this tour, the team hit a crossroad. As Gettemeier put it, after losing two games on the West Coast, which was considered a failure by the guys, "We had a come to Jesus meeting." After that, "We went on to never lose again that year, after that trip." Of all things, Gettemeier informed me that Guelker had recently suffered a heart attack and was coaching from the sidelines from a wheelchair during that trip. Rick Benben, who was Guelker's assistant, did a lot for the team as well.

Eventually, as the season came to a close, the NCAA Division I championship was in sight and taken home after a 3-2 final match victory over Clemson in Tampa, Florida. From the West Coast to the Southeast—SIUE wasn't to be stopped even by an older Clemson side that fielded a number of foreign players.

This historic team earned Hall of Fame honors at SIUE and the university has this unique achievement captured on its official website: "SIUE earned the 1979 NCAA Division I crown behind a plethora of talented players for Hall of Fame Coach Bob Guelker. Matt Malloy scored a hat trick as SIUE defeated Clemson 3-2 in the national championship game in Tampa, Fla. The 1979 men's soccer team includes Assistant Coach Rick Benben, Don Ebert, Tim Guelker, Ed Gettemeier, Mark Downar, Bob Bozada, Jeff Cacciatore, Tuaya Chiwanga, Tim Clark, Tom Groark, Joe Howe, Dave Hummert, Dave Hundelt, Pat Malloy, George Mishalow, Morris Mwongo, Steve Schell, Stuart Stevenson, Terry Trushel, and Mike Twellman."[59]

This would be Guelker's last legendary championship run. His accomplishments as coach, and his vision of the game, which touched lives across the nation, were cemented in the record books, and as time goes on it might just be an obscure fascination for future fans of soccer, though his presence is one that helped shape the game in a profound way long before the product that is before all of us today. As Gettemeier said, "He was a role model for all of us."

Furthermore, despite fielding high-quality teams over the years, with salient talents such as Steve Trittschuh and Joe Reiniger, the 1979 triumph is SIUE's only Division I national soccer title, to date. However, this solo stat is somewhat misleading as there were other strong performances.

Keep in mind, in 1975, SIUE finished second overall in the NCAA Division I tournament. That year, SIUE defeated SLU 2-1 in the Third Round and subsequently stepped past Howard 3-1 before losing to San Francisco in the final.

In 1977, the Cougars took third-place at the NCAA Division I tournament.

Lost in the archives of college soccer, you'll find that in 1982, SIUE lost a 1-0 nail-biter in the semi-finals of the NCAA Division I tournament to the eventual champion, Indiana.

Through the generations, SIUE has fielded some of the best talent in the nation. The list of SIUE players that played pro is voluminous.* A few would include the aforementioned Bob Bozada, Jeff Cacciatore, Don Ebert, and Ed Gettemeier, along with Mike Banner, John Carenza, Zach Bauer, Kevin Hundelt, Matt Little, Greg Makowski, Justin McMillian, John Stone, Tom Stone, Mike Twellman, Tim Twellman, Tom Twellman, and Greg Villa.

In view of the astounding history of coaching, players, and accomplishments, there's no denying that SIUE holds a special place in the vast history of St. Louis soccer. Second only to SLU. This has always been the case. SLU has the championships, and the prestige of representing *St. Louis proper*, while SIUE has been the *other* school across the river trying very hard to live up to the elite standard set by the Billikens, which, amazingly, was a standard established by Guelker before he even set up shop in the forest of the Metro East. Though, on a quest to do the impossible and outdo what only the Billikens have achieved so far, the Cougars have reached the mountaintop, at least once. There is hope for each new generation, however. When the Bronze Boot match comes around each year—the annual showdown between SIUE and SLU—it's but another opportunity to be number one, yet again.

ST. LOUIS COLLEGES RUN THE TABLE: 1973, THE YEAR OF NATIONAL CHAMPS!

SLU and SIUE: The top two legendary soccer colleges of St. Louis that bequeathed greatness to all native residents. One might think that was it...the glory of SLU and SIUE was the only game in town. Think again.

Somewhere, lost in the archives of American college soccer, is the insanely phenomenal year of 1973. In this year, as crazy as it sounds, St.

---

* For an extended list of players, which is lengthy, see the SIUE section in the Golden Vault.

Louis colleges won each national championship across-the-board! The NCAA Division I 1973 championship went to SLU. The NCAA Division II 1973 championship went to UMSL.

(The men's soccer championship for NCAA Division III schools apparently started in 1974.) The NJCAA Division I 1973 championship went to Florissant Valley Community College.

That's called *running the table*!

Pete Sorber—who happens to be the father of soccer-great, Mike Sorber (who played for the US in the 1994 FIFA World Cup)—was coach at Florissant Valley Community College from 1967-97. His overall record was 415-85-22 and his teams won 10 NJCAA championships. On five occasions Sorber earned NJCAA Coach of the Year honors. He is in the St. Louis Sports Hall of Fame and the St. Louis Soccer Hall of Fame. He's one of the greats in St. Louis soccer history and ranks up there with Bob Guelker and Harry Keough in the hierarchy of college soccer coaches.

Pete Sorber, UMSL, and SLU were part of the legendary 1973 year of champions.

"How is this possible?" You might ask. Well, somehow, someway, it is. It happened. As weird as it may be (though not totally surprising in the least), each St. Louis college won its respective national title. It's weird—if that's the right word—because something like this is extremely hard to accomplish. Having said that, if you were ever on the fence about St. Louis being the cradle of soccer in America, there's your proof; it's one more example of how dominant St. Louis soccer has been over the years. Indeed, 1973 was an epic soccer year for St. Louis colleges as never before or since.

ST. LOUIS PROS: PROFESSIONAL OUTDOOR AND INDOOR SOCCER IN ST. LOUIS

THE ST. LOUIS STARS

On MLS in St. Louis: "St. Louis finally has a team," said Tommy Howe, a former member of the St. Louis Stars, who was teammates with greats including Al Trost, Pat McBride, and Denny Vaninger. These players, and many others, played a unique role in what we have today, all around us. Given the vast amount of history leading up to St. Louis City SC, the inception of the St. Louis Stars (circa 1967-77) was really the legitimate starting point of pro soccer in St. Louis.

Most of us don't know what we want out of life before our early 20s and that's okay. Some of us, before our early 20s, know exactly what the plan is and that's okay too. Unless, of course, your voracious goal involves telling everyone how great you are when you only have one talent: telling people how great you are. Members of the Stars never suffered this affliction; each was great in many ways. The guys who were playing for the Stars, many of whom started with the team in their early 20s, seem to have been shuttled forward as entertainers, elite athletes expected to win, and pioneers of a sport. Little did they know of the big impact they would have on soccer in America over 30 years later. For most of the players, they were just young college grads starting out in life with a sport that was working its way through the *approval polls* of American fans, despite being a worldwide phenomenon.

As it turns out, practically every step the St. Louis Stars took was paving the way for St. Louis City SC.

The Stars first played in the NPSL (National Professional Soccer League) in 1967. Then from 1968-77, the Stars competed in the NASL (North American Soccer League). Headed by owner Bob Hermann (who the collegiate Hermann Trophy is named after), the Stars were a precursor to the exciting world of St. Louis City SC as we know it today.

The original NASL came long before MLS and lasted from the late 1960s into the mid 80s. It is easy to think of the original NASL only in terms of Pele—the world's biggest star—and the New York Cosmos.

For Pele, the Cosmos rollercoaster was a magical time floating in a post-retirement comeback as he had played his last game for Brazil in 1971; his third World Cup title had arrived in 1970. Then, at the club level, he had retired from Santos in 1974. Lounging in Brazil, he was approached by the Cosmos with a great offer, one that included millions of dollars—and American soccer would never be the same. Al Trost—who was a captain of the USMNT during the 70s—said, "The game dramatically changed when Pele hit the scene." The bicycle-kicking Pele graced the NASL with his presence from 1975-77. The league was booming wherever he went; it was like The Beatles on tour. Like few in the world, he was an ambassador for the game wherever he traveled, causing a stir, which was what the US desperately needed to help move things along for a sport trying to find its way within the American athletic landscape.

Yet, prior to Pele's massive and somewhat surprise arrival, the NASL was already a functioning league; sometimes, from a distance, it seems as if the NASL started with Pele's first Cosmos appearance and ended with his retirement, though it was around before and after the Brazilian legend's two-year jaunt.

The era of the NASL was a time, for sure, that saw the growth of the game, and St. Louis was one such place. Back then, soccer was a curiosity; papers would run stories which enchanted some with a game that was mythically obsessed over around the world but only gaining baby-steps in the US. Teams used creative promotions to draw people in such as this snippet from a St. Louis Stars game-day brochure ("Match Day, Vol. II, No. 2, Atlanta vs. St. Louis | United States vs. Jamaica | Busch Memorial Stadium, May 14, 1972"): "Punch. Trap. Slam. Crash. Kick. Punt. Block. Pass. These are the words that describe the exciting and sometimes violent action of professional soccer. See the St. Louis Stars go into battle against America's finest teams. Order your tickets today." Such a description—"Crash," etc.—seemed to be geared toward a portion of the population unfamiliar with the sport.

St. Louis, however, was a place in the US that encouraged the sport big-time. It should go without saying that soccer in the early 1970s was not at the level of baseball but there was certainly an undercurrent, one that was reverberating around the area; local St. Louisans appreciated soccer and embraced it.

Fans of the St. Louis Stars saw the team in action from 1967-77.

A few opponents included the Kansas City Spurs, Atlanta Chiefs, Rochester Lancers, Dallas Tornado, Washington Darts, Toronto Metros, and others. Even Santos, and Pele, traveled to play the Stars in 1968—a friendly game. Midfielder Pat McBride told me, "It was at Busch Stadium and I think we had close to 30,000."

One of the perks that went along with having the Stars included not only great players but also game-day brochures provided for by the team. Years later, these brochures are now valuable historic relics.

One such brochure from June 30, 1970, summed up the event in a simple thick-paper vanilla-colored pamphlet. The front cover read "ST. LOUIS STARS SOCCER CLUB" along with an artsy image of soccer action (with graphic art that screamed late 1960s); it was priced at 15 cents. On the back page, the Directors were listed (T.R.P. Martin, William V. Bidwill, Robert R. Hermann, Dr. Charles A. Thomas, Charles G. Houghton, Jr., John S. Childress, Edward J. Schnuck), followed by the Chairman of [the] Board (Robert R. Hermann), the President (Theodore R.P. Martin), the Treasurer (Glenn M. McNett), and the Staff which included the General Manager (Sumner S. Charles), Executive Secretary (Mrs. Nelda Devine), and the Team Coach (Bob Kehoe). To reach the team, an address was provided, which, back then, was located on Clayton Road in St. Louis. There was also a phone number. Below this information, still on the back page, was a nicely presented black and white advertisement from Anheuser-Busch, Inc., including (left to right) a can of Budweiser, a bottle of Michelob, and a bottle of Busch, with a message reading "GOOD TASTE RUNS IN THE FAMILY" thus accentuating the brand and the local appeal for a company based just down the road in south St. Louis. On the inside of this simple, elegant, and timeless brochure was the information of each opposing team, along with the St. Louis Stars. On the left included the team roster, along with the "STAR OF THE WEEK" which included a player's headshot and brief description; in this case, it happened to be one Steve Frank. Look to the right, on the other page, and you'd find the information for the visiting team, Hapoel Petah-Tikvah (roster included). Next to the visiting team's roster was a "SCOUTING REPORT" presented by the one and only Bob Kehoe. Coach Kehoe explained: "Hapoel Petah-Tikvah has been one of the top Israeli teams for years. In existence since 1936, they have won 6 first division championships, placed 2nd six times, and 3rd on one occasion. In 1970, they finished 4th in a sixteen team league, and placed three of their players on the Israeli World Cup team." He added: "I look for this team to be very fast with good ball control, and great understanding between players. They are very young, with the oldest player being only 26. Seven of these players have played for their National Team, while five others have been on the Israeli National Youth Team." Just below Coach Kehoe's description was the NASL League Standings, which included the Northern Division (Kansas City, Rochester, and St. Louis), along with the Southern Division (Washington, Atlanta, and Dallas). At the very bottom—combining both pages—was a pictorial guide depicting referee signals entitled, "OFFICIAL SOCCER SIGNALS."

Just a few months earlier, from May 3, 1970, the brochure included much of the same, along with a scouting report from Coach Kehoe for the opponent, Coventry City. The "STAR OF THE WEEK" was Stars defender, Mike Kalicanin (who, coincidentally, guarded Pele during the 1968 friendly with Santos).

On May 20, 1970, Hertha B.S.C. Berlin was the opponent, and the "STAR OF THE WEEK" was Tom Bokern.

It's the type of souvenir that you could take home, immediately place on a chest of drawers, with similar knick-knacks, then wait a few decades for Mike and Frank of *American Pickers* to drop by, look at your pamphlet in awe and then ask if you want to sell it. You suggest $25. Mike sincerely pauses, then says, "I think you're a little low at $25. I'm going to offer you, $3,000!" It's a common theme on *American Pickers*: Some things are way more valuable than you would think. You rejoice internally but hold back your outward emotions, thinking it best to keep the brochure because of its sentimental value, thus disappointing Mike greatly. After all, you like the way it looks on the chest of drawers: simple, elegant, historical.

By 1972, the team brochure had upgraded to more of a plastic, glossy, magazine look and feel to it, with additional pages as well. Perhaps a step in the right direction but it lacked the quaint beauty that the previous brochure had going for it. Sometimes, despite the time or age, a simple brochure for fans goes a long way. Moving on though, the brochure of July 22, 1972 (Vol. 11, No. 6) cost 50 cents. It had an artistic painting of soccer action (with an intense feel of the late 1960s and early 70s about it), including players and fans, with "St. Louis Stars" included. Below the photo was a brief description of the event: "MATCH DAY... JACK IN THE BOX NIGHT...TORONTO vs. ST. LOUIS...UNITED STATES vs. C.Y.C. ALL-STAR...Busch Memorial Stadium." A few pages in, you'd find the rosters of each team. At this time, the Stars were coached by Casey Frankiewicz, and Bob Guelker headed the United States Olympic Team. As opposed to the previous brochure of 1970, this updated edition was replete with advertisements of Busch, 7UP, and Jack in the Box, Carondelet Savings and Loan, Around the World Food at Chase-Park Plaza Hotel featuring Gourmet Gifts, Jacks or Better Fun & Family restaurants (with a promise of "All the Roasted Peanuts you can eat & They're Free!"), along with an anti-littering ad from Anheuser-Busch. Jim Leeker, one of the team's stars, was featured in the front of the brochure and on the back cover was featured a montage of photos entitled: "FOCUS, STRIKER—NO. 9, JIM LEEKER." Leeker was also included in the "PLAYERS OF SOCCER STARS" section within the brochure that provided other players, their photos, and brief biographies. Some of those teammates included James Draude, Steve Frank, Gene

Geimer, Larry Hausmann, Tom Howe, Pat McBride, John Pisani, and Gary Rensing. The team's President and Management group were also featured. The last page included a section of St. Louis Olympians called "FOCUS." It showcased a group of five players that included John Carenza, Buzz Demling, Al Trost, Joe Hamm, and Mike Seerey. Legendary Coach Bob Guelker was also listed. It was yet another timeless souvenir that reminded fans of the event, the grand stage of St. Louis, whether intended or not, and spoke to the growth of soccer throughout the nation, a small piece to the larger puzzle of the beautiful game in America, a sport on the rise.

Back in the early 1970s, the promise of what MLS has turned into—a truly spectacular league on the verge of being an international sensation—had not yet materialized. Players like Jim Leeker—who was featured on the back page of the aforementioned brochure—were admired by many in the St. Louis area, including local kids who found a passion for the game. Yet, the groundwork being laid down for American soccer was just that: groundwork.

It was a fascinating time for the history of soccer in St. Louis, and America at large. Players like Leeker were immersed in the game. They were on a quest for glory. And they were in the right place.

St. Louis was one of the cities in the US that provided an outlet for the world's most popular and beloved sport. In some cases, crowds were scant, while at other times attendance was quite full; yet people were well aware of the undercurrent that was sweeping the nation, even in this window of time, in the NASL which was slightly before the hurricane-like arrival of excitement that draped Pele wherever he and the Cosmos went during 1975-77. However 'aware' people may have been, though, soccer was still taking a serious backseat to baseball (still America's pastime at this point), basketball (which was growing in popularity), and football (also growing in popularity).

In one form or another, soccer had persisted in England long before the US dabbled with it (reluctantly, like a new international dish recently added to a restaurant's menu in Middle America). As Leo Robson pointed out in *The New Yorker*: "From its earliest days as a traditional English pastime, the game was a tribal affair—defined by one historian as 'more or less institutionalized violence between villages or different parts of villages.' By 1600, it had been banned by Edward II, Edward III, Richard II, Henry IV, Henry V, Henry VII, Henry VIII, James I of Scotland, James IV of Scotland, and Elizabeth I. Yet these edicts had little effect on the game's appeal or on its unruliness. In the sixteen-sixties, Samuel Pepys noted that London, one frosty morning, was full of footballs. In 1817, Walter Scott informed his friend Washington Irving, who was visiting Scotland, that it wasn't safe for local teams to play against each other: 'the old clannish spirit was too apt to break out.'"[60] The fabric of the game had already been embedded into the DNA of English society long before the US experimented with it. "As Tony Collins recounts in a brisk forthcoming survey, 'How Football Began' (Routledge), the game's transformation from folk pursuit to global industry began in the elite British schools of the nineteenth century, where Anglican educators such as Thomas Arnold, the headmaster of Rugby School, promoted sports as a way of harnessing youthful energies that had previously found rebellious outlets."[61]

This was long before kids like Don Ceresia and Bill McDermott—Mr. Soccer—were playing in churchyards in north St. Louis. Yet in the early 1970s, when kids like McDermott, Trost, and McBride were now young adults, soccer in America did not share the vast history it did in England.

As such, the 1970s proved to be an interesting time for the St. Louis Stars as soccer in America was finding its way.

Soccer in America had plenty of talented players but in terms of society embracing the game, it was like a small toddler, learning to crawl; it was not only navigating through the athletic forest of baseball, basketball, and football, but also that of bowling. Yes, oddly enough, bowling (of all things) was extremely popular during this time, one of TV's biggest sensations, as a matter of fact.

Interestingly, basketball and football were not quite in the place we know them today. Each sport was gaining in popularity, and, with the advancement of color TVs in the 70s, the Super Bowl and the NBA finals were capturing bigger audiences; not to mention, star players such as Dr. J, Magic Johnson, Larry Bird, Terry Bradshaw, Lynn Swann, Joe Montana, and Jerry Rice, who were starting to electrify the imaginations of people watching from home with new and ever-changing technology in their TV sets. Prior to color TVs was, of course, black and white technology. Prior to the 1970s, baseball and bowling were the big sports on TV. Baseball ran supreme. On black and white TVs, this seemed to work. On the other hand, within the realm of black and white TVs, basketball and football didn't 'pop' as much. Not to mention, baseball was already America's pastime. While basketball and football were popular, each sport was still catching up with baseball in terms of 'mainstream across-the-board adoration around the nation.'

Today, baseball has taken a backseat to basketball and football. (It's hard to pinpoint an exact 'date' but, generally speaking, as the 80s turned into the 90s, baseball was finding itself in third place.) Football, in fact, is top of the heap. It's America's 'passion.' Someone like Colin Cowherd, a FOX Sports TV host, will point out that if you look at a place like Twitter it would appear that basketball is the most popular sport; though, across-the-board, football is the leader. Yet it's important to remember that this shift, a shift that started to see baseball take a backseat to basketball and football, really started to take a turn in the 1970s and into the 80s. And it just so happened that color TVs were on the rise. (Around this time, especially in the 80s, video games featuring the aforementioned sports would begin to take shape in mainstream society as well.)

With all the change in technology that encapsulated the marvelous 1970s and 80s, along with a growing cultural interest in basketball and football, part of America was pushing soccer away, while other portions of the population were intrigued with and embracing it.

That's where the groundbreaking St. Louis Stars found themselves in the 1970s: stuck between other popular sports. Yet, there was always something with soccer that drew people in—a fancy goal, a well-known team or player. Or something else, altogether. One game against

Montreal—albeit in Montreal—saw around 75 fans attack the referee, Tom Bell, after awarding a penalty kick, even kicking him and landing a punch. Still though, apart from this deranged excitement (something many Americans gravitationally fall into like a submarine's torpedo seeking out its target), soccer was having a difficult time working its way into America's mainstream.

One reason that Americans insisted on pushing soccer away perhaps had something to do with it being an English sport. America had fought for its independence from England in the American Revolution and War of 1812. While England has been both an ally and foe of America over the years, there has been a complicated relationship in terms of cultural tastes. Americans have always wanted to differentiate themselves from England, and Europe at large. Cricket is a good example. Americans invented baseball as if to say, "You have cricket, we have baseball," which is essentially the same game with a few adjustments here and there. While England enjoyed rugby, Americans grew found of football, which is very similar. When it came to soccer, Americans never recreated it. Instead, soccer was viewed as "that sport foreigners with effeminate accents play." Much of American society shunned soccer, preferring instead the Big 3: baseball, basketball, and football.

On top of this, foreigners indeed looked down on American attempts to have a big presence in the world of soccer. Foreigners of all backgrounds saw American players as inferior. Many Americans were aware of this sentiment, especially those with a passion for the game. Foreigners knew that soccer was growing in America, which was common knowledge back in the 70s. From a piece in the "United States Soccer Football Association 1970 Yearbook," Erwin Single, President of USSFA (United States Soccer Football Association), wrote, "The 1970's seem certain to go down in American sports history as the decade in which soccer finally turned the corner and, at long last, was discovered by Americans." In the same 1970 Yearbook, successful businessman and soccer pioneer Lamar Hunt pointed out, "At present it [soccer] suffers from lack of exposure on a school level from such traditional American sports as football, baseball and basketball. This status is changing and will be a major factor in the successful growth." Hunt added "a major factor at this date will be the willingness of the press to devote coverage to soccer. Media people are basically not cognizant of the rules and fine points of the sport and tend to relegate it to the 'foreign game' niche." Even English soccer legend Bobby Moore recognized the interesting dilemma the US was in. In the "United States Soccer Football Association 1970 Yearbook," Moore wrote, "In a few months' time the finals of the 1970 World Cup competition takes place in Mexico. Once again, one of the biggest nations in the world, America, will not be represented. To me, this always seems one of the strangest facts on the world sport scene." He was absolutely right as he reflected during a World Cup year. He added, "Soccer is played virtually the world over...and yet in America, where sporting facilities are probably better than anywhere else, is still in its infancy."

So indeed, while Americans were turning the corner, people in Europe, South America, and elsewhere saw it as a weakness that created an interesting landscape in which foreigners were showing up to play in America equipped with an attitude of superiority. In fact, many Americans were perhaps annoyed by how foreigners viewed American soccer. From a 1972 pamphlet entitled "Match Day (Atlanta vs. St. Louis | United States vs. Jamaica | Busch Memorial Stadium)," in the section "SCENE SETTER," Greg Maracek wrote: "The single most significant result is that the American athlete is telling the world, 'We are ready to take the challenges of your sport and to prove Americans can compete with the world at their game, which is now OUR game of the future— SOCCER!'"

In a way, the early NASL teams, the St. Louis Stars among them, had added pressure to live up to the standards of baseball, basketball, and football, and also that of foreign opinion towards American soccer at large. There was a lot to prove.

As a result, the Stars and other early NASL teams around the nation— including the owners, coaches, players, and fans alike—were like early

American frontiersmen, taking a chance, settling the untamed land of the Midwest and West, with wagons, staking their claim (knowing deep down they were onto something big). As Pat McBride explained it: "Having the opportunity to represent St. Louis on a professional level…we were considered, back in the day, ugh, pretty much, the American players were pretty much soccer pioneers." It's amazing to think of it, yet this new untamed land was soccer. However, despite America's unfamiliarity with it, St. Louis had already been entrenched with the sport for many generations; subsequently the Gateway to the West served as a beacon for the rise in its popularity.

The Stars touched many generations. The same Dan King who won a state championship with St. Thomas Aquinas-Mercy, played on a US youth national team, suited up for two NCAA Division I titles with Indiana, played pro indoor, and wound up as head coach at UMSL, used to be a ball boy for the team, and he sought autographs from Pat McBride, Jim Leeker, and others. The players were a great inspiration to him and so many others.

The Stars weren't going to be denied a shot at greatness.

The team actually highlighted an interesting—and very unique— footnote for history. There was the all-St. Louis starting lineup put forth by Bob Kehoe in 1970, a revolutionary move at the time. The players included Tom Bokern, Steve Frank, Larry Hausmann, Jim Leeker, Pat McBride, Jerry Mueller, John Pisani, Paul Pisani, Joe Right, Gary Rensing, and Chris Werstein.

Leeker pointed out how proud Kehoe was of this lineup, a first of its kind in the NASL. Kehoe—who played for the USMNT in 1965 and became its coach in 1972—happened to be from St. Louis and he was the first NASL coach that was born in the United States.

Aside from this one-time arrangement, the Stars were no strangers to foreign players in the roster. In fact, the first year Pat McBride suited up with the squad there were a number of guys that barely spoke English. Though, as McBride explained, for the game of the all-St. Louis lineup, there were a few injured players so the opportunity was there and Kehoe took it. As McBride said, "He had the utmost respect from all the St. Louis players on the team."

Year by year, the Stars, these pioneers of American soccer, approached each game one by one in the wondrous unchartered terrain of pro outdoor soccer in the NASL.

SEASON-BY-SEASON RECAP: THE STARS

In 1967, the St. Louis Stars—with players Tom Basic, Casey Frankiewicz, Mike Kalicanin, and Pat McBride—had help in the coaching department from George Mihaljevic and wound up finishing 14-11-7, a good record for the first season.

For the second season in 1968, the team's record was 12-14-6. A few players included Casey Frankiewicz, Carl Gentile, Mike Kalicanin, Pat McBride, and Joe Puls.

In 1969, the Stars struggled to find wins with a 3-11-2 result. Some players on the field were Tom Bokern, Casey Frankiewicz, Larry Hausmann, Dave Jokerst, Mike Kalicanin, Pat McBride, Paul Pisani, Joe Puls, Don Range, and Chris Werstein.

In 1970, not much changed in the win column. The end result was 5-17-2. A handful of players included Mike Kalicanin, Jim Leeker, Pat McBride, John Pisani, Joe Puls, Don Range, and Gary Rensing. St. Louis was a team testing the use of a large amount of St. Louis talent on the field. In this year, the famous all-St. Louis lineup took flight. The fans were proud to have the representation. It was a gutsy coaching move by Bob Kehoe. By contrast, the Washington Darts fielded a team of all foreigners during a game against the Stars in 1970. According to the official game program of the Washington Darts—"WASHINGTON Darts I St. Louis Stars Soccer Club I Sunday, May 10, 1970 I OFFICIAL GAME PROGRAM 50 cents"—the Darts' team roster consisted of two players from Ghana, one from Haiti, one from Argentina, and the rest were from Trinidad and Tobago and Scotland.

At this time in the NASL, the Southern Section consisted of the Dallas Tornado, Washington Darts, and Atlanta Chiefs. The Northern Section included the St. Louis Stars, Kansas City Spurs, and Rochester Lancers.

This was a different time in sports, and American culture. Long before the movie *Blood Diamond*, which depicted the dark underbelly of the diamond trade, the Atlanta Chiefs' "Official Tara Stadium Game Program, Game Scorecard" on July 25, 1970—which featured the Atlanta Chiefs vs. St. Louis Stars—listed an advertisement from Ben Hyman that read "The Best Place to Select Diamonds is at Kimberly Mines, South Africa," followed by, "'The Next Best Place is At Ben Hyman's, Atlanta.'" Sure, it was an innocent ad; back then, few knew of the struggle that diamond-miners endured for their labor. A different epoch it was; this was during a time when cigarette ads were commonplace. The game-day programs from those days are an interesting reminder of how far America has come culturally. What used to be a normal ad—one that was simply trying to tell a story of 'beautiful diamonds'—is now viewed as politically incorrect in some circles.

In terms of soccer, Atlanta was proving to be an area with highly interested fans. Sponsorship in game-day programs—which took the form of Ben Hyman's diamonds, the Marriott, PAN AM, TWA, Delta Air Lines, Evans Toyota, and others—is a sign that there was commercial interest in soccer. Just as the Stars were leading the way in the name of American soccer, so too were the Chiefs. Eventually Atlanta United FC would emerge onto the MLS scene, playing its first season in 2017, with a huge following that saw games seat around 70,000 people throughout the year and beyond. Much of this excitement had roots in the path the Chiefs had created long before. Phil Woosnam had been a part of the Chiefs' 1968 NASL championship team. Woosnam—who was born in Wales—was a former Chiefs player and head coach. He also coached the USMNT in 1968, and then became the NASL Commissioner (1969-83). He definitely had a hand in the growth of the game in Atlanta and throughout America. He was one of the early pioneers of the American soccer experience and his efforts, in part, have paid off big-time as, magically, Atlanta United FC won the MLS Cup in 2018, and MLS is thriving to this day. Yet, back in 1970, the Chiefs and Stars were playing it game by game.

As the season wound up, 1970 turned out to be quite a year for a St. Louis forward: Following a hat-trick performance against the Atlanta Chiefs, Jim Leeker was named NASL Rookie of the Year. Furthermore, from a Rochester Lancers official program (circa 1970), Pat McBride was featured and Alan Grayson wrote, "McBride attributes most of his skill to George Mihaljevic." Referring to Mihaljevic, McBride said, "'He'd explain to me how great soccer players like Stanley Matthews, Puskas, or Didi did things. It wasn't that he was trying to impose their style on mine. But he brought these things to me and let me pick up what I wanted.'" While McBride had a sophisticated education of the game, he was also noticed beyond NASL circles. Grayson noted, "According to Zlatko Cajkovski, coach of West Germany's crack Bayern Munich team: 'McBride could easily play on any first-division team in Europe with a few months of training.'" Quite a compliment for an American player in the early 1970s. Given the all-St. Louis lineup, Leeker's Rookie of the Year award, and McBride's notable performances, St. Louis was right in the thick of things.

The following year of 1971 saw a 6-13-5 record. A few key players included Tom Bokern, Steve Frank, Casey Frankiewicz, Jack Galmiche, Gene Geimer, Carl Gentile, Larry Hausmann, Mike Kalicanin, Jim Leeker, Pat McBride, John Pisani, Paul Pisani, Dragan "Don" Popovic, Joe Puls, Gary Rensing, Willy Roy, and Chris Werstein.

In Toronto, the visiting Stars were entering familiar territory. In 1971, Toronto was a new team to the NASL, so to speak. This was long before the fanatical support of Toronto FC. (Canada—a nation fixated on hockey— was slowly embracing soccer.) In the match-day program (which sold for 25 cents), William G. Davis, whose letterhead read, "PRIME MINISTER OF ONTARIO," spoke to the exciting times for soccer in Toronto in his official, printed, letter to the Toronto Metros team President, John Fisher. As William G. Davis wrote on May 12, 1971, "Soccer has long been one of the most popular sports in the world, and it is encouraging to know that Toronto Metros will be competing against some of the finest professionals." He added, "I am sure all Canadians will likely develop an appreciation of a sport not now too well known in this part of the world." On this road of soccer-discovery, which evidently was taking place in Canada as well, the Stars received recognition as six members of the team—Jim Leeker, John Pisani, Dragan Popovic, Casey Frankiewicz, Pat McBride, and Joe Puls—were featured inside the program next to a "CAPRI TRAVEL AGENCY" (of Toronto) advertisement for the 1974 World Cup. In addition, there was an Adidas shoe display for the "Adidas 2000" (a very elegant, simple, and timeless black shoe with three iconic white stripes) that was corroborated with a "MEXICO 1970" description that pointed out: "84 out of the 95 World Cup Goals were scored with ADIDAS." Whether it was Toronto, Washington D.C., Atlanta, Dallas or elsewhere, the schedule of the Stars navigated the team through its corner of the soccer kingdom yet it was part of the grand picture of international soccer.

As it turns out, 1972 was a turnaround year as the Stars captured a much needed 7-4-3 finish. Player and Coach Casey Frankiewicz led a classic roster—whose white jersey's featured blue trim and read "St. Louis" in blue cursive letters across the front that hovered over a red-colored number—that included Jim Draude, Steve Frank, Gene Geimer, Larry Hausmann, Tom Howe, Jim Leeker, Pat McBride, John Pisani, Paul Pisani, Joe Puls, Gary Rensing, John Sewell, Wilf Tranter, and Mike Winter.

Things leveled out a bit the following year in 1973 as the team earned a 7-7-5 record. Player and Coach Casey Frankiewicz was leading the way again with familiar players and a few new additions that included John Carenza, Buzz Demling, Steve Frank, Gene Geimer, Larry Hausmann, Tom Howe, Dave Jokerst, Yao Kankam, Pat McBride, Joe Puls, Gary Rensing, Willy Roy, Al Trost, Denny Vaninger, and Mike Winter.

To date, the team had contributed many USMNT players, such as Buzz Demling, Steve Frank, Carl Gentile, Gene Geimer, Gary Rensing, Pat McBride, Willy Roy, and Al Trost.

Interestingly enough, McBride and Trost grew up in the same St. Louis neighborhood. As Trost said, "Pat McBride lived across the street...in north St. Louis just a couple blocks from Fairgrounds Park." As it turns out, McBride was a few years older and had previously played sports with Trost's older brothers. Like others on the team, both had also attended SLU and were NCAA national champions. As fate would have it, on the Stars, McBride and Trost were paired up in midfield together—a true St. Louis combination. While these two riddled opponents with a one-two punch, there was a lot of ancillary talent on the field worth its weight in gold in the form of Demling, Frank, Howe, Rensing, Roy, and Vaninger. As usual, much of the talent pool was St. Louis based.

Then in 1974, the record rolled into 4-15-1.

By this time, forward Jim Leeker—who eventually became President of the St. Louis Soccer Hall of Fame—had departed the team. His time with the Stars was from 1970-72. Years later, with a multitude of grandkids (19) participating in an annual holiday backyard soccer match, Leeker looked back fondly on all the experiences he and the others had had. The practices, commitment, games, travel, and support from fans added up to a phenomenal ride. For Leeker and other local players, it was an honor to represent St. Louis soccer, especially at a time in America when outdoor pro soccer was creating a unique place for itself. While Leeker stepped away from the Stars and was subsequently on his way to starting a family he also played with the senior team of Kutis, which allowed for a less demanding schedule.

At this juncture, in 1974, the Stars were about three years away from closing up shop in St. Louis. Those having kept the ship moving forward included Jim Bokern, John Carenza, John Garland, Gene Geimer, Denny Hadican, Larry Hausmann, Tom Howe, Dave Jokerst, Bob O'Leary, Bob Matteson, Pat McBride, Joe Puls, Gary Rensing, Willy Roy, Mike Seerey, John Sewell, Al Trost, Denny Vaninger, and Mike Winter.

In this year, Denny Vaninger would represent the USMNT and despite having two former Hermann Award winners (Trost and Seerey), the team encountered the grim reality of pro soccer that wins are hard to come by. In the larger scheme of things, the season of 1974 was a FIFA World Cup year—in which West Germany won the title—and soccer excitement was in the air. The season may have been low on wins but the Stars were actually in the middle of a storm that was the growth of soccer in America; the mid 70s was a turning point and the wave of popularity that soccer created nationwide was only getting bigger, thanks in part to NASL teams like the Stars.

The year 1974 also brought with it the arrival of Dettmar Cramer as coach of the USMNT. Prior to taking the job, Cramer was an assistant coach for West Germany during the 1966 FIFA World Cup; right after his brief stint with the USMNT, Cramer became the coach of Bayern Munich. It was a great moment for American soccer to have such an accomplished mind guide the USMNT, albeit for an ephemeral period of time. Cramer was known in some circles as Napoleon—due to his approximate height of 5'2"—and the Football Professor, thanks to his eye for detail. During the German Napoleon's voyage in the US as skipper, a handful of St. Louis players—such as Buzz Demling, Pat McBride, Al Trost, and Denny Vaninger—were members of the USMNT and Cramer's influence was felt in St. Louis and around the nation as people from that era, such as legendary Coach Gene Baker, can attest.

Things would pick up in 1975 as the Stars came roaring back with a 13-9 turnaround season, which was a big relief for everyone involved. This was also the year Pele joined the New York Cosmos. Subsequently, the soccer atmosphere in the US exploded. Members on the squad during this exciting time were Jim Bokern, Peter Bonetti, Dennis Burnett, John Carenza, Steve Frank, Gene Geimer, Larry Hausmann, John Hawley, Dave Jokerst, Bob Matteson, Pat McBride, Bob O'Leary, John Pisani, Gary Rensing, Mike Seerey, Al Trost, Dennis Vaninger, and Roger Verdi.

As for 1976, the Stars found a 5-19 record, featuring players such as Jim Bokern, L. James Bond, John Carenza, Joe Clarke, Keith Fear, Larry

Hausmann, Bruce Hudson, Dave Jokerst, Bob Matteson, Pat McBride, Bob O'Leary, Gary Rensing, Mike Seerey, Al Trost, Dennis Vaninger, and Roger Verdi, to name a few.

As the team approached the 10-year mark, it was becoming clear that this experiment of pro outdoor soccer in St. Louis was coming to a close.

The final season for the St. Louis Stars came in 1977 as the team rallied to put together a 12-14 record, and the attendance that year was the best of all with an average of 9,126 at the gate. Players for the last hurrah included, among others, Peter Bennett, Fred Binney, Steve Buckley, Steve Cacciatore, Joe Clarke, Terry Daly, Ray Evans, John Jackson, Dave Jokerst, Bob Matteson, Steve Moyers, Bob O'Leary, Gary Rensing, Barry Salvage, John Stremlau, Al Trost, Dennis Vaninger, Roger Verdi, and Peter Wall.

Incidentally, in 1977, the New York Cosmos welcomed yet another international great and World Cup champion, Franz Beckenbauer; the NASL was at its peak. However, the NASL was soon to decline, and the following year saw the St. Louis Stars switch over to the California Surf. (Sound familiar—St. Louis Rams to LA Rams?) Al Trost was a player that went with the Surf, then he found himself playing for the Seattle Sounders, and New York Arrows. (Despite not playing for the Stars, St. Louis-native Dan Counce, a former SLU Billiken that won the Hermann Trophy and represented the USMNT, played with the Surf as well.) Gene Geimer, a former Billiken who also suited up for the USMNT, played forward for the Chicago Sting and Cincinnati Kids, among others. Other Stars players scattered about, playing for this or that team and so it went. It would've been nice if the Stars had continued. Having said that, it would've been nice had the NASL continued. But sometimes things have to end.

All in all, it was a good run for the St. Louis Stars, a team, and, to some extent, a *movement*. These pioneers were part of a mobilized effort to spread soccer throughout the nation by means of pro outdoor soccer. The *idea* was to join the world of soccer. In hindsight, the *idea* was to get where MLS is today.

Team owner, Bob Hermann—a smart St. Louis native who attended St. Louis Country Day School, Princeton University, and also served in the Navy during World War II—captured the excitement of soccer as best he could given the era in which he was working, and the overall circumstances in terms of the game's popularity from coast to coast, and at home.

There wasn't yet a soccer-specific stadium for the Stars to call home. Many games were played at Francis Field,† a geographically well-situated, classic, simple, somewhat bijou yet small stadium at Washington University in St. Louis. Games at Busch Memorial Stadium that had big attendance numbers still had a hard time filling the entire place, so the look was that of being half empty (an issue that early MLS franchises in the late 1990s were grappling with).

As a result, the Stars and other NASL franchises were learning along the way. Compared to established European powers—Liverpool, Manchester United, Bayern Munich, Real Madrid, Barcelona, and Juventus—the ownership groups in the United States—which were equipped with smart, well-connected, ambitious people—were essentially taking pro outdoor soccer "baby steps" through no fault of their own as things were just getting started and coming together on the fly. Though it was pro soccer after all, and with that comes a lot more than just putting players on the field. Marketing is a huge endeavor that franchises deal with every year until the bitter end.

Why did the NASL eventually fold? It's hard to say. From the outset as the NASL purported to be the next great league, it was suffering internally. Things were not meant to last. The veneer of what it wanted to be, a magical league on par with any goliath counterpart of its ilk in Europe, was simply spurious in the end. Partially, I suppose, one could

---

† The stadium materialized in the early 1900s. The location was used for the 1904 Summer Olympics. In 1984 the capacity was decreased to around 3,000 people whereas it previously held approximately 19,000. Today the stadium is known as Francis Olympic Field.

blame the stadiums—or lack thereof in terms of actual soccer-specific stadiums—for the downfall. In some instances, teams were playing on American football fields which didn't come across as legitimate, and hence—at times—it felt like a pseudo-soccer experience. Then, of course, many stadiums were just too big for the occasion and empty seats left a less than desirable feeling for the fans. On another note, perhaps the league and teams overspent. However, often overlooked was the rise in popularity of basketball and football, thanks to exciting new players and more color TVs in the 1970s which trickled into the 80s—the combination sent a shock wave of electricity throughout the sports world, and, in particular when ESPN formed in 1979, these sports (along with baseball) were emphasized over soccer for decades. You had Dr. J, Magic, Bird, Terry Bradshaw, Lynn Swann, Earl Campbell, Joe Montana, and Jerry Rice. While basketball and football were competing with the established almighty baseball, soccer got lost in the shuffle. As soccer was fighting hard for approval with mainstream America, essentially traditional American sports won out. Despite soccer's growth in the 70s, it was still a time when Americans were very suspicious of the sport and some even had outright contempt for it, summing it up with pithy responses such as, "No thanks."

It would take the 1994 FIFA World Cup to help boost morale for soccer again, in a tremendous way; the host United States proved it was ready for soccer as it set records for attendance during this World Cup. After MLS got started in 1996, it would take a few years for it to really take off (as we know it today).

Bottom line: It's been a struggle for soccer in America. The NASL was a necessary step—albeit a challenging one—to get to where we are today in terms of popularity of soccer in America. Luckily for fans, MLS today is everything the original NASL set out to be.

Still though, back in the day, as the NASL worked its way into retirement, there was a new dawn rising.

MISL AND THE ST. LOUIS STEAMERS: THE FALLEN STARS LEAD TO THE ST. LOUIS STEAMERS

Soccer in the 1970s and 80s was engaging with America like never before. Thanks to the popularity of Pele, the NASL was looking like a thing that might stay. However, this dream—as enticing as it was— soon faded. Following the retirement of Pele (1977), the NASL slowly lived out its last days, which somewhat pathetically trickled into 1984. While this was taking place, teams like the Stars would fade. Though, on a different front, which happened to be professional indoor soccer, teams like the St. Louis Steamers were riding the wave of excitement created by 'the Pele league' and Americans were enchanted yet again with the world's greatest game, albeit inside arenas in which the players were thrust against one another essentially in shark-tanks with green AstroTurf thrown on top of thawed out hockey rinks as fans followed an orange-and-black ball# bouncing off the walls, along with quick-moving players. The indoor game was exciting, full of skill, with a lot of goals and physical play that, at times, bordered on outright violence. In other words, perfect!

Fans soon fell in love with the MISL (Major Indoor Soccer League). In fact, the MISL first kicked off on December 22, 1978. The first game was between Cincinnati Kids and New York Arrows, with baseball legend Pete Rose—co-owner of the Cincinnati Kids—initiating the official first kick before the game. Buzz Demling—a St. Louis native that played with the USMNT in the 1970s—went in the record books: "Buzz Demling was assessed the first penalty when Referee-in-Chief Dr. Joe Machnik whistled the Cincinnati defender for tripping at 7:44 of the first quarter. New York did not score on the man-advantage."[62] The New York Arrows were stacked with talent and would eventually win the first four MISL championships. One such player in this historic opening game was an iconic star in the making, Steve Zungul. Zungul, a forward for the New York Arrows, eventually became "...the first man in MISL

\#   Often made by Spalding or Voit.

history to score 100 goals,"[63] and in the inaugural MISL match against Cincinnati, he, "...tallied four goals and was named Star of the Game."[64]

Similar to today's MLS teams (such as Portland, Seattle, and Atlanta), the MISL teams provided excitement and energy. Fans would walk into an indoor arena and the playing field sparkled with electricity. Each game provided a festive atmosphere with light shows, misty fog, and rock music for team introductions. Advertisements echoed products on the playing walls. The concessions offered soda, beer, large baked pretzels with different dipping sauces, nachos with jalapeno peppers, popcorn, and other snacks sure to increase the odds of a high cholesterol count. Team posters and brochures and flags and other souvenirs were abundant.

The weird thing about indoor is that critics, in all their glory, will tend to ridicule it for not meeting the standards of outdoor. Perhaps they'll argue that professional indoor talent, whether foreign or domestic, does not live up to top-level outdoor talent. This couldn't be further from the truth. Indoor has proven itself to be something special altogether. In fact, more often than not, most indoor players will likely be very good outdoor players, however, not all outdoor players will be good indoor players. In outdoor, players can hide so to speak. On the other hand, indoor puts an exclamation point on all your weaknesses as a player. There's no hiding. It's five against five in a small space that demands skill. This translates to high entertainment value. As a result, more often than not, fans left pro indoor games in a stir, with their soccer-thirst quenched.

THE 1970S AND 80S: THE ST. LOUIS STEAMERS

The St. Louis Steamers were in the middle of the action. During the late 1970s and into the 80s, the MISL provided fans everything you might want out of a game: action, shots on goal, rivalries, high-level talent, along with personalities like Branko Segota, Steve Zungul, and Brazilian-born Tatu (who would typically throw his jersey into the crowd after a goal; he had plenty of extra jerseys on hand). These were a handful of the star players the Steamers would go up against.

The Steamers had stars of its own. Many lineups placed on the field by the Steamers were typically overflowing with St. Louis-born talent. There were great international players as well. To try and name all of them would take quite some time.[§] In brief, the Steamers' lineups would include the likes of Ty Keough, Daryl Doran, Carl Rose, Sam Bick, Tony Bellinger, Pete Collico, Dan Counce, Eric Delabar, Don Doran, Tom Galati, Kevin Handlan, Mark Mathis, Bob Robson, Frank Schuler, Paul Turin, Scott Vorst, Bob Bozada, Danny McDonnell, Bob O'Leary, Jeff Sendobry, John Stremlau, Joe Clarke, John Hayes, Dan Muesenfechter, Dennis Vaninger, Sean Mulqueeny, Mike O'Mara, Jeff Cacciatore, Don Droege, Larry Hulcer, Steve Moyers, Jim Tietjens, Tim Walters, Ed Gettemeier, Greg Makowski, Greg Villa, Perry Van der Beck, Pat Baker, Don Ebert, Mike Hylla, Steve Pecher, Bill Stallings, Mark Frederickson, Jim Kavanaugh, Manuel Cuenca, Tony Glavin, and Slobodan Ilijevski, to name but a few.

DARYL DORAN: A LEADER FOR GENERATIONS

Throughout the halls of history that is pro indoor soccer in St. Louis, there were a number of greats that wore jerseys for the Steamers, Storm, and Ambush.

Though, outside of Ty Keough, Steve Pecher, Don Ebert, Rick Davis, Steve Trittschuh, Perry Van der Beck, Preki, and certainly a few others, one player stood out above the rest.

Daryl Doran—the Cal Ripken of pro indoor soccer—was an icon in the indoor scene (in St. Louis, obviously, and around the country as well). He encompassed practically every pro indoor era, playing for the St. Louis Steamers, Storm, Ambush, Steamers (part II) and Illusion; he even snuck in some time with the Los Angeles Lazers, once upon a time. Dating back to the original Steamers run, within a team-oriented structure, he was one of the centerpieces around which everyone else revolved.

---

§   See the Golden Vault for an extended list of pro indoor rosters.

If you were to take an NFL linebacker and an Olympic gymnast and mix them in a drink you'd have Daryl Doran. Built like a brick house, he provided a unique combination of strength and skill. On the field he was known for hard tackles and firm defensive ability, along with deft touch and vision, perhaps an indoor soccer version of Brazilian legend Dunga; yet it could be argued that Doran was more skillful that Brazil's previous coach and World Cup captain. Doran was an exquisite talent that—as a leader of soccer in the area—a myriad of players looked forward to siding up with. I was fortunate enough to practice with him on a couple of occasions where I saw his skill up front. Along with great juggling ability with immaculate technique, and a technically sound shot, on one occasion he sent a forward—who was straight ahead of him with no angle to play with—a through pass with the outside of his right foot, on turf, that was perfectly placed in front of the player for a one-on-one with the goalie—it was quite a Brazilian touch indeed. Ron Jacober, who spent much time with the St. Louis Storm, calling games for the radio, said: "Daryl Doran was maybe the best indoor player ever from St. Louis. Really tough guy. His feet were bad for 20 years of his life but he still played. And he was one tough son of a gun, he really was." Doran had arthritis in his big toes and oddly enough the indoor surface was more forgiving than outdoor grass pitches. Through this hardship, he persevered.

As a decorated All-Star, Doran became synonymous with St. Louis indoor soccer during his lengthy career—coupled with substantial service as a player-coach—that spanned over 20 years which included a championship season in 1994-95 with the Ambush. This championship was the first professional indoor soccer title for St. Louis, and the first pro sports championship since the Cardinals won the World Series in 1982. In all, Doran played 828 pro indoor games. That's astounding. That would not count games played with the US national futsal team in 1999. In many ways, Doran—who previously attended CBC and St. Louis University—kept pro indoor soccer going in St. Louis and for his time involved with season after season, generation after generation, for all intents and purposes, he *was* indoor soccer in St. Louis—a truly iconic figure in the sport.

PROFESSIONAL INDOOR SOCCER HAS A SPECIAL PLACE IN ST. LOUIS

The beauty of the MISL was that it was like a buffer zone between the NASL and MLS.

It's vastly important to remember the first year for MLS was 1996. Prior to this monumental historic event, local players—from St. Louis and the Metro East—had to contend with the fact that professional outdoor soccer—which in Europe was the equivalent of Major League Baseball—just wasn't readily available for US talent. Not yet, anyway. Give it time people would say, give it time. Fast forward to November 13, 2020, on the eve of St. Louis City SC materializing into a tangible product on the field, and its sporting director Lutz Pfannenstiel said in a *St. Louis Post-Dispatch* story: "'One of our main aims is to have a big circle of players in our community in line prepared to become professionals.'"[65] This is where academies play a valuable role alongside a professional franchise. That's the world of St. Louis City SC via 2023 and beyond. Yet, in the 1980s and early 90s, the idea of professional outdoor soccer in the US flanked by academies was like traveling to the moon; pro outdoor soccer had been done before, it was possible, but everyone knew a return visit was very challenging, if not unlikely. If it were to occur, the finest minds in the world had to be on the same page, after years of work, and, even then, somewhat of a miracle had to take place in order for a successful launch.

However, while pro outdoor soccer in the 80s and early 90s was a thing of dreams, indoor soccer had taken off in America—in a big way, thereby providing a pro soccer outlet, entertainment, and inspiration. Though, as you may have guessed, there was a time limit for it. Back in the good old days (the late 1970s to the mid-1990s), for one reason or another, the patience of the American public would only go so far. In short, here's why: baseball, basketball, and football. Or, the Big 3 as I like to call them. In spite of soccer taking a backseat to traditional

American sports, for about 10 years, believe it or not, indoor soccer was knocking on the door of the Big 3; some may question the magnitude of the knock itself, which is a legitimate question, but nonetheless there was a knock at the door. The NASL, also known as the Pele league, had paved the way for soccer in America with the New York Cosmos; Pele had led the way along with a handful of other international stars (such as Franz Beckenbauer, Johan Cruyff, and George Best). Excitement was huge and Americans were warming up to soccer. While the NASL essentially existed from 1968 to 1984, with big moments, thanks to Pele, Beckenbauer, and a few others, if you can believe it, a strong argument could be made that the true dynamic league was the MISL.

This is where the St. Louis Steamers, Daryl Doran, Ty Keough, and others, stepped in to fill the void when the NASL was ebbing its way to retirement. The MISL, which definitely got a boost from the NASL, started attracting large crowds in the late 1970s and early 80s—call it the "golden era" of indoor soccer in America. When Pele retired in 1977, the MISL, which formed in 1978, was riding the wave of popularity the Brazilian legend had stirred up. It was perfect timing.

It's hard to deny the buzz you sense when you walk into an indoor soccer arena; you realize very quickly that excitement is in the air. Because of the smaller field, with skillful and physical play, along with a lot of goals, Americans were satisfied. Indoor soccer was a new fascination, one that was taking off.

For frame of reference, when Michael Jordan signed with the Chicago Bulls in the early 80s the Chicago Sting—owned by Lee Stern—were actually getting bigger attendance for games.

As the MISL was in full swing there were a number of teams, including but not limited to the New York Arrows, Baltimore Blast, Cleveland Crunch, Dallas Sidekicks, San Diego Sockers, and not to mention the St. Louis Steamers.

To say these teams were a big deal is putting it mildly. It can't be said enough, the MISL was phenomenally popular around the country (particularly in San Diego, Dallas, Kansas City, and Baltimore, just to name a few). It was a celebratory atmosphere during games. As for the nightlife, players would party like Blues standouts Brett Hull and Tony Twist after a hat-trick and KO. However, it should be pointed out, the league had trouble expanding and sustaining (whereby modern-day MLS is going up and up). Having said that, the MISL had a few hubs around the country, stronghold hubs. And for a time, call it the golden era of pro indoor soccer, the league was electric.

While this may have been true, soccer was still going through an 'auditioning period' with Americans at large.

Yet, for the most part, St. Louis was all in. The St. Louis Steamers had passionate fans, regular fans—fans that believed in soccer during a time when soccer was trying desperately to be cool. In effect, soccer was auditioning like a well-known European play touring a nation that happened to be obsessed with baseball, basketball, and football (American football that is). Soccer was trying to get as many of those obsessed fans to share their attention and passion with the world's chosen sport. Meanwhile, these Steamers fans, along with fans of the Sockers, Sidekicks, Comets, Blast, and others, were really into indoor soccer and loved how exciting it truly was.

As things kicked off for the Steamers in the 1979-80 MISL season, the team was coached by Pat McBride. McBride coached from 1979-81 and 1985-87. Al Trost was coach from 1981-83. Dave Clements led the team from 1983-85. And Tony Glavin was the coach from 1987-88.

Influential St. Louis Coach Dave Berwin said McBride was arguably the best US player of all time. Along with his accolades as a player, McBride was also fortunate enough to assist coaching legend Bob Guelker at SIUE.

Now McBride had a front row seat to one of the most exciting venues in town, albeit as a head coach. Given the historic nature of the original St. Louis Steamers, I was excited to speak with McBride about his experience as conductor of the team. Here I was, talking to one of the great players in St. Louis soccer history who had played for SLU, with great success, for the St. Louis Stars, and the USMNT. As an interview,

Pat was one of the best because he talked very clearly and slowly which made taking notes easier than others. He was very forthcoming too. I thought, *this is great, now I can get some inside info on the Steamers*—something off the beaten path, so to speak. I asked him about any game-day rituals he might've had as coach, during the glory days when crowds were off the charts and the team was like a rock and roll band—like did he go to a special diner and get the same meal from the same waitress kind of thing. I assumed (and hoped) his answer would be something along those lines and then he responded "No, I really, no, not that I can put my finger on." It was a great response though, very nonchalant: *Egh, we just sorta showed up to the game, you know.* It was very plainspoken, as though he were recalling what groceries he just brought home.

As McBride explained, when the Steamers logo was unveiled—which Bill McDermott helped design—there were maybe a handful of people there. The thought was: This indoor soccer thing isn't going to take off. Rather, skeptics thought locals would remain obsequious to baseball and football. For the first game, there were 15-16,000 people in attendance. The second game had to be stalled because there were up to 4,000 people in the lobby being sorted out; it was mayhem, a sensation. McBride explained how the pre-game introductions made them feel like they were 10 feet tall...there was the PA announcer and "the people are just going crazy." Tim Leiweke put together the whole affair, ahead of his time. McBride praised Tim's ingenuity and pointed out: "Just the way it was put together, it was, and the steam itself, you know, the whole presentation I think was, it was great to be a part of. I don't know how else to say it. It was, it really was." Back then, as McBride said, to the best of his knowledge there weren't any professional teams "that were having introductions like that." He added, "In terms of the steam, and, you know, the players running through the steam." He pointed out, "Laser lights, the whole presentation, it was unbelievable. And it was copied by the NHL, it was copied by, you know, by everybody. Really, the NBA, I mean, I think that would be a story that's waiting to be told." There was a pulse, the fans were loving it, electricity was in the air. While Leiweke was putting on a show for the ages, McBride left the presentation wizards to their magic as he was concentrating on the coaching front: "I wasn't involved in any of those kind of meetings. You know, I mean I just had the team ready to play and boom, so."

The team was off and running. For lack of a better word: spectacular!

In the early 1980s, the massive attendance numbers for the Steamers were even averaging around 17,000 in 1981-82, under Coach Al Trost. As Trost said, "It was phenomenal, it was great." He added how the arenas had "14-to-20,000 people and they were pretty much all full, you know, all the time." Legendary St. Louis sports commentator Ron Jacober said, "In the early days of the Steamers they drew huge crowds." St. Louis was buzzing. "It was just amazing," Trost said, reflecting on the crowds at the arena. "Even after the games were over they'd never go home...waiting outside the stadium for all of the players to leave, just lined up waiting to get autographs."

In those days, Trost attested to the fact that the team was comprised mainly of St. Louis talent, 80-85% by his estimation, born and raised. This helped boost attendance. Another reason for the popularity was, according to Trost, the indoor season filled in that gap of time—winter through early spring—"before baseball really kicked in." You couldn't have asked for a better setup, quite frankly. Schedule-wise, the golden era of indoor soccer was essentially just competing with the NFL, which has two days a week for games, and the NBA; therefore, thousands of people had a void to fill in respect to sports entertainment; the excitement St. Louis felt for the original Steamers made it a truly historical time. Moreover, St. Louis Cardinals legend Stan Musial was an owner of the Steamers and some pre-game meals were held at his restaurant Stan Musial and Biggie's. This association with Musial gave the Steamers even more credibility, a magical boost. Mainstream St. Louis bought in: the Steamers were cool.

It was a first-class operation with perks as Trost had a club-leased four-door Ford, blue color, that he drove from his home in Ellisville—where he lives to this day—to practices held largely in Chesterfield (at a facility called Castle Oak), and occasionally in Webster Groves (at a place called the Soccerdome), then to games at the renowned Checkerdome right by Forest Park. In the off-season, he took a drive with his family back to Seattle where he had previously played for the Sounders and got a chance to see some great national parks, like Yellowstone—he threw the bags on top of the car and hit the road, an Al Trost version of *National Lampoon's Vacation*. "That was all done in the Steamer-leased car!" he said, laughing fondly about a good memory. This would be his post-playing life, just a few years removed from when he represented the US national team against Poland circa 1973 in a game held in Connecticut—when a cross came into the box and "Gene Geimer kind of headed it back out to me, so I was outside the box"—where Al cracked a half-volley into the far upper-corner for a 1-0 winner. Poland, by way of the 70s and 80s, had a high-level team (as it does today). This was a unique, very mysterious, and intriguing time for the US national team back when the adidas uniforms were recollected for reuse—sometimes for a few years—as Al cracked up laughing over the thought of it. (To say soccer was competing with baseball, basketball, and football back then is no joke after all!) Be it the national team, St. Louis Stars, California Surf, Seattle Sounders, or New York Arrows...Trost was a top-class player and individual. Then, which often occurs, players retire and pick up leading the next generation from the sideline just as Phil Woosnam, Bob Kehoe, Gene Chyzowych, Gordon Bradley, Dettmar Cramer, Walter Chyzowych, Bob Gansler and others had done.

Back in coaching mode, Trost and assistant Tim Rooney would figure out the lines for the team before matches, with an eye on important opposing threats, so the players knew what was expected of them going in. The Steamers Booster Club—which consisted of die-hard fans, "probably a couple hundred of them"—would hold various parties after games at different restaurants for players, staff, fans, and the like. "It was just a fantastic time," Al said.

As a front and center franchise during this golden era of indoor soccer, St. Louis had serious talent.

Steve Pecher—a defender that was awarded the 1976 NASL Rookie of the Year with Dallas—was a mainstay with the Steamers for years and led as captain. Additionally, the stabilizer, the big frame of Pecher's, with a pep in his step, bouncing on the ball's of his slightly outward pointing feet, hesitated at nothing to mix it up with a propensity for hard tackles, slide tackles—a one-man wrecking crew with an eye to distribute the ball as he had a knack for reading the field. He was just plain a gamer. Initially, Pecher played for the Florissant Cougars and Normandy High School where he became an All-American and Missouri state champion in 1974. Eventually, after playing at Florissant Valley Community College, where he won the NJCAA national title and was named NJCAA All-American, he joined the Dallas Tornado of the NASL and then subsequently toured pro indoor soccer with the St. Louis Steamers, Kansas City Comets, and Los Angeles Lazers. He also was called up to the USMNT (1976-80) where he went toe-to-toe with the Mexican national team in legendary, revered, and daunting Mexico City; and, as a natural leader, he was named captain (1978-80) where his tough play earned a couple red cards over the course of time. As for the Steamers, Pecher, an MISL All-Star, played from 1979-84 and after some time with the Kansas City Comets he returned to the Steamers again from 1985-87.

The Steamers were lucky to have another team leader, the versatile, resilient, and soccer-savvy Ty Keough (from 1979-85). Keough, who possessed great touch and accuracy, was also a member of the USMNT for a couple years (1979-80) and shared the field with Pecher, a dynamic duo. (The year 1979-80 also saw Keough's former SLU teammate Pete Collico, a talented forward, join the Steamers.)

Sam Bick was with the Steamers throughout the magical years (1979-87). As a St. Louis native, Bick went to De Smet and eventually had success at Quincy University as he was part of multiple NAIA national championships in the 70s. Subsequently he acquired two caps with the USMNT (in 1976). His experience was extremely valuable with the Steamers and he eventually became captain when Pecher went down with an injury in 1984.

Dan Counce—who won the Hermann Trophy while at SLU—was a celebrated forward that represented the USMNT (1974-76) and scored 21 goals in 30 games for the Steamers (1979-80).

The power-punching didn't stop as the team also had forward Greg Villa at its disposal. Villa, a former SIUE sensation and a USMNT member (1977-80, where he scored five goals), flurried with the Steamers in the 80s (1980-82 and 1985-86).

Tough defender Greg Makowski, who was an SIUE Cougar and member of the USMNT (1978-80), helped keep things in order with the Steamers (1979-82 and 1985-86).

A few other SIUE legends that lit up the field for the Steamers were Don Ebert (1980-86), a scoring dynamo who earned MISL Rookie of the Year in the season of 1980-81; Bob Bozada (1980-82), a versatile threat; the spry, dazzling footwork of Jeff Cacciatore (1981-87); the reliable forward and midfielder John Stremlau (1980-83); and Granite City sensation Steve Trittschuh (of the USMNT from 1987-95) made his first pro appearance with the Steamers (1987-88).

Tony Bellinger—a defender and midfielder who played for the USMNT (from 1977-80)—was a standout with the Steamers (from 1979-87), a great talent.

Midfielder and SLU star Larry Hulcer jumped from the New York Cosmos (1980-81) to the St. Louis Steamers (1981-85). The multi-talented Hulcer also represented the USMNT for eight games (from 1979-80).

The experienced and amazingly good defender Don Droege—another SLU standout that was also on the USMNT (1977-79)—joined the Steamers (from 1983-85) at the end of his long professional voyage.

Kevin Handlan—a defender and midfielder from SLU—had a run with the Steamers during the team's first season (1979-80).

Denny Vaninger—a prominent forward who previously played for the St. Louis Stars in the 70s and the USMNT (1974-75)—joined the Steamers in the early 80s (from 1980-83).

Midfielder Ricky Davis—who was a longtime member of the USMNT (1977-88), not to mention playing the role of captain as well—was a featured attraction for the Steamers (from 1983-86), where he racked up 90 goals. In fact, Davis tallied up 123 games for St. Louis, the second most in his career. Only with the New York Cosmos (1978-84) did he play in more games, with 136.

Honduran international forward Armando Betancourt—winner of the Hermann Trophy in 1981 while at Indiana University—showed off his attacking skills for the Steamers (from 1984-86).

Even crafty and wily veteran Angelo DiBernardo—winner of the Hermann Trophy in 1978 while at Indiana University—made his last professional stop with the Steamers (1986-87).* The Argentinian-born attacking midfielder had previously landed with the Los Angeles Aztecs, New York Cosmos, Kansas City Comets, and USMNT (1979-85). He only played six games with the Steamers but spread his wealth of skill and knowledge on the field for fans while adding to the already illustrious list of past players.

As one can see, the golden era of the Steamers essentially *was* the USMNT. It was a carnival of limitless talent.

One can't forget Slobodan Ilijevski, a popular goalie with fans, who won the MISL Goalkeeper of the Year award in 1981-82 and 1983-84. Slobo, as he was known, first had an unsuccessful tryout in Chicago, but someone gave Pat McBride a call and said you need to look at this goalie, he's pretty good. Apparently McBride said he didn't need one at the time but took a look nonetheless. Slobo arrived in St. Louis with only $25 to his name, and made the team. Ron Jacober, who called games over the radio for the original Steamers, St. Louis Storm, and original St. Louis Ambush said, "He had nothing when he got here. So they worked him out and said 'oh this guy can play' and they signed him." After having some pre-game snacks with Slobo, Jacober recalled, "His pre-game meal was Apple Pie à la Mode, that's what he had before games." As a goalie

---

* This information came from *Stats Crew* online, accessed January 5, 2021. There is other information online that listed DiBernardo's time with the Steamers for the years 1987-88.

flopping around on the turf, Slobo was said to use just about anything to compensate for his body, including ointments and even onions and tomatoes for his knees. (Tough life, goalies.) Loved by the fans, Jacober added, "Interesting guy. He was kind of eccentric, but a wonderful, wonderful human being."

In addition, defender and midfielder Tony Glavin (1980-87), who was all over the field, was a steady source of scoring, and like many teammates he was an MISL All-Star.

Balancing all this out, with a knockout punch, would be the aforementioned Daryl Doran. A few other dazzling talents that helped steer the ship during these years included the forward prowess of Manuel Cuenca (1979-81), Steve Sullivan (1980-81), John Hayes (1981-83), Dan Muesenfechter (1981-83), and Tim Walters (1982-85); midfield maestro and USMNT member Perry Van der Beck (1987-88); the defensive steadiness of Carl Rose (1979-86), Joe Clarke (1981-82), Jeff Sendobry (1980-84), and Chris Kenny (1985-88); along with the goalkeeping exploits of Eric Delabar (1979-84), Manny Schwartz (1980-83), and SIUE legend Ed Gettemeier (1984-86).

And, lo and behold, Jim Kavanaugh, an owner of St. Louis City SC and one of the prominent reasons MLS landed in St. Louis, graced a Steamers uniform in the late 80s (1986-88).

Things were rolling.

In 1980-81, 1981-82, and 1983-84 the Steamers placed second overall in the MISL.

But, mysteriously, indoor soccer went from boom to 'almost bust.'

Despite big attendance in the early 80s, the box office numbers gradually faded downhill in the years after that. In so doing, teams hung around, living off the good old days of the early 80s. In 1985, a move was made to bring local favorite Pat McBride back in as coach. Bringing McBride back was popular for sure, as he was a hometown icon that St. Louis embraced. In addition, the Steamers held on to a sustainable amount of cachet with its top-flight players, such as Tony Bellinger. In 1986, Soccer Digest (February/March issue) informed readers that

"Bellinger, the St. Louis Steamers' dependable defender, holds the distinction of being the only player to have participated in all six MISL All-Star Games."

Into the late 80s, the rock and roll atmosphere lingered. Look no further than Nebo Bandovic, who played for the Steamers alongside his brother, Boki. As Dave Luecking pointed out in a 1988 *Soccer Digest* publication, the Yugoslavian "Nebo is the Oscar Madison of the two—seemingly disheveled at all times. He's a wild and crazy guy, flamboyant on and off the field. He says he likes money, fast cars, and fast women. He describes his friends as 'gangsters.'"[66] On some levels the good times were rolling indeed.

Though, in the late 80s, the Steamers were about to fold.

Actually, it should be pointed out that pro indoor soccer never technically busted but fizzled out of popularity as the late 1980s turned into the 90s. Essentially, the MISL was around from 1978 to 1992.

Since the close of the original MISL, as many people know, the top pro indoor soccer league has changed names a number of times. Most fans didn't care either way; they just wanted pro indoor soccer; the name by which the league was administered was irrelevant—so long as teams were in place and competing.

As the 1990s were nearing, pro indoor soccer was in dire straits, especially in St. Louis. Would there be a team? Would there not be a team?

DR. ABE HAWATMEH SAVES THE DAY

The St. Louis Steamers: The Late 1980s

The team is about to finish its run. Toward the end of this wondrous escapade, enters a passionate soccer fan named Abe Hawatmeh. As most people know him, Dr. Hawatmeh was born in Jordan where he first enjoyed soccer as a boy. Dr. Hawatmeh—who has a confident, energetic, Jordanian accent—pointed out, "I was a good *soccer* player in Jordan," and he moved to Italy, where, as he said, he soon enjoyed soccer more from the bench. As time went on, he became a surgeon and Urologist. After he moved to St. Louis, the dazzling doctor began meeting people here and there, one thing led to another, and he got a call from St. Louis Mayor Vincent Schoemehl, who informed Dr. Hawatmeh he was going to own a soccer team, the Steamers; the team was in the last few years of its existence at that point.

Unfortunately, the Steamers folded shortly after Dr. Hawatmeh's involvement. In 1988 the Steamers closed shop.

Next up, however, came the St. Louis Storm, and Dr. Hawatmeh—also affectionately known as Abe—was an owner.

The St. Louis Storm, 1989-92.

The St. Louis Storm, as many know, had a brief, though exciting, tenure. Abe was present as the Storm benefitted through contributions from an assortment of players, including the likes of Fernando Clavijo, Daryl Doran, Kevin Hundelt, Slobodan Ilijevski, Mark Moser, Preki, Mark Santel, and Branko Segota.[†]

Attendance gradually increased each year. One reason likely had to do with goal-scoring sensation, Preki. The Yugoslavian-born attacking midfielder unleashed outright havoc on keepers with 68 goals in the 1990-91 season, followed by 45 in the 1991-92 season. Since his sojourn with the Storm, Preki has represented the USMNT in the 1998 FIFA World Cup and also has become the only player so far to win the MLS MVP award on two occasions. In 2016-17, he returned to coach Saint Louis FC for a brief stint.

The sure hands of Ilijevski, the speedy Clavijo, the all-around ability of Doran, the goal-scoring Moser, the crafty quick feet of Santel, along with the experience of MISL legend Segota also led to fan approval.

There were some interesting times in the Storm days, for sure. One away game in Tacoma, Washington, saw Ron Jacober—the legendary St. Louis Cardinals announcer who Abe calls "the best radio voice in

---

[†]   For an extended list of St. Louis Storm players, visit the pro indoor soccer section in the Golden Vault.

the business"—relay the entire broadcast by telephone back home for radio listeners, thanks to some technical difficulties. According to Ron, it wasn't the most pleasant performance of his career.

As the team entertained fans on the road and at home, this little-known venture of the Storm featured a lot of top players. But it should also be noted, they were top players in the prime of their careers. Preki, Clavijo, Santel, and Doran certainly were displaying top-level soccer. Such a group is an owner's dream come true. According to Abe, the Storm even went to Europe for indoor soccer games and had great success. Abe said that "...we beat them" and the crowd was chanting for the team; it was a true testament to the talent of the Storm, a group of guys not to be taken lightly.

Yet, as good as times were, there were difficulties in keeping the Storm in the black. For practically any sport, it's an issue with which every pro team around the nation has to deal at one point or another. Aside from Abe, who was well-regarded, there was another owner who didn't carry as much standing in the eyes of others. A reliable source indicated that he skipped out owing money all over town. Unfortunately, for soccer fans in St. Louis, the Storm was soon to pass.

The St. Louis Ambush, 1992-2000

Indoor soccer in St. Louis (the longtime hub of soccer nationwide) was, perhaps, beginning to look like a thing of the past. This is where Abe stepped up and made a bit more history.

One day the NPSL commissioner, Steve Paxos, called and said (according to Abe), "Dr. Hawatmeh, I want to come down to St. Louis, if it's okay with you, tomorrow or something, and I want to have a dinner and talk to you." The two had dinner on the Hill (the classic St. Louis Italian-style neighborhood replete with casual and elegant family-friendly restaurants). There was a lot riding on pro indoor soccer at the time. St. Louis, the nation's longstanding bastion, was potentially going to sit the next few plays out. This would have been a major blow to the league and the city of St. Louis in terms of finances and morale. Abe was hesitant to jump in again as owner; the Steamers had folded; the Storm had done the same, unfortunately. So much was at stake—Abe's life and career could've potentially gone down the drain. Regardless, according to Abe, "After dinner I bought the Ambush!" he said, chuckling. He couldn't help himself. He added, "I gave him a check," and it went from there.

As it turned out, Abe knew everybody—governors, mayors, sponsors, local officials. It was a busy, lively, and exciting time. As owner, Abe wore many hats including fundraiser, high-five cheerleader *à la* Mark Cuban, bill-payer, party organizer, and politician. According to Abe, he'd go back and forth from his game suite—where he'd wine and dine with sponsors—to the locker room, where he'd encourage leading scorers like Joe Reiniger and Mark Moser to get a goal for him. Abe, being the sophisticated doctor he was, would enthusiastically swoop in with words of encouragement that perhaps reflected more of a bourgeoisie charm. On one occasion, team leader Daryl Doran had some friendly advice for how to communicate with the players on a colloquial level. According to Abe, "I used to go down and I said, 'hey gentlemen.' He said 'Abe, what the hell is with gentlemen?'" Abe added that Doran told him how to speak to them, in proper locker room fashion. Abe—who took everything in stride—loved it and was living out a true fairytale fantasy with a professional soccer team for the sport he loves.

The Ambush had some standout years in the 1990s; the teams were remarkably good and there were plenty of wins.⸸

In addition, a longtime writer for the *St. Louis Post-Dispatch* and member of the Naismith Memorial Basketball Hall of Fame, Dave Dorr, told me, "Abe paid the players well and on time."

Everything culminated for the Ambush (and professional soccer in St. Louis at large) in 1994-95 when the Ambush earned the league championship. Abe proudly said, "We could've beaten any indoor soccer

---

⸸   For an extended list of St. Louis Ambush players, visit the pro indoor soccer section in the Golden Vault.

team ever." It was the first pro soccer league championship for St. Louis... like a diamond.

One player's story perhaps speaks a little louder than others. He was part of the 1994-95 championship run with the Ambush. Indeed, few can claim the high standing of one Steve Trittschuh. For those who think that indoor is inferior to outdoor, look no further for proof of indoor being legitimate than Trittschuh's participation during his prime. During 1987-88 with the Steamers and 1994-95 with the Ambush, Trittschuh was a game-changing defender that was on top of the soccer pyramid as a member of the USMNT (1987-95).

When I spoke with Steve over the phone I realized what a genuinely nice guy he is. In fact, there's something about Granite City guys. Granted, Gene Baker, another genuinely nice person, isn't originally 'from Granite City' yet he was there long enough to have some of it undoubtedly rub off. Throughout my life, including the tournaments I participated in as a guest player for the Granite City Elks, I've met many Granite City guys and maybe their genuine niceness, which is always straddled by a fist ready to punch, comes from generations of steel workers that pass down what seems to be a trait known as "we work together in dangerous conditions which means we have to watch out for one another." Whether that's an actual thing or not, Trittschuh—a true Midwesterner, a good guy to hang with, someone that's easy to talk to—was known as quite a tough customer in his day. Take away the soft veneer and this hard-tackling Granite City native perhaps has reached the highest plateau of American soccer, even among his cohorts from the most elite inner-circle of St. Louis soccer.

Indeed, Harry Keough was on the field in World Cup 1950 when the underdog USMNT took down mighty England 1-0. Mike Sorber was in World Cup 1994, including the highly televised Round of 16 1-0 loss to Brazil that saw Tab Ramos dramatically leave the field from a cheap shot he took on the side of the head from the elbow of Leonardo. Steve Ralston, once a regular USMNT member, who quietly made a name for himself in MLS over the years, is, after all, the second all-time assist leader in MLS (second only to Landon Donovan)—not bad, not bad at all. What's more, Taylor Twellman, as talented as he was, won the MLS MVP award in 2005, and rightly so. The list goes on, by the way. Al Trost was captain of the USMNT, as was Steve Pecher. Ty Keough, Chris Klein, Brad Davis, Tim Ream, and Josh Sargent have all represented the USMNT, and, the list goes on.

Yet, Trittschuh, who was a member of Busch, Scott Gallagher, and a standout at SIUE, was also a regular member of the USMNT throughout the late 1980s and early 90s who played in World Cup 1990. Lo and behold, he has the distinct honor of being on the field in arguably the biggest USMNT game in history, or as it's simply known: the 'shot heard round the world.'

This was an epic 1989 showdown between the US and Trinidad and Tobago, in Trinidad and Tobago, in front of a sold-out home crowd where almost every fan was wearing a red shirt. Furthermore, it was a must-win game for the USMNT; a tie or loss wouldn't have done it; the US literally had to win in order to qualify for the 1990 World Cup. You could feel the tension in the air. As if there wasn't enough pressure, a young Dwight Yorke, arguably Trinidad's greatest all-time player, would play in this game. As an article from *The San Diego Union-Tribune* pointed out: "It is the last place you'd expect to be the crossroads of U.S. soccer."[67] Interesting observation. (Can't say I agree with the syntax but that's aside the point.) Trinidad and Tobago, of all places, doesn't seem like the gateway to a World Cup.

But there was more history regarding a previous USMNT in Trinidad and Tobago than this one game in 1989. In fact, Trittschuh and his teammates were landing in a place that previous US players had been many years earlier. "Port of Spain, Trinidad and Tobago's diverse capital, is where the U.S. national team made one of several airline refueling stops on its way to the 1950 World Cup in Brazil, where they shocked England and the rest of the world with a 1-0 victory against a team that some London bookmakers had installed as a 12-goal favorite—a result many rank among the most improbable upsets in sports history."[68] (This was the same 1950 US team that featured numerous St. Louis players, including Harry Keough.)

Back to 1989, when another 1-0 victory was looming in the air. Somehow, someway, the USMNT was back in Trinidad, with a chance to make history. Most remember this 1989 game for Paul Caligiuri. History tends to remember the goal-scorer. Though, as Caligiuri would likely admit, he was flanked by a team full of talent, patriotic pride, and raw emotion for a game that was meant for greatness. Trittschuh was in the starting lineup as a defender with teammates Tony Meola, Mike Windischmann, John Doyle, Paul Krumpe, Brian Bliss, John Harkes, Tab Ramos, Paul Caligiuri, Bruce Murray, and Peter Vermes. The field wasn't in the best condition, in part because it had rained a few days earlier and the ground was somewhat unkept (causing the ball to take unsteady bounces). As a result, Trittschuh explained, "It was kind of hard to play the game." He added, "It wasn't the prettiest game." Yet it was one of those games that, if it were on TV right now, I'd likely set everything aside and watch because the tension was unbelievable, the stakes were so high, and history was made in a big way. First of all, one must remember that prior to World Cup 1990, the USMNT had not been in a World Cup since 1950. That's worth repeating: since 1950. That's 40 years. As a result, the US men's soccer program had been trying to find its way all that time, with plenty of ups and downs. As it turned out, the USMNT had tied Trinidad and Tobago 1-1 in Los Angeles prior to this showdown. Trittschuh scored that game. Also, in St. Louis at Soccer Park, the USMNT had a so-so performance against El Salvador. So the team had dug a hole for itself. The table was set for one final game in Trinidad and Tobago. One final game for a chance to enter World Cup 1990. Because of points the US had to win. A tie or loss would've seen Trinidad advance to World Cup 1990. The Trinidad fans knew without a doubt how important this match was. In fact, in honor of the game, the Trinidad government announced a national holiday. The stakes were so high that when the USMNT arrived at the airport, approximately 48 hours before the match, local fans had lined the streets from the airport to the hotel, yelling and throwing things at the team, trying to psych them out. Come game day, the USMNT arrived at the stadium about two hours before kickoff and Trittschuh pointed out, "It was packed, I mean it was full." Fans were singing. "It was just a crazy atmosphere." Trittschuh said, "But it wasn't anything that we weren't used to." As he recalled, for games in El Salvador, Guatemala, and Costa Rica, it was even crazier. Back in the 80s, fans in El Salvador were known to throw bags of urine. It was all good practice for this showdown in Trinidad.

Prior to kickoff, covering the game for ESPN, John Paul Dellecamera said, "This is the most important 90 minutes in the history of the players on the US national team."

For what seemed like an unbelievably difficult task—to defeat a very talented T&T squad on home turf in front of fanatical fans—the team was getting ready, the whistle was about to blow. Then it just started to happen.

Steve Trittschuh was standing his ground, doing what he could to relieve pressure from a mounting T&T attack. The shot that won the game, of course, came off the boot of Paul Caligiuri, a miraculous volley from distance. With that goal, along with a team effort that rallied for the duration of the game, the USMNT won 1-0 and entered the 1990 World Cup for the first time since 1950, 40 years earlier. As Trittschuh said, the end of that game was "a relief." He added, when the team arrived in Miami, the press was waiting.

In a way, this game was like a launching point for the USMNT program, a rebirth of sorts. For all intents and purposes, with ups and downs, the USMNT has entered a whole new realm of popularity today, with a ton of success and improvement along the way. Much of the popularity, success, and improvement has been due to this epic achievement in Trinidad. After all, a nation that reaches the World Cup is a nation relevant in the world of soccer. Trittschuh and the USMNT put the US back on the map and for American soccer things have improved continually ever since.

Subsequently, Trittschuh was a member of that 1990 FIFA World Cup squad in Italy, which turned out to be a brief escapade, and played in the opening game against Czechoslovakia.

As we return to the St. Louis Ambush, with Trittschuh as a featured member, it is abundantly clear how talented the team was. Certainly a highlight of Trittschuh's career came a few years after the 1990 World Cup in the 1994-95 NPSL championship season with the St. Louis Ambush; as he said, it was one of the best times he's had playing on a team.

In a way, he kind of stumbled into the situation. In the late 80s, he'd suited up with the Steamers. Then he branched out. In between teams, Trittschuh—who played in a number of places throughout his career, including stops with the Tampa Bay Rowdies and Sparta Prague—thought he'd make a return to indoor. He probably recognized he'd only be with the team for a short time, called Daryl Doran—who was a player-coach at the time—and said he had a few open months.

Fast forward to 2020, when Trittschuh was inducted into the St. Louis Sports Hall of Fame as part of "The 2020 Induction of Southern Illinois Sports Legends" and was referred to as "St. Louis soccer royalty" by longtime St. Louis Cardinals announcer, Ron Jacober. Steve commented about his time bouncing around from team to team, Europe to the US.

Back to the mid-1990s. When Trittschuh joined the Ambush, for convenience sake, he stayed at his mom and dad's place in Granite City, just a short drive from practices which were held in north St. Louis near 270, and games which were downtown. This was a very significant time in Trittschuh's career and for St. Louis soccer. From 1979 until 1994, St. Louis had not won a championship in pro indoor soccer.

This 1994-95 St. Louis Ambush team was special. Trittschuh and the Ambush took home the championship in style.

Team owner Abe Hawatmeh was jubilant and proud of his team that he was certain could defeat any other "indoor soccer team ever."

Mark Moser had a stellar year with 89 goals.

In the championship, the Ambush took down the Harrisburg Heat, of Harrisburg, Pennsylvania, with a four-game sweep that featured a 14-11 win in the final match.

This was a huge deal for St. Louis soccer. It's still remembered years later. For purists that think outdoor is the only way to play soccer—well, there's a strong argument to be made that indoor is more demanding than outdoor. As I like to say, indoor puts an exclamation point on all your weaknesses as a player. If you can succeed in indoor you're doing something right. And this Ambush team was number one. To win a championship with the Ambush was, in fact, a spectacular achievement for Trittschuh and his teammates.

Looking back 25 years, Joe Lyons, of the *St. Louis Post-Dispatch,* wrote: "In the finals, the Ambush won 19-9, 18-8 and 12-7 to set up its dramatic title-clinching win in Harrisburg. 'That season, everything just seemed to come together for us,' said Doran, who runs Doran Fitness in O'Fallon, Mo., and who recently became the women's soccer coach at St. Charles Community College. 'A key, obviously, was being healthy at the end of the year, something that limited us in other seasons. But the really great thing about that season was how well we played together. We had Moser and Reiniger up top who were always so dangerous, and our midfield, with guys like Steve Kuntz, Scott McDoniel, Steve Maurer and John Klein, did a phenomenal job of playing the game at both ends of the floor. And we also got some great play from guys in the back like Steve Trittschuh and Chris Kenny, which allowed Kevin Hundelt and me to move forward and contribute in the attack."[69] Additionally, in true St. Louis form, Lyons pointed out that "...a key to the title team's success may have been the squad's North vs. South games in practice"[70] which were arguably even more competitive than actual games. As it turns out, the very competition from their youth—North vs. South rivalries—that pushed them to where they were, helped put them over the top.

It was groundbreaking to be the first pro soccer championship for St. Louis. For Abe, Steve Trittschuh, Daryl Doran, Mark Moser, Jamie

Swanner, Joe Reiniger, and company, the 1995 championship represents a special epoch of St. Louis indoor soccer.

As 1996 came around so too did MLS, its inaugural year. Yet, no St. Louis. While MLS was making strides and getting off the ground, St. Louis was surging forward with pro indoor soccer by way of the Ambush, hoping for a boost in attendance to the levels of the early 80s and the high-flying Steamers.

When it comes to getting people in seats, teams are always on the lookout for players with a spark. The type of players that make owners like Abe wake up early in a fantastic mood, ready to jet over to the arena all while risking a handful of speeding tickets to see a world-class performance.

By the late 1990s, the St. Louis Ambush had a true legend walk through its midst. As so many great players had come and gone over the years, one more joined the list: Kenny Snow. As a four-year first-team All-American at Indiana University, Snow also won the Hermann Trophy on two occasions (1988 and 1990); in 1988 he was featured on the front cover of *Soccer Digest*—a magazine typically reserved for pro players—with the caption: "Indiana's KEN SNOW | College Soccer's Super Scorer." Eventually he tallied up two games with the USMNT. On paper, Brian McBride—St. Louis' 'adopted son' by way of St. Louis University—could easily make a claim as Chicago's best all-time player, though, if you truly know soccer it would have to be Kenny Snow. All of 5'9" (give or take), Snow may not have played in the EPL or a World Cup, but this could theoretically be chalked up to playing in a different era when coaches at higher levels—particularly in regards to the EPL and USMNT—preferred forwards that were over six feet tall (for a style of play that largely revolved around crossing the ball into the box). This is all speculation of course, but the bottom line is that Snow's craft and guile around goal were uncanny. And someone like Brian McBride would likely hasten to agree. As a kid at Indiana Soccer Camp, myself and other campers looked up to Snow, our elder, college legend, and perhaps reluctant camp counselor. Jerry Yeagley praised his talents, placing him in a category of rare air.

Way back when, while visiting St. Louis, on a lark I stopped by the arena—in downtown St. Louis, the same location as the Blues—and viewed what was probably my one and only St. Louis Ambush game in the 1990s. In-between pro indoor teams, there was Snow, making a brief stop in St. Louis. Somewhere in the game his perfect scoring technique was on full display as a teammate—perhaps Joel Shanker—chipped a through pass over his shoulder, down the left wing. With a defender chasing on his right side, Snow ran onto the ball, which bounced high maybe twice. About 10 or 15 yards outside the corner of the box, with the ball around head and shoulder height, with his left foot Snow connected on a full side-volley, on the move no less.§ The form of Snow was perfect. The ball went from his left foot—practically above his head—to the far upper right hand corner, crashed into the net for a goal. Perfect technique—so quick, sound, immaculate. It left anyone in the stands, even with the slightest amount of soccer expertise, gawking at such a difficult and perfectly struck shot. That was Kenny Snow, a finishing genius that could score with the best of them from around the world. Unfortunately, he died during the COVID-19 pandemic in 2020. Though for a brief year or so in St. Louis, Snow dazzled onlookers with some 56 goals in 28 games.

There were good strides made in the 1990s, including the Ambush championship of 1995 coupled with the appearance of highly renowned players such as Snow and Trittschuh. However, there was a problem: the St. Louis Rams.

Despite good years with the Ambush, Los Angeles was about to send a football team to the Midwest. The 1995 introduction of the St.

---

§   Very Brazilian; I recall seeing the first team of Internacional in a stadium in Porto Alegre when I was 14 and a player scored a similar volley inside the box, with his back to goal; it's a move you might see in Thai kickboxing as the Brazilians have a lot of interplay in the box to allow for such a thing.

Louis Rams—competing in the soaring NFL—signaled the beginning of the end for Abe's run as owner. Dave Dorr informed me over the phone: "Because once the Rams came then the media in this town just completely turned all of their attention to the Rams. And that took away many of Abe's sponsors." The new Rams gathered up all the attention; obviously, not to mention, the Cardinals and Blues were still around; it was a tough market space for the Ambush. As Dorr said regarding Abe's venture: "He lost a lot of money when he owned the Ambush. But he kept it for all those years just because he loved soccer" and one of Abe's dreams was to own a pro soccer team, which he did. In many ways, Abe was a true hero for soccer in St. Louis. He put it all out there, and despite some ups and downs, he got a lot in return. According to Dorr, "He had great years and it was a fun time for the town, and so it was worth it."

It came down to getting fans in seats. In the larger scheme of things, the struggle for pro soccer in St. Louis persisted as the original Steamers transitioned to the Storm which transitioned to the Ambush and then back to the Steamers again as 2000 came around.

In many ways pro indoor soccer in St. Louis was in a fight for its life as each ownership group was banking on big attendance numbers, like in the early days of the Steamers, yet, despite good showings here and there, this wasn't materializing as hoped. Soccer heavyweights like Daryl Doran were steering the ship, as best they could, to keep pro indoor soccer extant. Doran—who essentially was like the Cal Ripken of indoor soccer—persisted through the 1980s, 1990s, and 2000s. Around his orbit, many others from St. Louis and around the world came and went. From 1989 through the 2000s, whether it was on the Storm, Ambush, or the second run of the Steamers, players, many of whom were local, included Steve Trittschuh, Shane Battelle, Terry Brown, David Brcic, David Eise, Steve Ralston, Mike Laposha, Pat Mann, John Klein, Mark Santel, Kevin Hundelt, Chris Kenny, Steve Kuntz, Mark Moser, Kirk Moser, Joe Reiniger, Joel Shanker, Tim Henson, Tim Leonard, Matt Caution, Kevin Kalish, Matt Little, Pat Barry, Jeff Davis, Jeff DiMaria, D.J. Newsom,

Kevin Quigley, Joe Smugala, Brandon Gibbs, Justin McMillian, Mike Kirchhoff.

ST. LOUIS KNIGHTS & ST. LOUIS STRIKERS: ALONG FOR THE RIDE

Alongside the indoor soccer scene there were a few attempts at pro outdoor soccer that took flight from time to time in lower-level leagues with teams such as the St. Louis Knights (1994-95), and the St. Louis Strikers (2003-04). The St. Louis Knights were presumably part of the Second Division of the USL. The St. Louis Strikers competed in the USL's Premier Development League, the fourth tier of what was known as the 'American soccer pyramid' at the time.

The St. Louis Knights didn't last long—a team caught in the 90s as American soccer was finding its way toward MLS. The coach was Jim Bokern, formerly a standout player with SLU, St. Louis Kutis, and the St. Louis Stars.

As for the St. Louis Strikers, it was managed by Sterling Wescott, who played with D.C. United, and subsequently with the second launch of the St. Louis Steamers. The Strikers played home games at Soccer Park in St. Louis (which makes sense) and also (for some strange reason) in Springfield, Missouri—which is not exactly nearby.

The tricky thing about lower-level leagues in American soccer over the years is that they often have changed names, even so subtly. For example, "United Soccer Leagues" changed to "United Soccer League"—oy vey. And they often had very ephemeral lifespans. Having said that, there were very good players in such leagues, and through no fault of their own, the leagues have been quite unpredictable in nature.

Regardless, the indoor teams in St. Louis had the most prominence.

THE REINCARNATION OF THE ST. LOUIS STEAMERS

The St. Louis Steamers, Part II, 2000-2006.

As the 1990s drifted away, so too did the Ambush.

In the early 2000s, the St. Louis Steamers had a reincarnation of sorts. Part II was about to begin, with Daryl Doran leading the way.

The second attempt at the St. Louis Steamers technically occurred between 1998-2006. The team was founded—or as one might say, "Re-founded"—in 1998. Essentially, the second incarnation of the Steamers generally represented St. Louis on the field from 2000-2006. In 2002 the team had a year off—these things get convoluted sometimes.

Attendance levels for the second St. Louis Steamers were not quite as expected as the team averaged around 4-5,000 per game. The days of the golden era of indoor soccer in St. Louis, which included massive attendance levels, were long gone. The reasons are somewhat mysterious. Essentially, pro indoor soccer at large—across the country—was very popular in the early 1980s, but declined in attendance levels in the years to follow. My theory, which is just a theory, is based on the Pele factor. Pele's arrival in the US during 1975-77 caused a colossal stir. He and other illustrious members of the New York Cosmos—by way of the NASL, in which the St. Louis Stars had competed—created huge excitement and there was natural spillover as the MISL—founded in 1978—got off the ground. Times were great for the MISL at first, but gradually people lost interest. Furthermore, as the second incarnation of the St. Louis Steamers was in motion there was an interesting phenomenon occurring. Pro outdoor soccer was underway in the form of Major League Soccer, which kicked off its inaugural season in 1996. In the early days of MLS, franchises were working hard to consistently get bodies in seats; things hadn't quite exploded across-the-board yet. (Soccer was still auditioning for mainstream approval in America and big changes would occur throughout the 2000s and especially after 2010 when the USMNT had exciting moments at the FIFA World Cup in South Africa.) As MLS action was underway, taking on a battle of its own to find success in America, the St. Louis Steamers found itself in a difficult position in terms of attracting large crowds. Interestingly, the NASL—and the Pele factor—seemed to boost the early days of the MISL, with natural spillover. However, MLS didn't seem to provide the same for pro indoor soccer. One reason might have had something to do with *curiosity*. In the early days of the MISL, in addition to natural spillover from the Pele factor, there was *curiosity for this new game: indoor soccer.* Indoor soccer had an electric vibe about it. People were curious, they were drawn in. Perhaps this love affair was nothing but a brief dalliance. Certainly the attendance figures for the Steamers Part II were suggesting as much. Yet people were showing up. At times, crowds were big. Yet it wasn't substantial enough to rival the old days when the team was treated as though it were Valentino Rossi in the late 90s returning to Italy after a victorious race.

In 2000 and 2001 the Steamers rolled into losing seasons.

Then 2002 saw a year off for the Steamers as ownership issues behind the scenes were getting sorted out.

As 2003 swung around, the Steamers were ready to go, yet again. However, despite having a talented roster, it was another losing season in 2003-04. Yet with a 14-22 record there was something to build on.

As for 2004-05, the Steamers managed to tumble into a 20-20 record.

In the final 2005-06 season, the Steamers had a great year. The team record was 23-7. That team included the quickness of Jamal Beasley, the skill and passing organization of Jeff DiMaria and Sterling Wescott, the lightning bolt Shaun David, the rocket shot of Joe Reiniger, and the goalkeeping exploits of Brett Phillips. When you have a shot that's powerful and accurate (and typically low) like Reiniger's, along with the speed of David, things should work out well. Guys like me like to tell you how fast they were. Maybe I was as quick (so I'd like to think), but when it comes to speed, this guy David was "from another planet" fast.

Just having a fast guy or two on a team is one thing, but it all has to come together with a little gamesmanship, passing and organization, etc. The Steamers of 2005-06 had a mix of everything as the team made the championship game and eventually came in second place to the Baltimore Blast in a close contest.

D.J. Newsom—who is originally from north St. Louis and played center mid for Norco, Busch, and Rosary High School—eventually joined the Steamers as a defender from 2000-02, then spent a year with the Cleveland Force, with Hector Marinaro, and rejoined the Steamers from 2003-06. Newsom, sturdy in build, an affable guy, eventually became a police officer in the Florissant area for around 10 years; following that he was in personal security in the realm of Fortune 500 clients. Reflecting on his time with the Steamers, he pointed out: It was a talented team that really came together during its final season, falling just short of a championship. Following the 2006 loss in the final to Baltimore, which was at home, Newsom said, "We knew the owners were both from Philadelphia and they were, you know, they were taking their money and not having the team again."

So it was, the end of an era...again. The Steamers, Part II, folded.

ST. LOUIS LIONS MAKE STRIDES

In 2006, under the leadership of Tony Glavin, the green and white St. Louis Lions set forth. As of 2021, the team was competing in the USL League Two, known as the fourth tier in the realm of the American Soccer Pyramid. It's known as a developmental league under the umbrella of USL.

ST. LOUIS ILLUSION, ILLINOIS PIASA, AND ST. LOUIS AMBUSH (PART II)

After the St. Louis Steamers made a curtain call, pro indoor soccer continued with the arrival of the St. Louis Illusion, Illinois Piasa, and eventually the St. Louis Ambush, Part II.

The St. Louis Illusion, 2008-10: Glen Carbon, Illinois

As the St. Louis Illusion set forth, from an indoor arena in Glen Carbon (known then as The Game Arena), the echo of SIUE greatness lingered as the famous soccer-grounds of the Cougars were just up the road—a short drive, perhaps a mile or so—in Edwardsville. The owner and coach was Jamie Swanner...a good goalie from the days of the original Ambush. This venture had but a brief moment, yet made a claim for winning the 2008-09 United States Open Cup for Arena Soccer. Then, as things ended (almost as soon as they began), the team was followed up by the Illinois Piasa.

Illinois Piasa, 2010-14: The Metro East
Illinois Piasa had roots in the Metro East area and played some games in the Illinois locations of Granite City, Pontoon Beach, and Glen Carbon.

From 2008-2014, pro indoor soccer in St. Louis was represented by the St. Louis Illusion (2008-10), and Illinois Piasa (2010-14). These two teams played a crucial role in preserving the pro indoor legacy of St. Louis.

AC ST. LOUIS MAKES A SPLASH
Amid the musical chairs of pro indoor soccer, in 2010, AC St. Louis—a pro outdoor team—took shape in what was the NASL, USSF Division 2 Professional League.

The team was coached by St. Louis area native Dale Schilly though it didn't last long. Sometimes, as we've seen in American soccer, the names of teams and leagues can get confusing. *Wikipedia* described the attempt of AC St. Louis in pro outdoor soccer in the following way: "AC St. Louis was an American professional soccer team based in St. Louis, Missouri, United States. Founded in December 2009, the team played its first and only season the next year in the NASL Conference of the temporary USSF D2 Pro League, the second tier of the American Soccer Pyramid. With plans to join the new North American Soccer League the following season, the club folded in January 2011 under unmanageable financial strain."[71] As the article pointed out, there were plans to join the "new North American Soccer League the following season" yet it had competed in an umbrella league of the NASL. Be that as it may, the team had a good run however brief it was.

In fact, Steve Ralston joined the squad at the end of his career.

Another highlight of the team arrived in the form of the U.S. Open Cup. After being hired, it didn't take long for Dale Schilly, the type who wakes up in a good mood, to get going as coach. "I'm on a plane to Los

Angeles in my second game ever as a pro coach to coach against the Los Angeles Galaxy," Dale recalled. "We played at Home Depot Center against Bruce Arena and Dave Sarachan" and lost 2-0. However, for a team that emerged out of nowhere it was quite an experience.

AC St. Louis, in all of its short and sweet glory, actually was the offshoot of a plan to bring MLS to St. Louis by attorney Jeff Cooper with the help of Schilly. The valiant but failed attempt was circa 2008-10.

THE REINCARNATION OF THE ST. LOUIS AMBUSH

As the St. Louis Illusion, Illinois Piasa, and AC St. Louis were surging forward, the St. Louis Ambush, like the previous reincarnation of the Steamers, were waiting in the wings, ready to launch Part II.

In 2013, the St. Louis Ambush (2013-present) took flight, yet again. Though, the takeoff for the Ambush would be fickle, at best. When an ownership group re-launched the Ambush—in St. Charles, Missouri—the idea was to win games, like in the old days. Things started up again, that's for sure. Just one problem: Things didn't really go as planned. From 2013 to 2019-20 the team surrendered a losing season every year. Yes, that's right, hold your horses, during that time, the Ambush—ipso facto a legacy of the great indoor teams from yore—had a losing season every year. In fact, you can't make this up: In 2016-17, the team endured a record of 1 and 19. That's not a clerical error. Online at *Just Sports Stats*, a summary of the 2016-17 Major Arena Soccer League season was listed as the following: "The St. Louis Ambush of Major Arena Soccer League ended the 2016-17 season with a record of 1 wins, 19 losses, finishing fifth in the MASL's Central Division."[72] One might say, "Tough year, back to the drawing board, put some ice on it, walk it off, take a lap, see yah next year." I see the spirit of what they were doing; it just wasn't working. Tough times, that's for sure.

As for 2020-21, the team finished the regular season with a record of 8-7. From the official website of the St. Louis Ambush, on April 10, 2022, it read: "The Ambush finished with a record of 8-7 in the abbreviated 2020-21 season. This is the first winning record for the Ambush since the team started in 2013. The Ambush finished 4th in the standings, of the 7 teams which played in the 2020-21 season. Several of the league teams were unable to play due to COVID-19 restrictions in their home cities. The Ambush also made their first playoff appearance since returning to indoor soccer in 2013. The Ambush lost both games of a 2 game series to the Kansas City Comets in March 2021." Given the two playoff losses, this set the team back to an 8-9 record, overall.

For the 2021-22 season, the Ambush suffered a 10-16 overall record (playoffs included).

But indoor soccer in St. Louis has survived. It's stuck it out, fought the good fight, with a few punches along the way and some knockouts, but it's stayed the course, somehow. A lot of it has to do with how strong soccer has been in St. Louis for generations; people will remain interested, get in their cars, drive, park, pay for tickets, and show up for a game or two, regardless the score.

With this in mind, St. Louis City SC should have a sigh of relief going into the first few seasons knowing that, after all, St. Louis fans are demanding yet forgiving.

SAINT LOUIS FC LAUNCHES PRO OUTDOOR SOCCER
Saint Louis FC, 2015.

A few short years after the fall of AC St. Louis, a new professional outdoor team emerged. Saint Louis FC—which was in the USL Championship and played games at World Wide Technology Soccer Park—would represent Scott Gallagher as its pro team; it became the ceiling of the club so to speak. A few key players included Mike Ambersley, Bryan Gaul, Christian Volesky, Kyle Greig, and Sam Fink.

From first to last (in terms of chronology), coaches were Dale Schilly, Tim Leonard, Preki, Anthony Pulis, and Steve Trittschuh.

Saint Louis FC outlasted its predecessor (AC St. Louis) yet the party wouldn't last too long. In 2020, as the COVID-19 pandemic grew in strength, it was announced that Saint Louis FC would fold after the season's end. Financial challenges that revolved around getting people in seats had already accompanied past seasons and with the onset of the pandemic it became clear that the team would have to conclude its run. By this time, Steve Trittschuh—who had previously been coached by St. Louis legends Bob Kehoe and Bob Guelker—had departed Colorado and returned home to coach the side. On January 25, 2020, right on the edge of the tumultuous year that 2020 proved to be, the *St. Louis Post-Dispatch* featured an upbeat article on Trittschuh and STLFC which read: "The team begins workouts this week. 'It's a talented and a deep group and I'm excited to get everybody together to start working toward the start of the season,' Trittschuh said."[73]

In September 2020, the *St. Louis Post-Dispatch* reported, "With St. Louis City SC scheduled to begin play in Major League Soccer in 2023, STLFC decided to shut down operations at the end of this season."[74]

Around the same time, just about two months before November 2020, the *St. Louis Business Journal* stated, "The ownership group said the club, which plays one tier below Major League Soccer in the United Soccer League Championship, decided it wasn't feasible to return next season and cited the Covid-19 pandemic as a reason for its exit."[75]

Despite the bad news, Saint Louis FC had built quite a following in the form of the supporters' group the St. Louligans (also known as Louligans). In 2020, the group, the largest of its kind in the St. Louis area, was "...registered as a 501(c)3 nonprofit, a status it says helps formalize its growing charity efforts."[76]

The Louligans, who intend on supporting St. Louis City SC, have roots that go back to the days of AC St. Louis, in which things started to come together. St. Louligans co-founder Mitch Morice is quick to point out the group doesn't have titles, rather, everyone helps with different tasks. In a title-less world, for lack of a better description, Mitch agreed he'd be quantified as a co-founder, along with Brad, who also has been there from the beginning. In the early days of AC St. Louis, with games held at Soccer Park, Brad was known for wearing a tacky chicken-head hat which rallied others around him as somewhat of a geographical marker. One might ask, "Where are you guys?" Followed by, "We're by the guy with the chicken hat!" As Mitch noted, in the AC St. Louis days, circa 2010, there were a number of smaller groups, such as the Bosnians and others from this place or that place (such as a group that was linked to the Amsterdam Tavern by Tower Grove Park). According to Mitch, "At the time we said, 'You know what? We really need to kind of get some unity here.'" Brad, a co-founder, came up with "Louligans" and it took.

As of November 19, 2020, the St. Louligan's Facebook page read, "The Louligan umbrella houses most if not all members of the Laclede's Army, Eads Brigade, River City Saints, Chickenhead's Coalition, DayPints Club, Henry Shaw Collective, STL Ultras and United Knights." As one from England might affectionately say, "They're maniacs, they're mad, they've gone mental!" and they love their team. Games at Soccer Park (currently World Wide Technology Soccer Park) were passionately attended by Louligans and the trend will certainly march forward as St. Louis City SC officially navigates through the treacherous waters of MLS.

With immediate rivals, Kansas City and Chicago, the Louligans will have plenty to work with. During the Saint Louis FC days, Mitch reflected on how the Louligans established a strong presence in Louisville, Kentucky. The fans of Louisville were just outmatched. Mitch and company, who already had experience from the days of supporting the St. Louis Lions and AC St. Louis, took three buses down there with approximately 150 people and "We show up with drums and chants and flags and banners and we're ready to go...and they were not." The Louligans were louder and "out-chanted" the Louisville contingent. Mitch added, "It was a men against boys kind of thing in terms of fan support."

As the St. Louligans and gazillions of fans prepared for the arrival of St. Louis City SC there was much activity behind the scenes to have the team, stadium, jerseys, and a myriad of other necessary steps ready for launch.

A strong argument could be made that nothing in the history of St. Louis soccer would compare to what St. Louis City SC was about to do, and the owners, fans, and the like could barely contain their excitement as time rolled closer to the first season.

As Saint Louis FC ended, St. Louis was one of the last cities to gain an MLS franchise within the framework of America struggling to accept soccer for so many years.

SOCCER IS FINALLY COOL!

And so it was: During the 2000s and from 2010 onward, the United States was embracing soccer across-the-board as never before.

The idea of the United States catching up in soccer on the world's stage is somewhat unique to America in the modern era. For decades, in fact, mainstream America essentially shunned the sport, and, as a result, it took a long time for the game to gain popularity around the country. Meanwhile, the rest of the world—places such as England, Netherlands, France, Germany, Spain, Italy, Brazil, and Argentina—had a massive head start both in terms of national team play and professional leagues.

In a round about way, the US, and its lack of interest in keeping up with the international soccer sensation in the years prior to 1996, emulated England in the early days of the sport.

Once upon a time, when soccer was gaining a foothold around the far-reaches of the globe, England saw itself as high and mighty (nothing new there), and, in turn, it didn't much respect the efforts of foreigners organizing the sport—the very sport England had invented. After all, when FIFA formed in 1904, there were seven members and not one was from the F.A. (the Football Association, which formed in England in 1863, which set rules for the sport). England was very dismissive and figured it would be okay residing within its own soccer borders. Leo Robson wrote in *The New Yorker*: "By 1930, the year of the first FIFA World Cup, in which the U.S. competed but England did not, Jimmy Hogan, an English former player who had spent his coaching career abroad, complained, 'We are absolutely out of date.' Soccer, as played in its mother country, remained primitive in technique and tactically complacent, with an emphasis on moral fibre that had begun to look increasingly quixotic."[77]

In its own way, the United States, which lacked a viable and sustainable pro outdoor soccer league for generations, was isolating itself from international soccer as well.

Basically, every decade before the inception of MLS in 1996 represents a time in America when soccer was that *other sport*. Why was that? You know, it's a funny and fascinating topic: Why did pro soccer take so long to blast off in America? It's a topic worth reexamination, one that will likely be studied at greater length far into the future, by very curious students and aficionados of the game.

So then, why was soccer that *other sport*?

Well, maybe a quote from Richard Feynman's book, *QED: The Strange Theory of Light and Matter,* could sum this up aptly. Referring to complicated subject matters and his physics grad students, Feynman wrote: "What I am going to tell you about is what we teach our physics students in the third or fourth year of graduate school—and you think I'm going to explain it to you so you can understand it? No, you're not going to be able to understand it. Why, then, am I going to bother you with all this? Why are you going to sit here all this time, when you won't be able to understand what I am going to say? It is my task to convince you *not* to turn away because you don't understand it. You see, my physics students don't understand it either. That is because *I* don't understand it. Nobody does."[78] True to form, American soccer exists in a mysterious world all its own, too.

Despite St. Louis being one of those cities that was a beacon of hope for soccer, interestingly, the sport certainly has taken a backseat in America for years.

To get to the root of why soccer was that other sport in America, you have to understand a few things. And that would be: baseball, basketball, football, bowling, golf, and tennis, to name a few. There's no 'set law' to explain it. It just is what it is. Things have changed recently, but soccer in America has been battling with these other more accepted sports for years. You have to remember, prior to MLS, for a large part of the 20th century, soccer was a far cry from what it is today. In layman's terms, "Soccer sucked." Many Americans, but not all, did not like it. End of story. Part of the reason had to do with the United States breaking away from England long ago. England, of course, had cricket. The US essentially tweaked cricket into baseball. Rugby, it could be argued, was tweaked into American football. In terms of sports, the US, a global political, military, and financial power, isolated itself presumably out of arrogance. The idea emanating throughout society was, 'You have your sports, we have ours.' After all, baseball and American football are very niche games that are pretty much restricted to the US (with few exceptions outside of a small grouping of nations here and there; whereas, soccer has always had a global following; interestingly, basketball has increased in international popularity over the years). Here's the short end of America's isolation policy in the world of sports: Soccer took a backseat for many generations while most people in the greater continental US got swept up in baseball, basketball, football, bowling, and so on. Therefore, pro soccer in the United States never really got a fair shot.*

Now that soccer is so popular in America—with sold out games in Seattle, Portland, LA, Atlanta, and elsewhere—it seems very clear that for years, with conflict between mainstream America and the subculture that adored the beautiful game, soccer was stolen from the public for so long.

Many Americans today are exorbitantly passionate for soccer, yet some—granted, a smaller number these days—still aren't sold. Even a sector of society that holds onto disdain for it has come around to accept that it is a "thing" that is universally cool. (This dwindling crowd might not think it's cool but accepts it is cool to others; ipso facto, this acknowledgement has allowed a resonating wave of acceptance to take

---

* Even during the NASL days, soccer was going through an awkward 'auditioning process' with Americans.

hold in more circles.) ESPN has helped in this regard. For many-many years ESPN essentially shunned soccer, thus giving gung-ho American critics a platform to stand on; gradually, ESPN has increased its highlights and games aired which has grown into more extensive soccer segments for panels to discuss things and more games aired. Thus, if ESPN is on board, America is too. Furthermore, with FOX on board as well, it's a solid one-two punch that instills a sense of calm in Americans when they see men kicking a ball as opposed to outright cynicism, contempt, and methodical, organized, lambasting.

In turn, like continental drift, since the 1994 FIFA World Cup and the inception of MLS in 1996, soccer has gone from audition phase to a straight up party.

The road to MLS and the new St. Louis City SC franchise has been a long, tedious, and fascinating affair. The roots of this journey are vast. Now that soccer has turned the tide, St. Louis is in the driver's seat.

Everywhere you look there are supporters' groups across the nation, from state to state, city to city, with Presidents, Vice-Presidents, managers, with intricate organization, headquarter-bars, guys and gals drinking beer, wearing the team shirt, marching, car-pooling, banging drums, chanting, competing with other groups, talking ad nauseam on podcasts, blogging, posting, adorning scarves for God's sake (yes, team scarves have gotten way-cool!), and the St. Louligans are right in line as a powerhouse supporter group for the 28th team in MLS history. Can a sports fan ask for much more?

"Finally" is the key word. While Kanas City and others were flaunting their stuff in MLS, St. Louis, the original giant of soccer in America, didn't have a team? Everything seemed wrong and out of place. As St. Louis waited for the arrival of an MLS team (from 1996 until very recently), time seemed to stand still.

If this is the case, if time could stop, then, to the delight of some, Daryl Doran—who encompassed at least three decades as a player— might live on forever. I recall sitting at a bar the night before departing for Dallas, Texas, with the St. Louis Illusion. A guy, from perhaps Iowa or Quincy, Illinois (one of those parts), introduced himself to some of the guys, and, in so doing, locked on to me. I have no idea why, but I was the brunt of his one-sided conversation for an indeterminate amount of time. He began expressing his aspiration of trying out for the team, then he began rattling off Doran's stats from long, long ago...something on the level of Stump the Schwab. He asked about Doran's gym. Dazed by a barrage of stats and questions about Doran, I said, "I don't know," and turned to Vedad Alagic—a player from Bosnia, a former Billiken— and got the answer from him. Then, after a while, the guy just sort of disappeared. (I've since had to fastidiously research all this material; this guy would've come in handy! But that's not an invitation for him to re-emerge.) I can't say exactly, but that was a glimpse of many moments from decades of pro soccer in St. Louis that have led to what is now a new epoch in the making. Certainly, in the future, plenty of fans will arrive at this location or that one with fanciful ideas of playing someday, fully charged with stats of this icon or that. That's when you know a team—a movement—has arrived.

HOW MLS GOT TO ST. LOUIS: THE FINAL TURN

EVERY GOOD TEAM NEEDS GOOD OWNERS: THE STRUGGLES OF PRE-ENTERPRISE ATTEMPTS AND THE LONG WAIT

As anyone can see, St. Louis soccer is like a time capsule waiting to be opened to share its entire splendor from the past. What better stage on which to do so than an MLS team? To get this show up and running, many efforts were made before Jim Kavanaugh and Carolyn Kindle Betz crossed the finish line, and history was made.

Initially, circa 1996, there wasn't in place a united group to invest and produce a franchise.

Over the years, many cities—St. Louis, Nashville, Austin, and Sacramento, to name a few—have been approaching Don Garber, the head honcho in charge of MLS, for entry into the growing league. Commissioner Garber has toured multiple cities and received many pitches from experienced marketing teams. It's a long process, one that has high stakes.

In this process there are certain things that might be cause for concern. In fact, certain things might sway a commissioner to have a moment of pause...and to ask the question: "Is this really a city to trust with an MLS franchise?" Garber undoubtedly heard stories that might *not* have reflected very well on St. Louis, that being: "St. Louis earned the title of deadliest city in America with a murder rate of 60.9 per 100,000 in 2018. In that year, 186 were slaughtered in the city of a population of about 318,000."[79] That's right: According to Fox News, St. Louis was the murder capitol of America in 2018. In 2019, CBS News ranked the most dangerous cities in the United States in an article called "Murder map: Deadliest U.S. cities,"[80] and St. Louis was still ranked number one. Not Los Angeles, Chicago, New York City, Washington D.C., Detroit, Baltimore, nor Miami. Nope, none of those. Oddly enough, Louisiana had three in the top 10—Shreveport, Baton Rouge, and New Orleans. But St. Louis, good old St. Louis, came out on top. The number one murder city in the nation. Wow. That's astounding. There are some violent cities in America yet St. Louis is number one. Unbelievable.

If St. Louis could talk, it might have told Garber, "Mea culpa. Look, let's not dwell on this or that. Everything's gonna be fine! It'll all work out! Trust me." Garber, in all of his wisdom, likely had some trepidation about St. Louis and its reputation.

Yet, despite this cultural phenomenon, the market of which St. Louis has apparently cornered, there was always that tantalizing feeling that, indeed, rightly so, the Gateway City would someday have an MLS team. In 2019, from a story published by Fox Sports Midwest, the leader of MLS was quoted saying: "'St. Louis is a city with a rich soccer tradition,' MLS commissioner Don Garber said, 'and it is a market we have considered since the league's inception. Our league becomes stronger with the addition of the city's deeply dedicated soccer fans and the committed and innovative local ownership group.'"[81]

Having said that, St. Louis experienced some struggle along the way.

Jeff Cooper, a local attorney, launched a strong effort with the help of local coaching guru Dale Schilly around 2008-10. MLS felt uneasy with the investor-group and declined.

Then around 2014-15, another effort was put forth, again with the involvement of Dale Schilly. A stadium and strong investor-group were paramount for success; however, this maneuver, yet again, fell flat.

These were noble efforts. Stadiums were drawn up. Local politics were set in motion. Numerous news stories were published regarding the complicated nature of building a stadium, along with business proposals, business tax, tax credits, non-tax credits, the Board of Alderman, the governor, votes...it was basically a soccer version of C-SPAN that played out incrementally over a long course of time. Yet failure.

Then in 2016, something peculiar happened: The St. Louis Rams departed for Los Angeles. Just as the arrival of the Rams had halted the progress of the St. Louis Ambush in the 1990s under the ownership of Abe Hawatmeh, the subsequent departure of the Rams was lending a hand to an MLS franchise birth in St. Louis. People were lamenting the loss of the Rams; they couldn't believe the beloved days of Kurt Warner, Marshall Faulk, Orlando Pace, Isaac Bruce, and Torry Holt, circa late 1990s-early 2000s, were going to be a footnote for a franchise in LA; St. Louisans collectively owned a piece of that history[†] and did not want to let go. Yet it was done. The Rams were gone. People were upset. On the other hand, people got excited. Soccer fans started to sense something was afoot. Mayor Herb Roach of O'Fallon, Illinois, said, "When the Rams left, the NFL football team, that left a gap." That void could be filled.

[†]   Incidentally, when the Rams were riding high, led by Warner, Faulk and company, the team wore the soccer powerhouse-brand Puma jerseys in the NFL...how times have changed. You can't turn anywhere these days without the sight of Nike.

ENTERPRISE SAVES THE DAY

Around 2017-18, things started brewing again. After different groups had been cajoling commissioner Garber for an extended amount of time, the reality of an MLS team joining the storied franchises of the St. Louis Cardinals and Blues was beginning to form.

Part of the big process of attaining an MLS franchise came down to a potential stadium. A stadium was always front and center. According to Fox Sports in 2019: "The prospects of a Major League Soccer franchise ever calling St. Louis home appeared to have died two years ago when voters turned down the use of a business tax to finance a new downtown stadium."[82]

In 2017, a proposal for a stadium (set for $200 million) in downtown St. Louis went forward and at first was accepted by city officials; in fact, city tax revenue ($60 million) would help ease construction costs. Yet, some locals didn't like the idea and Kurt Erickson of the *St. Louis Post-Dispatch* reported, "In April 2017, St. Louis voters rejected a referendum asking if they supported funneling $60 million in public funding to build a soccer stadium."[83]

Missouri Governor Mike Parson was originally thought to be an ally of the ownership group. "But when it came time to turn talk into walk, Parson pulled a disappearing act. He didn't just strand the St. Louis leaders who considered him an ally. He embarrassed them,"[84] explained Ben Frederickson of the *St. Louis Post-Dispatch* in a 2019 article. The change of heart from Governor Parson presented itself in the midst of haggling over stadium tax credits. The idea of 'welfare for millionaires' (propagated by former Missouri Governor Eric Greitens in 2016) was something citizens of Missouri—a very conservative state—weren't too fond of. Frederickson pointed out: "The soccer plan Greitens shredded was shut down not by the short-time governor, but by city voters who rejected a previous ownership group's plan, one that included an ask of $80 million from local taxpayers and $40 million from the state. It was from that derailed effort that the MLS4TheLou ownership group emerged,"[85] which united the "Taylor family of Enterprise Holdings with Jim Kavanaugh of World Wide Technology in an effort that has been praised both regionally and nationally for its primary reliance on private dollars, its narrowly tailored requests for city and state tax breaks, and its dedication to becoming a vibrant contributor to the Downtown West district beyond simply hosting soccer games."[86]

This was huge. St. Louis needed a boost. In 2019, Dave Skretta of Fox Sports pointed out: "Led by members of the founding family of car rental giant Enterprise, the city began to work anew last fall on its pitch for a professional soccer team. On Tuesday, the league officially announced that St. Louis would become its 28th club when it begins play for the 2022 season."[87] (This report was prior to the COVID-19 pandemic that set St. Louis City SC back to 2023.) In fact, the Enterprise ownership group turned out to save the day. Carolyn Kindle Betz, who is the granddaughter of Jack Taylor (Enterprise founder), said, "'St. Louis is home to the first official majority female-led ownership group in MLS.'"[88] Pretty exciting stuff. Incidentally, the original headquarters of St. Louis City SC happened to be in the Enterprise offices located in Clayton, Missouri. Enterprises' offices have been in Clayton—one of the highest regarded cities around St. Louis—since the company's inception. Michelle Harris, the respected mayor of Clayton, is very involved in the community and as she said: "I'm very proud that Enterprise calls Clayton home. I just have the utmost respect for them and what they do for our region." Harris added: "As a woman mayor, I really admire the leadership and grit of women who play soccer as well as those who are leading our community to do innovative things that can fuel growth for St. Louis." Fox Sports pointed out: "Six other female members of the Taylor family are part of the ownership group, along with businessmen Andy Taylor and Jim Kavanaugh, a soccer insider who was part of the first failed ownership team."[89]

And it became so. In 2019 the big announcement came thundering in. With billionaires Carolyn Kindle Betz and Jim Kavanaugh the dream became reality.

What about the Busch family? Where were they? One might think with all the soccer involvement from Busch in the past they'd be involved with St. Louis City SC. So where were they? Well, among other things, they were busy with an MTV reality show that eventually aired in 2020, so. You might have missed the episode "Texas Size Drama"—there was a lot of work that went into that. A camera crew and everything. Don't forget "Gussie's 23rd Birthday"—oh yeah, now we're talking! There was a lot going on—these things happen. People make commitments and that's just how it goes. (It would be nice if the Busch family would press the pause button and reintroduce Busch Soccer Club. Maybe someday. But that's another story altogether.)

The bottom line is: the other billionaires came through.

Throughout this long journey, one can't underscore enough the importance of the stadium. As it turns out, talk of a proper stadium, one that would impress MLS and generate millions in cash flow, has become something of a legend in the struggle for St. Louis to have a seat at the table that is MLS.

In the past, Collinsville, Illinois, was suggested as a prime location for the potential stadium. As a suburb of St. Louis just across the river on the Illinois side Collinsville has good access to the interstates. That's a plus; there's a start. Michael Stipe, the singer of R.E.M., once worked at the Waffle House in Collinsville. Not bad, pretty cool. There are also interesting local features such as a racetrack (World Wide Technology Raceway at Gateway) and the Cahokia Mounds (a national jewel). Another plus. That's great, right? Well, you see, both are within close proximity to a massive waste dump that happens to be obscured from sight by a large hill. There were other potential drawbacks. Perhaps, had Collinsville been awarded the stadium, fans could've sauntered over to a place just below South Roxana and Roxana proper known as historic downtown Granite City, for a tour of large, intimidating, smokestacks that pollute the area like something out of the Soviet Union's Five-Year Plan in its rise to industrialization in the 1930s. After that, fans could hastily venture throughout Madison, Venice, Brooklyn, National City,

Fairmont City, Washington Park, or East St. Louis.[†] Take your pick. These places look like they were hand-decorated by John Waters. On their best days, considering random garbage scattered on the ground and dilapidated buildings, it looks as though WWIII ended about a week prior. In laymen's terms, from the viewpoint of a commissioner, these are places that completely "stop a project dead in its tracks." There's no way around it. They're mostly small towns known for crime, strip clubs, and abandoned tires. This is the undeniable, gritty, subculture that lurks around cities throughout America; it's a factor that can't be ignored, one that flourishes in the Metro East.

In summary, Collinsville had an upside, given its central location in the Metro East along with easy access to interstates, but, overall, it wasn't equipped with the most ideal surroundings for a stadium. Tempting, but notwithstanding it was obvious that a St. Louis location—near Busch Stadium, the Enterprise Center, and St. Louis Union Station—would be much sexier.

And there it was. Given the setbacks of a downtown St. Louis stadium initially being denied and a Collinsville, Illinois, stadium falling short of glamorous, the question as to how St. Louis could join MLS became a prominent one. When the problem was solved by the guidance of the Enterprise-led ownership group, a stadium in downtown St. Louis became the ultimate destination. As Fox Sports posted: "The new soccer stadium, which is planned for Market Street just west of Union Station, will be the centerpiece of a major development project in the city's Downtown West district. It will include a mix of secondhand retail, restaurants, and gathering spaces open year-round to the public, and is expected to continue a downtown revitalization effort that includes Busch Stadium—home of the St. Louis Cardinals—and the Enterprise Center, the home of the Stanley Cup champion St. Louis Blues."[90] The complicated process of acquiring space for a stadium—the political

---

[†] These are all locations that residents of Clayton and Ladue likely have on a list called, "Places I will avoid for Christmas shopping."

wrangling for such a venture (along with building rights, business proposals, and legal contracts)—finally came to fruition. Despite every obstacle, and to the delight of St. Louis area soccer fans, the stadium was moving forward. As *KSDK 5 On Your Side* reported in 2020, "The stadium was designed by St. Louis-based architecture firm HOK and Julie Snow of Snow Kreilich Architects."[91] It yields a modern, high-tech, intimate feel, in the form of a classy disconnected square meets rectangle shape as seen from above; where, if you view it from a certain vantage point, it's like the Arch resting on a platform.

The result is yet another historic St. Louis landmark will be erected. The list of iconic architectural places in St. Louis is quietly impressive.

The Eads Bridge, which used Carnegie steel and dates back to 1874, was a huge deal in its time. As a result of this bridge being constructed, St. Louis was really becoming the 'Gateway to the West' for which it's known to this day. As a matter of fact, after completion, in ceremonious fashion, the organizers marched an elephant across the bridge to show the public how safe it was.

Of course, there's the world-famous Arch, which first made an appearance back in the 1960s.

Near the Arch, just south a little distance, actually, would be the Anheuser-Busch Brewery (with roots going back to 1875), which is like a town all in itself.

Next to the Anheuser-Busch Brewery rests the old Lemp Brewery (an impressive establishment that was built from around 1840 through the 1860s), a leading beer company in its day, with legendary stories of wealthy family members battling over this, that, and the other for a company that would eventually fall apart.

Then, in the downtown area, there's the Enterprise Center (where the Blues play), Busch Stadium (where, of course, the Cardinals play), and St. Louis Union Station, all of which are within walking distance—more or less—of the new MLS stadium.

The announcement of the team becoming a real thing, along with the stadium, was big news in 2019. Local TV and radio stations talked about it (which is worth noting as soccer was rarely discussed). As Mayor Harris of Clayton said: "I think that St. Louis is such a sports city. I'm a huge Blues fan and Cardinals fan too. We're just known for our teams and we're known for our fan base, and so I think this is just going to add to the professional sports level that we have here and bring more excitement to town." As for the new stadium Mayor Harris said that "it looks fantastic to me and will transform the areas around it."

In addition, Mayor Herb Roach of O'Fallon, Illinois—a geographically strategic Metro East suburb where visitors often stay while attending Cardinals games and the like—voiced his thoughts on the new stadium saying it "is beautiful" and "I think the location that they've selected out there, right off the interstate, is just a great location, I mean as far as the surroundings, as far as being able to get there by MetroLink, being able to get there by bus, by car—there are so many plusses to it."

St. Louis City SC has electrified the St. Louis sports scene in a profound way. Just as it was about to launch, excitement was in the air. History was being made. MLS had arrived.

COVID-19 THROWS A MASSIVE CURVEBALL

St. Louis City SC was set to play in the 2022 MLS season. Just as things were taking off, a curveball threw everything off-balance.

Around Spring 2020, thanks to the coronavirus—COVID-19—there was mayhem practically everywhere. Sports leagues—MLS, NBA, MLB, and others around the world—had suspended operations. Everything was at a stand still. Not long after the Enterprise group had announced the arrival of MLS in St. Louis, the COVID-19 pandemic was taking hold. There were stay-at-home orders around the US; in some cases, gloves and masks were required for people to engage in public. Life had completely changed. Schools had shut down; millions of Americans were losing their jobs; millions were filing for unemployment; the federal government was actually paying people to stay home with stimulus checks. There was talk of the NBA, for instance, finishing its season in front of empty arenas. To say life had changed was an understatement.

The St. Louis City SC stadium was under construction and nerves were rattling. Would everything have to stop with construction? Would the team even come to fruition?

Some experts on networks like CNN, MSNBC, and elsewhere, were suggesting that perhaps coronavirus would carry into 2022—the planned arrival of MLS in St. Louis.

Despite talk and the reality of doom and gloom, in April of 2020, the downtown stadium continued construction. The *St. Louis Post-Dispatch* caught up with owner Carolyn Kindle Betz who explained: "We are in constant contact with our construction partners, who are taking the necessary steps to protect every member of the team. They also remain in close conversation with health and government officials for the latest updates to best assess how to safely manage this project, and will be ready to adjust course at any time."[92]

By this time, Sam Cosner, leader of Public Relations and Communications for the soon-to-be team, was part of an excited group that, according to Cosner, had set up shop in "Jack Taylor's old office" at Enterprise Rent-A-Car which had been converted to suit the needs of the ongoing efforts of St. Louis City SC. Cosner—who was born and raised in St. Louis, and attended Parkway North High School and UMSL— grew up playing outside back and looked up to Philipp Lahm as a player. At the age of 31, he was less focused on kicking a ball around and more geared toward producing a team, literally from scratch. As he explained, the working situation was in a normal office, not much bling. It sounded reminiscent of *The Larry Sanders Show*, one of HBO's most popular sitcoms in the 1990s that didn't have fancy signs around set announcing where people were (as many hit shows do). The makeshift Enterprise office space was not intended to be permanent, rather it would suffice until the time came to switch over to the official offices that were part of construction alongside the new stadium in Downtown West. At this time, during the coronavirus pandemic of 2020, it was all happening, step-by-step. It was in motion.

With everything going on in terms of forming a brand, finding a team name, the colors, crest and all that, and starting a team from scratch, Cosner, who wakes up, checks email, gets coffee, and rolls from there, said, "It's definitely a once-in-a-lifetime opportunity, obviously, for everybody working on it."

As years go by, St. Louis City SC will be the apotheosis of pro soccer in St. Louis. To think, the long struggle to join MLS was met by yet another setback—COVID-19. St. Louis City SC may have been temporarily derailed, but the end goal was in sight just as the world-famous 20th century explorer Colonel Fawcett sought a mythical lost city of gold in the Amazon; there may have been a setback or two, but the journey would continue. Whereas Colonel Fawcett—working on behalf of the British Royal Geographical Society—was seeking to make a myth materialize into a tangible collection of treasure, St. Louis City SC was much closer to the finish line with a very realistic objective, one that was highly reliant on time. It was just a matter of waiting.

Around May 2020, despite COVID-19 cases and fatalities remaining high, there was a glimmer of hope for sports down the road. An article in the *St. Louis Post-Dispatch* pointed out on May 7, 2020: "Four Major League Soccer teams took the first small step toward returning to play Wednesday by allowing players to use team training fields for individual workouts."[93] Prior to this, weeks had gone by with no action allowed for players. In a bold step, "Sporting Kansas City, Atlanta United, Orlando City and Inter Miami let players in for vigorously controlled voluntary workouts on the first day they were permitted by the league."[94]

To illustrate how serious the coronavirus was, it was pointed out that "MLS protocols for the individual workouts include restricting facilities to essential staff, disinfection of all equipment after each session, screening measures including temperature checks, and staggered player and staff arrivals and departures, as well as designated parking that ensures proper distancing."[95]

Apparently locker rooms were off limits.§ Things were moving quickly with the league slowly reopening. Strict health measures were being taken to ensure safety for players. "They must also wear personal protective equipment such as masks upon arriving and departing from the fields, while staff will be required to use such equipment at all times. Staff must maintain a distance of 10 feet from players at all times."[96]

It wasn't just soccer. The gradual return to sports in 2020 was moving forward. "Other North American sports are poised to follow MLS. The NBA is opening facilities for small groups Friday in places where local restrictions are eased. NASCAR is bringing back live racing at Darlington Raceway on May 17 without fans in attendance. UFC will host the first of three shows without fans in Jacksonville, Florida, starting Saturday. The National Women's Soccer League has also started to allow individual workouts."[97]

Eventually, in the summertime of 2020, MLS and the NBA conducted playoffs and crowned champions for each league in the controlled confines of the ESPN Wide World of Sports Complex near Orlando, Florida, with no fans in attendance. (Incidentally, the champions for each respective league were the Portland Timbers and LA Lakers.)

Then, because of the coronavirus pandemic, a decision was made to postpone the opening season of St. Louis City SC by another year, so instead of 2022, it was decided to launch the inaugural season in 2023.

What did this really spell out for St. Louis' efforts with regard to MLS: Shaky times afoot. That was the bottom line. It was terrible timing for St. Louis entering the league for the first time ever (after waiting so long in the first place). This was all piling on as St. Louis was poised to enter the league just a year or so away. Then in late 2020 the vaccine for COVID-19 came to fruition. Talk about nerves and stress for the

---

§   Just the following day, regarding MLS teams, it was reported that, "Indoor facilities are limited to staff and players who require rehabilitation treatment," in an article by Ben Frederickson, entitled, "MLS offers hope and a daunting reminder," *St. Louis Post-Dispatch*, SPORTS, published May 8, 2020, p. B4.

ownership group. The stadium, of all things, was building up mounds of dirt just off I-64 as construction was slowing moving forward.

From one owner to another. As Jim Kavanaugh and Carolyn Kindle Betz of St. Louis City SC surged forward with a new stadium and team, an iconic figure made headlines in the *St. Louis Post-Dispatch* on April 13, 2020. "Former St. Louis Man of the Year, Citizen of the Year and member of the National Soccer Hall of Fame, Robert Ringen 'Bob' Hermann died at his home in Ladue Monday at the age of 97."[98] Hermann, of course, owned the groundbreaking St. Louis Stars.

As it turns out, the passing of Bob Hermann, Bob Guelker, Harry Keough, and Bob Kehoe wasn't the end of soccer in St. Louis, rather it was the marking of a new era that each man helped shape. Now, with the birth of St. Louis City SC, the legacy of Hermann, Guelker, Keough, Kehoe, and a myriad of others, lives on. Their spirit carries on with each touch of the ball, with each roll of the ball.

PART II
PLACES OF INTEREST AROUND THE NEW STADIUM

LOCAL ATTRACTIONS: SOCCER BARS, RESTAURANTS, THINGS TO DO ABOUT TOWN

Amsterdam Tavern
3175 Morganford Rd.
St. Louis, Missouri

Located in the heart of Tower Grove (right next to Tower Grove Park where you can find a pickup soccer game or two), Amsterdam Tavern serves an atmosphere of soccer on top of soccer. A Google search (circa November 22, 2019 and April 12, 2022) provided the following information about it: "European-style sports bar with a soccer focus, offering craft brews, cocktails & a beer garden." Soccer fans from around the area flock here to check out an assortment of games, both club and international.

Also nearby is the Missouri Botanical Gardens, which is what it sounds like, an extremely popular St. Louis attraction.

There is also Local Harvest Grocery, a unique neighborhood grocery store that serves nearby residents and people that arrive from all over the St. Louis area to get high-quality local products.

Close neighbors: Alpha Brewing Company, Tower Pub, Destination Café, Three Monkeys, The London Tea Room.

J Smugs
4916 Shaw Ave. (at Kingshighway)
St. Louis, Missouri

For beer, drinks, and food, look no further than J Smugs off of Kingshighway. It's a relaxed, cozy, and upbeat place—piano included—to stop by to unwind and get a taste of St. Louis nightlife. Joe Smugala—a former player for the St. Louis Steamers—is a member of the ownership team along with JB Anderson—who, coincidentally, yours truly earned a U16 Holland Cup championship with back in 1991—and J Smugs also has ties with Matt Stelzer of Amsterdam Tavern.

The Arch
The Arch came to fruition in the 1960s and is an iconic symbol not only of St. Louis but the whole country. It's the Gateway to the West. It's one of a kind, sitting large and silver, overlooking the mighty Mississippi River. Can you ride up to the top of the Arch? Yes, you can. There's also a gift shop below.

Busch Stadium
A few USMNT games have been held here. Though, without a doubt, Busch Stadium is known primarily for the St. Louis Cardinals, which, outside of the New York Yankees, happens to be the team with the second most World Series titles in MLB history. So, for most Cardinals fans, Busch Stadium is holy ground. In operation since 2006, it's a beautiful outdoor stadium with an open layout—played on natural grass—that also features Ballpark Village (the drinking and eating party zone).

Incidentally, the previous Busch Memorial Stadium, which launched in 1966 and had a circular shape, was home to some St. Louis Stars games.

The Enterprise Center
The Enterprise Center, named after the same Enterprise Holdings that is behind the new St. Louis City SC franchise, is home of the Stanley Cup

champion, St. Louis Blues. Just outside the stadium, you'll find statues of former Blues players Brett Hull, Al MacInnis, and others.

In years past, this arena has changed names and it used to be home to the St. Louis Ambush. It's also a staging ground for concerts and related events. The Enterprise Center is well located and it's very close to the MLS stadium. Along with Busch Stadium, Enterprise is a true St. Louis landmark. Excitement awaits.

St. Louis Union Station

From the old train station, Union Station was transformed into a popular mall. While the new St. Louis MLS stadium is under construction nearby, Union Station has been focusing on revamping its image, with new stores and attractions, to bring in a new wave of customers.

The Central West End

Just west of the new MLS stadium, in what is considered one of St. Louis' trendiest places, is the Central West End, full of bars, restaurants, and interesting shopping options. The Wyndam Apartment Terrace is where Tony LaRussa allegedly lived while he coached the Cardinals. Just down the road is Mansion Row—on Lindell Street—which is a grouping of large mansions that overlook Forest Park and the St. Louis Art Museum. Remember the infamous McCloskey incident from 2020? That took place just up the street.

The Hill

Another of St. Louis's must-see places is The Hill. It's subtle. Notwithstanding the Italian flags on the streets, you might miss it at first glance. The Hill is a section of St. Louis known for numerous Italian restaurants that flourish in a brick-home neighborhood. A bit west of downtown St. Louis, The Hill rests just south of Forest Park and a little northwest of Tower Grove Park, essentially off of S. Kingshighway Blvd. and Manchester Ave., which are near Interstates 44 and 64. The Hill rides the wave of classic St. Louis. There are many places to eat and enjoy a beer or wine, a few of which include Charlie Gitto's On the Hill, Dominic's, Rigazzi's, Favazza's, Guido's Pizzeria & Tapas, Zia's, Anthonino's Taverna. When it comes to soccer, Italians know their stuff. You'll be right at home in The Hill, which certainly has a few TVs available for viewing some games.

The Saint Louis Zoo

It might seem odd to mention a zoo in a soccer book. Sure, it doesn't make much sense. However, as far as zoos go, if you're a tourist viewing a soccer game, have a little time on your hands, and happen to like zoos, then look no further: The Saint Louis Zoo—which is a few miles west of downtown—is world renowned. It's high-quality, well-organized, with a wide range of animals, including an array of reptiles, and, across-the-board, it's a must-see.

The Saint Louis Science Center

Again, like the St. Louis Zoo, this doesn't have anything to do with soccer but it's worth mentioning in regard to the overall ambience of St. Louis. For tourists visiting St. Louis for a soccer game (and perhaps you have some time on your hands), turn left before the zoo: The Saint Louis Science Center is phenomenal. (If you haven't guessed, it happens to be right by the zoo.)

LOCAL SOCCER STORES: PAST & PRESENT

Soccer Master

Soccer Master, the grand deluxe of soccer stores, a child's dream come true. With multiple locations throughout the St. Louis area, Soccer Master has been the go-to destination for soccer equipment for generations.

OMG Soccer
Located in St. Louis, OMG Soccer offers a range of soccer equipment.

Johnny Mac's Sporting Goods
Johnny Mac's, the myth, the legend, a store from yesterday, had high-quality soccer gear (along with equipment for just about any other sport). When I lived in Carbondale, Illinois, I recall getting a pair of Puma cleats at Johnny Mac's, the ones with the white bottoms that Maradona wore in the 1986 FIFA World Cup. They turned out to be one of the best pair of shoes I owned. They didn't get me off to a good start though. After purchasing them, later that day we had a game against my future teammates, the Collinsville Untouchables—in Collinsville, Illinois—and they decimated us 3-0. Regardless, Johnny Mac's had provided equipment, like the shoes I purchased, to players for years. Unfortunately, in recent times, circa 2019, the local store chain began to dwindle away. However, Johnny Mac's should be remembered as a truly historic outpost of sporting stores in the St. Louis area.

The Collinsville Soccer Store
To the best of my memory, there was a Collinsville, Illinois, soccer store operated by Dawn Hunt's dad, which was situated right near the Collinsville Ketchup Bottle factory on the south entrance of the town. Who is Dawn Hunt you might ask? Well, she wasn't a soccer player, that's for sure. Dawn's dad, as I mentioned, ran the soccer store, and she happened to be a high school classmate of mine; we shared homeroom together; her older brother was a member of Suede Chain, a band from the Metro East; he and other members had also played soccer for Collinsville High School.

This store, in similar fashion to others, was a product of the soccer boom during the 1970s and 80s in St. Louis and around the country.

These stores serve as a testament as to how popular soccer has been in St. Louis. Each has played a valuable role in both the soccer tradition and growth of the game around St. Louis.

St. Louis Soccer Hall of Fame

You will likely need to make reservations ahead of time for the annual induction dinner celebration hosted by the St. Louis Soccer Hall of Fame. Each year new inductees, honorees, and future stars are recognized at a big event and this has been going on for over 40 years. The organization's website—under its name—administers updates about upcoming events and historical matters relating to St. Louis soccer.

On October 11, 2019, the 49th Anniversary Induction Dinner was held at the Union Station Grand Ballroom in St. Louis, Missouri.

In 2020, the 50th Anniversary Induction Dinner was interrupted by the COVID-19 pandemic and rescheduled.

As of 2020, valued members of the soccer community that made up The Board of the St. Louis Soccer Hall of Fame included President, Jim Leeker; 1st Vice President, Bud Oldani; 2nd Vice President, Joe Carenza Jr.; Treasurer, Marty Templin; Secretary, Chuck Zoeller; and Reverend Chris Dunlap. Members of the Committee included Bill Becher, Bill Daues, Mike DiRaimondo, Larry Donovan, Mike Gallo, Joan Gettemeyer, Janice Gettemeyer Sansone, Tom Groark, Gary Guarino, John Hayes, Jim Kersting, Bill McDermott, Tim Putnam, and John Schneider. Those serving under the title Emeritus included Ed Cody, and Ray Puricelli.

There is a prerequisite to be inducted as a member. Typically, past members have been confined to important soccer figures with roots in St. Louis, Missouri, that were involved with outdoor soccer. For years now, discussions—or perhaps debates would be more apt—have taken place regarding whether or not to induct important soccer figures from the Metro East Illinois side of the river, and those with professional indoor experience. Members of the public with interest in such things can find announcements which are often posted at the organization's website and Facebook page.

Members inducted into the St. Louis Soccer Hall of Fame represent generations of soccer in St. Louis that go back before World War II. The organization has proven to be a unique and integral part of the ongoing

American soccer story that features the best of the best from St. Louis, the headquarters of American soccer.

A FEW OTHER ATTRACTIONS AS RECOMMENDED BY INFLUENTIAL MAYORS

Around St. Louis are amazing wineries, such as Chandler Hill Vineyards, along with many suburbs with history, dining, shopping and nightlife including but not limited to St. Peters, St. Charles, Wildwood, Fenton, Town and Country, Des Peres, Frontenac, Ladue, and trendy Clayton.

Mayor Michelle Harris of Clayton pointed out how her city is a great place to walk around, shop, and have dinner. As she says, "Clayton is the destination for fine dining and has exceptional outdoor dining." She added, "I'm hoping that people who come to soccer games will then travel on to Clayton for dinner, and that people from out of town will stay in our many hotels." Referring to the arrival of St. Louis City SC, she pointed out, "I hope it really will contribute to the real economic resurgence in the region but also in Clayton." Referring to St. Louis at large, Mayor Harris said: "We have the best combination of cultural amenities that any city has and that would be the Zoo, the Art Museum, the Science Center, the History Museum and the Botanical Gardens."

On the Illinois side of the river in the Metro East, there are a number of suburbs, for instance, historic Alton, along with Edwardsville, Maryville, Collinsville, Caseyville, Belleville, and Fairview Heights, where travelers may find lodging and excellent restaurants. There are many other Metro East towns such as Imbs (well, we already covered Imbs, and it's better left alone), but one stands out: the centrally located and very affable O'Fallon, Illinois. (Not to be confused with O'Fallon, Missouri, on the St. Louis side.)

Mayor of O'Fallon, Illinois, Herb Roach commented: "Will people come here and stay here because of our proximity to St. Louis? They'll do it for two reasons. They'll do it because of the buildup of youth soccer that's coming here, but we have an awful lot of people that come for the Cardinals' games and will stay here. We've got over 1,200 hotel rooms, and over 50 restaurants, that, you'll find people that are coming here and staying here for a lot of different recreational activities, outside, that are coming to St. Louis to visit but they'll want to stay outside of the metropolitan area." Mayor Roach also stressed the convenient MetroLink that swiftly takes patrons from the Metro East to areas around St. Louis.

PART III
THE INAUGURAL ST. LOUIS CITY SC

WHAT ARE THEIR CHANCES OF WINNING
THE MLS CUP?

To win the MLS Cup, St. Louis City SC has a monumental task ahead. Some would argue, however, that getting fans in seats is a more pressing and immediate issue.

In terms of finding success at the box office, St. Louis City SC should be a success.

But many experts I've spoken to have pointed out that traditionally St. Louis fans have shown a strong interest in soccer at all levels—club, high school, college, pro, and international—for games that are free or kind of a one-time affair. But it remains to be seen if they will pay for and support a team—such as the St. Louis Cardinals—over a sustained amount of time. The St. Louis Stars had some very good showings. As did the original St. Louis Steamers. The old Bronze Boot showdowns between SLU and SIUE had mega-attendance numbers in the late 1970s and early 80s. But then things tapered off a little bit. International games at Soccer Park or Busch Stadium have generated extreme excitement as well; but these are sporadic in nature.

For the next century, and then some, St. Louis City SC will need to bank on support that rivals that of the St. Louis Cardinals and Blues, bedrock organizations with devout followings.

While there has been some speculation about filling seats on a regular basis, most would agree that this should not be a major problem for St.

Louis City SC. MLS is a huge deal; in my opinion, it's right on the verge of becoming the world's next super league; this is a historic moment for St. Louis, America, and international soccer.

The good news is pretty straightforward: I think the overall craze for MLS will be victorious over time. St. Louis will likely be a powerhouse MLS franchise in the long run. There is also an added advantage of having Busch Stadium which could be used for big games from time to time.

Of note, Seattle has an interesting situation. The passionate fanfare out there is almost unrivaled around MLS. To put it lightly: Seattle Sounders fans are bonkers. They exude passion like few other fan bases in the world. Can St. Louis match that? Again, St. Louis City SC will likely get plenty of seats filled, but will the fans be as bonkers as those in Seattle? That's certainly a serious question.

As Ben Frederickson of the *St. Louis Post-Dispatch* wrote, "St. Louis, check out Seattle."[99] This was in November of 2019 as "The Sounders have made their way back to the MLS Cup final. Again. It's the third time in four years they've been there."[100] Frederickson added: "The city is juiced on more than caffeine. An estimated 70,000 are expected"[101] in attendance. That's some serious fanfare. Essentially, that's the equivalent of the St. Louis Cardinals selling out Busch Stadium in the World Series, with hysteria in the air...mass hysteria in the air. Seattle is a good comparison for St. Louis. Can St. Louis do it? Can the Louligans and fans alike strum up an atmosphere equal to or greater than the thunderous anthem that beats in the Pacific Northwest?

As Al Trost and others can attest, the Sounders have been pulling in big attendance numbers since the 1970s.

Frankly, Seattle Sounders fans come across as single men in their 20s, 30s, and 40s who work at a microbrewery by day that support their team by night with an allegiance to a greater cause that borders on hysteria. Nothing wrong with that. But it's definitely a vibe worth pointing out. In fact, listen up Seattle guy: Many people are jealous of you; there's something noteworthy about what you're doing out there.

On the other hand, St. Louis has more of a family-oriented vibe when it comes to live sporting events. You know, the wife is involved, kids have to be attended to. There's a long lineage of dads from the 1980s who wore the classic St. Louis look of "short-sleeve polo shirt tucked into khaki shorts (belt, optional) with Somerset loafers, no socks"; this look conveyed a strong moderate message of "hey, we sell insurance, cars, or work as a lawyer; we're into the game but we're not going to run around like a bunch of hooligans"; this vibe has carried on over time. Despite always having a beer in hand, St. Louis fans are very conscious of their behavior. They have to be—it's a family affair. (As for Blues games, it depends who they're playing. If it's Chicago or Detroit, everyone's yelling: men, women, grandmas, grandpas, vendors—all bets are off.)

Given the vast amount of former soccer players in St. Louis that understand the game at a high level, the result of fanfare will likely resemble the support of the St. Louis Cardinals: very passionate but subdued with a strong dose of intellectual curiosity for the quality of play on the field at all times.

EXTRAVAGANT PREDICTIONS

As for winning the MLS Cup: It's very possible. In fact, given the extreme sporting prowess with which St. Louis has been endowed over the years, it's very likely.

Right out of the gate, the chances of St. Louis City SC winning the MLS Cup, just as Atlanta did early on, will be based in large part on the sporting director and coach. These two will have to find the right players and then coach them the right way. Who are the "right" players and what is the "right way" to coach them? Well, this is always up for debate. Many times, coaches find the wrong players and coach them the wrong way. In 2020, St. Louis City SC, led by sporting director Lutz Pfannenstiel, was gearing up for the challenge as the *St. Louis Post-*

Dispatch reported, "The MLS expansion team, which will begin play in 2023, announced Thursday the addition of Tim Twellman, Charles Renken and Elvir Kafedzic under the title of sporting community relations consultant, a position with a couple roles as the team looks to have at least one academy team up and running in 2021."[102] Regarding Tim Twellman (the dad of Taylor Twellman), the article pointed out that "he and his two brothers played in the North American Soccer League in the '70s."[103] Tim's experience adds another layer of wisdom to the opening days of the franchise. The challenge for St. Louis City SC will be to find the right formula, establish a strong, attractive, style of play, and look for long-term success as a result. In doing so, St. Louis City SC, just as former St. Louis teams of the past (at all levels), will likely have highly skillful, smart, experienced players that exude brilliance in dribbling and passing, coupled with short passing, strong possession, organized defense, and a vibrant attack. The academy system as it is today, which is constantly improving, will be a valuable asset.

In the first 10 years of existence, will St. Louis City SC win the MLS Cup? Yes.

Within the next century, in terms of notoriety and accomplishments, will St. Louis City SC become the next Manchester United, Bayern Munich, and Barcelona? Yes.

Within the next century, is it possible for St. Louis City SC to become the next Wolverhampton Wanderers? That is, will the team have a decade or two of greatness, then fall off the face of the earth only to live off its past reputation and eventually get pulled out of the garbage heap by a Chinese investor? This is very possible. Though, in the next 100 years, I'm sensing more of a St. Louis Cardinals type of organization which is akin to Manchester United, Bayern Munich, and Barcelona in the ways of steadiness and consistency.

Will the rivalries between St. Louis City SC, Chicago, Kansas City, and Nashville be all that it's cracked up to be? Yes and then some. (That was an easy prediction!)

In 2036 St. Louis City SC will have the leading scorer in MLS.

In 2054, St. Louis City SC will win its fourth MLS Cup.

In 2072, St. Louis City SC will have the world's highest paid player on its roster. He will be from Brazil. He'll have a funny one-word name that everybody loves.

RECAP

Interestingly, within the realm of American soccer, which is on a path to winning a men's FIFA World Cup, there are plenty of egos. As such there are esteemed coaches, players, and fans scattered about, where one might generally refer to them as New Jersey guy, New York guy, Virginia guy... well, you get the point. There are a lot of guys. Some of which would also include Massachusetts, D.C., Pennsylvania, North Carolina, Georgia, Florida, Ohio, Chicago...they don't consider the rest of Illinois legitimate so leave it there; ask Paul Simon. Where were we? That's right, Michigan, Wisconsin, Arizona, Texas, California, Washington state, Idaho, Iowa, and Minnesota. Hold on. Not so much with Arizona, and definitely not Idaho and Iowa; it was a test to see if you're paying attention. As for the others, you might think you're better than St. Louis—that's a hard no. You're good, in some cases you're great, but you're not St. Louis. However, having said that, on the topic of MLS, you obviously have a case there, and, not to mention, a colossal head start (Seattle, Portland, LA, New York, and so on). But keep in mind, it's the whole package that's involved. This is not arrogance, it's simply fact. Here's the thing: The United States is not only on course to winning the men's World Cup someday (its last athletic frontier), it's also continually producing the world's next super league: MLS, which is getting closer to the likes of Serie A, EPL, and Bundesliga, as we speak. So it goes without saying, yet worth pointing out all the same, that many people in America are eager to grab some of the credit (if not all) for this "movement" that's underway. All of the aforementioned locations have a place and have achieved quite a bit, in fact, though St. Louis continues to hold the throne, both past and present as things are only getting started with St. Louis City SC.

St. Louis is the place where American soccer essentially started; it's the place where soccer developed; it's the place where soccer took off; it's the place where soccer is—and always will be—quality of the highest order. So now, after all that, let's recap.

At the club level, St. Louis teams—Seco, St. Paul, Kutis, St. Philip Di Neri, Imo's, Busch, and Scott Gallagher, to name a few—have gathered an overwhelming number of national championships.

Within the high school ranks, St. Louis teams—such as St. Thomas Aquinas-Mercy, CBC, Vianney, St. Mary's, De Smet, and others—have dominated the state of Missouri for as far back as anyone can remember. On top of that, St. Louis has put forth a myriad of nationally ranked teams and All-Americans.

In terms of college competition, St. Louis is still the undisputed champion of NCAA Division I titles as SLU sits on top of the throne with an astounding 10 championships (from back in the days when the UCLA Bruins, led by Coach Wooden, and Boston Celtics, led by Bill Russell, were similarly gathering trophies left and right). On top of that you have the incredible year of 1973 in which St. Louis colleges ran the table on national championships. Furthermore, you can't forget the 1979 NCAA Division I championship earned by SIUE.

Then you have professional soccer in which the St. Louis Stars—that fielded distinguished St. Louis-area talent such as Pat McBride, Al Trost, Jim Leeker, and Dennis Vaninger—were clearing out a path on the vast frontier of American soccer for future participants to follow; that path would be tread upon by thousands of youth, high school, and collegiate players, not to mention the litany of pro indoor teams that subsequently followed in the years to come, including the St. Louis Steamers, St.

Louis Storm, St. Louis Ambush (1995 champions), St. Louis Illusion, and Illinois Piasa, along with the professional outdoor presence of AC St. Louis, Saint Louis FC, and, finally, of course, St. Louis City SC.

PART IV

THE GOLDEN VAULT: BONUS MATERIAL

THE 1950 WORLD CUP USMNT

Before we enter the detailed world of St. Louis club, high school, college, and pro soccer, we should first give homage to the fabulous 5 that started for the USMNT in the 1950 World Cup victory over soccer giants, England.

The 1950 World Cup
United States vs. England
1-0
The St. Louis Contingent
As it turns out, for this colossal game in US soccer history, the goal-scorer was Joe Gaetjens, who was originally from Haiti. Though, as many people know, five players in the starting 11 were from St. Louis.[104] (That's a lot!) Here they are.

Frank Borghi
Position: Goalie
Borghi represented the USMNT from 1949-53. He also played for St. Louis Simpkins-Ford.

HARRY KEOUGH

Position: Defender

Harry Keough played for the US national team from 1949-57. As an adult, he also played for St. Louis Kutis, St. Louis Raiders, St. Louis McMahon, Paul Schulte Motors, and the San Francisco Barbarians.

Charlie Colombo

Position: Center Midfielder

Colombo played for the US national team from 1948-52. He also played for St. Louis Simpkins-Ford.

Gino Pariani

Position: Inside Right[*]

Pariani played for the USMNT from 1948-50. He also had experience playing for St. Louis Simpkins-Ford, along with a few others.

Frank Wallace

Position: Forward

Wallace was with the USMNT from 1949-50. He also played for St. Louis Simpkins-Ford, along with a few others.

For soccer aficionados, here is the full starting lineup.[†]

GK	Frank Borghi
RB	Harry Keough
LB	Joe Maca
RH	Ed McIlvenny (c)
CH	Charlie Colombo
LH	Walter Bahr
IR	Gino Pariani

---

[*] According to the *Wikipedia* page entitled "Gino Pariani" on December 14, 2019.

[†] According to the *Wikipedia* page entitled "United States v England (1950 FIFA World Cup)" on December 14, 2019.

IL	John Souza
OR	Frank Wallace
OL	Ed Souza
CF	Joe Gaetjens

Manager:
William Jeffrey

CLUBS

This section of the book is very important. Within the history of St. Louis soccer are multiple branches, including club, high school, college, and pro soccer. While it may feel like we're going off path, we're not. The whole collection of club, high school, and college soccer experiences are connected to the overall professional soccer environment of St. Louis. Without the passion and success of its club, high school, and college teams St. Louis would very likely not have an MLS team. Basically, it's all connected, and it's all a part of the overall soccer experience that lines up neatly with MLS finding a perfect home in St. Louis.

So let's have a closer look at the famous world of St. Louis club, high school, college, and professional soccer.

We'll begin with clubs. It's amazing how special it's been over the years. (Keep in mind, since the SLYSA era, the mid-1970s onward, club soccer looks a little different than the pre-SLYSA days when parishes were the norm. By club we're referring to youth and amateur soccer across the board.)

Legendary Club Teams of St. Louis

St. Louis Simpkins-Ford	St. Paul
Schumacher Juniors	Kutis
Seco Juniors	Im. Heart of Mary of St. Louis,
St. Engelbert	MO

St. Williams

St. Philip Di Neri

St. Bart's

Seco

Florissant Celtics

Florissant Cougars

7UP

Big Four Chevrolet

Imo's Pizza

Busch

Scott Gallagher

Coke

Pepsi

Norco

Johnny Mac

Lou Fusz

Legendary Club Team Note

Each team listed has so much to say, yet, one stands out as unique.

Kutis was a flat-out powerhouse. Pat McBride mentioned to me that Kutis played on behalf of the US national team for World Cup qualifying. Even *Wikipedia* captured this interesting tidbit of American soccer history: "The club gained its greatest prominence in the 1950s when it dominated both St. Louis and national soccer competitions. In 1958, the United States Soccer Federation used Kutis, with a few guest players, as the U.S. national team in two World Cup qualifying matches."[105] Strange, right? That's how good Kutis was.

Under-16 National Titles (Boys)

St. Louis titles: 6

Starting from 1976

For a comparative look, here are all the winners, nationwide, with St. Louis teams in bold. (The information was accessed online from championships.usyouthsoccer.org on November 27, 2019.)

BOYS UNDER-16 US YOUTH SOCCER CUP [FORMERLY LARRY HARMON CUP]

1976 Ruiz Soccer Club, Florissant, MO

1977 Annandale Boys Club, Annandale, VA

1978 Busch Gardens Soccer Club, St. Louis, MO

1979 Club America, Dallas, N-TX

1980 Busch Gardens Soccer Club, St. Louis, MO

1981 Montgomery United Ponies,

MD
1982 Columbia Kick, MD
1983 Goalpost, Federal Way, WA
1984 Vista Red Hawks, VA
1985 Blau-Weiss Gottschee,
Intermediate "A", Forest Hills,
E-NY
**1986 Liebe Soccer Club,
St. Louis, MO**
1987 Columbia City United, MD
1988 Busch Soccer Club, MO
1989 Busch Soccer Club, MO
1990 Livonia Metro Magic
Wolves, MI
1991 F.C. Delco Demons, E-PA
1992 NHBFC Black, CA-S
1993 Vardar III, MI
1994 Texans, S-TX
1995 Chicago Soccers, IL
1996 Nomads SC, CA-S
1997 Javanon '81, KY
1998 Vardar III, MI
1999 Chicago Magic, IL
2000 FC Westchester, E-NY

2001 Sockers FC, IL
2002 Atlanta Fire, GA
2003 Southern California United,
CA-S
2004 Casa Mia Bays, MD
2005 Arsenal FC, CA-S
2006 Baltimore Casa Mia Bays,
MD
2007 Real So Cal, CA-S
2008 Dallas Texans 92 Red,
N-TX
2009 Dallas Texans 93 Red,
N-TX
2010 Slammers FC, CA-S
2011 Concorde Fire Elite, GA
2012 Michigan Jaguars 96 Green,
MI
2013 Smithtown Arsenal, E-NY
2014 Baltimore Celtic 97/98, MD
2015 Baltimore Celtic, MD
2016 Loudoun Red, VA
2017 Tampa Bay United, FL
2018 Arlington SA 2002 Red, VA

Here are the consolidated St. Louis national champions from Under 16:

1976 Ruiz Soccer Club,
Florissant, MO
1978 Busch Gardens Soccer Club,
St. Louis, MO
1980 Busch Gardens Soccer Club,
St. Louis, MO

1986 Liebe Soccer Club, St.
Louis, MO
1988 Busch Soccer Club, MO
1989 Busch Soccer Club, MO

Under-19 National Titles (Boys)

St. Louis titles: 22
Starting from 1935
For a comparative look, here are all the winners, nationwide, with St. Louis teams in bold. (The information was accessed online from championships.usyouthsoccer.org on November 27, 2019.)

BOYS UNDER-19 JAMES P. MCGUIRE CUP

1935 Reliable Juniors of New Bedford, MA

1936 Hatikvoh Juniors of Brooklyn, NY

1937 Hatikvoh Juniors of Brooklyn, NY

1938 Lighthouse Boys' Club of Philadelphia, PA

1939 Avella Juniors of Avella, PA

1940 Avella Juniors of Avella, PA

1941 Mercerville Juniors of Trenton, NJ

1942-44 No competition-travel restricted because of war effort

1945 Hornets of Chicago, IL & Pompeii Juniors of Baltimore, MD, co-champions

1946 Schumacher Juniors of St. Louis, MO

1947 Heidelberg Juniors of Heidelberg, PA

1948 Lighthouse Boys' Club of Philadelphia, PA

1949 Lighthouse Boys' Club of Philadelphia, PA

1950 Harrison Juniors of Harrison, NJ

1951 Seco Juniors of St. Louis, MO

1952 Kollsman S.C. of Brooklyn, NJ

1953 Newark Boys Club of Newark, NJ

1954 Hansa S.C. of Chicago, IL

1955 Schwaben of Chicago, IL

1956 St. Engelbert of St. Louis, MO

1957 Lighthouse Boys' Club of Philadelphia, PA

1958 St. Paul of St. Louis, MO

1959 Ukrainian of New York, NY

1960 St. Paul of St. Louis, MO

1961 Hakoah of San Francisco, CA

1962 Schumacher Juniors of St. Louis, MO

1963 Kutis of St. Louis, MO

1964 Kutis of St. Louis, MO

1965 Im. Heart of Mary of St. Louis, MO
1966 St. Williams of St. Louis, MO
1967 Lighthouse Boys' Club of Philadelphia, PA
1968 St. Philip Di Neri of St. Louis, MO
1969 St. Philip Di Neri of St. Louis, MO
1970 St. Bart's of St. Louis, MO
1971 Seco of St. Louis, MO
1972 Seco of St. Louis, MO
1973 St. Elizabeth S.C. of Baltimore, MD
1974 Florissant Celtics of St. Louis, MO
1975 Imo's Pizza of St. Louis, MO
1976 Annandale Boys Club Cavalier of Annandale, VA
1977 Santa Clara Broncos of Santa Clara, CA
1978 Imo's Pizza of St. Louis, MO
1979 Imo's Pizza of St. Louis, MO
1980 Fremont Celtics, CA-N
1981 Scott Gallagher of St. Louis, MO
1982 Annandale Boys Club of Annandale, VA

1983 Montgomery United, MD
1984 Scott Gallagher of St. Louis, MO
1985 Columbia Jays, MD
1986 Fram-Culver of Culver, CA-S
1987 Union Lancers of Union, NJ
1988 Union Lancers 69 of Union, NJ
1989 LaJolla Nomads of LaJolla, CA-S
1990 Spartan Randolph Blackhawks of St. Paul, MN
1991 NHBFC Black, CA-S
1992 Vista Hurricanes, VA
1993 MVLASC Shooting Stars, CA-N
1994 Baltimore Spirit, MD
1995 Countryside Lightning, FL
1996 Scott Gallagher of St. Louis, MO
1997 Clearwater Chargers, FL
1998 CISCO Flames, AZ
1999 LaJolla Nomads, CA-S
2000 FC Delco Dynamo, E-PA
2001 FC Delco Black, E-PA
2002 Texans '82/83, S-TX
2003 FC Delco Arsenal, E-PA
2004 HSC Bulls '85, HI
2005 Sockers FC, IL
2006 Javanon SC, KY
2007 Dallas Texans 88 Red,

N-TX
2008 Solar SC, N-TX
2009 Baltimore Casa Mia Bays, MD
2010 Crew Juniors, OH-S
2011 Baltimore Bays Chelsea, MD
2012 Crew Juniors, OH-S
2013 Lehigh Valley United 93,

E-PA
2014 Concorde Fire Elite, GA
2015 Massapequa Arsenal, NY-E
2016 FC Golden State, CA-S
2017 Challenger Crew Jrs Gold 98, OH-N
2018 Baltimore Celtic SC Christos, MD

Here are the consolidated St. Louis national champions from Under-19:

1946 Schumacher Juniors of St. Louis, MO
1951 Seco Juniors of St. Louis, MO
1956 St. Engelbert of St. Louis, MO
1958 St. Paul of St. Louis, MO
1960 St. Paul of St. Louis, MO
1962 Schumacher Juniors of St. Louis, MO
1963 Kutis of St. Louis, MO
1964 Kutis of St. Louis, MO
1965 Im. Heart of Mary of St. Louis, MO
1966 St. Williams of St. Louis, MO
1968 St. Philip Di Neri of St. Louis, MO
1969 St. Philip Di Neri of St. Louis, MO
1970 St. Bart's of St. Louis, MO

1971 Seco of St. Louis, MO
1972 Seco of St. Louis, MO
1974 Florissant Celtics of St. Louis, MO
1975 Imo's Pizza of St. Louis, MO
1978 Imo's Pizza of St. Louis, MO
1979 Imo's Pizza of St. Louis, MO
1981 Scott Gallagher of St. Louis, MO
1984 Scott Gallagher of St. Louis, MO
1996 Scott Gallagher of St. Louis, MO

In the competitive areas of U16 and U19, St. Louis teams have been national leaders. Historically speaking, this is an amazing number of youth national championships for a city that has long been regarded, rightly so, as the king of soccer, and the heartbeat of soccer in America. In addition, Scott Gallagher won the U23 National title in 2006 along with various other titles. The most fitting examples for competition under the age of 23 are the U16 and U19 results.

U.S. OPEN CUP

For years, the U.S. Open Cup has been a leading adult tournament in the United States and to this day it allows a chance for amateur teams to compete against top professional teams. Since the 1990s, MLS sides have pretty much dominated the tournament. Yet, dating far back in history, St. Louis clubs have staked a claim to the trophy. Here are past winners of the U.S. Open Cup from St. Louis.

U.S. Open Cup (St. Louis Winners)

1920 Ben Millers	1948 St. Louis Simpkins-Ford
1922 St. Louis Scullin Steel F.C.	1950 St. Louis Simpkins-Ford
1933 Stix, Baer and Fuller F.C.	1957 St. Louis Kutis S.C.
1934 Stix, Baer and Fuller F.C.	1986 St. Louis Kutis S.C.
1935 St. Louis Central Breweries	1988 St. Louis Busch Seniors

How is this possible? With all the teams throughout the nation it's hard to win even one national title! But, with club and the U.S. Open Cup combined, St. Louis has won over and over throughout the years. Truly remarkable. It's a testament to St. Louis' stellar ability with soccer over the ages.

HIGH SCHOOL: A RICH TRADITION OF CHAMPIONS

HIGH SCHOOL TEAMS IN ST. LOUIS, MISSOURI

There are myriad St. Louis high school teams that deserve front and center attention. Top of the list would be St. Thomas Aquinas-Mercy and CBC. These were two teams that were feared by everyone. Dare not mess with these guys; it seemed that every year each school was nationally ranked and even the players on the bench were likely D1 college talents. Also, a school that deserves much attention is Vianney, among many others that are listed next. From 1968 through 1984, Missouri had one high school soccer champion. Eventually, in the 1985 season, Missouri switched to Class 1A-3A (small schools), and 4A (big schools). In the 2002 season, Missouri switched to Class 1, 2, and 3 ("3" being the biggest schools). As of 2014, Missouri tumbled into Class 1, 2, 3, and 4 ("4" being the biggest schools).

St. Thomas Aquinas-Mercy
Missouri State Championships: 11
1975, 1977, 1985, 1988, 1989, 1990, 1992, 1993, 1996, 1997, 1998
Did you know? This school was initially known as St. Thomas Aquinas, but hereafter we shall refer to it as St. Thomas Aquinas-Mercy and/or Aquinas-Mercy. St. Thomas Aquinas-Mercy, which was near Rosary High, eventually combined with Rosary High and turned into Trinity Catholic High School. (However, in 2021, Trinity announced it would shut down due to low enrollment.)

Here's the thing: When you think St. Louis high school soccer, if you're like me, you immediately think of CBC and Vianney, the powerhouses. Well, don't forget about St. Thomas Aquinas-Mercy, who, as of 2021, leads all of Missouri high schools in soccer titles.

Legendary coach: Vince Drake. As a player, Vince, who was an outside defender, was a member of SLU during the glory days, and, once upon time, he played for Bob Guelker on a US youth national team in Guatemala back in 1964. At the Missouri State High School

Activities Association website (circa 2021), Drake is listed with 10 state championships which makes him the all-time leader for coaches in Missouri. Coach Drake humbly credits his large pool of talent for getting so many titles.

A former player, Dan King (known by many as "Dipper," who was a US youth national team member), said of his early days around Vince Drake and the powerhouse program, "He had some big-time teams, man." In that era "they were big." King added: "Kids these days, a freshman comes in, he goes 'well, you know, I should make Varsity,' right. When I went, you didn't even think about Varsity because when I was a freshman, you're looking at Perry Van der Beck, Bob Bozada, Steve Sullivan on the Varsity" and as King said, you're not going to get a chance with those great players because in reality "you paid your dues on the 'B team' and you were glad to do it!" That's saying a lot as King transitioned from being a high school state champ to playing straight away as a starting freshman defender at Indiana University under Coach Jerry Yeagley. King—who was extremely skillful—would eventually win two national titles at IU (1982 and 1983) and then moved onto play pro indoor ball. Recently, since the late 90s, he's been doing some coaching of his own at UMSL, certainly applying lessons learned from Coach Drake (who King gives credit for getting him to Indiana). Incidentally, his dad was a well-regarded referee, and, as a kid, Dan was a ball boy for the St. Louis Stars.

It would be impossible to include every great player that wore a St. Thomas Aquinas-Mercy jersey, but here are a few of them...

Steve Sullivan—who later played forward for the St. Louis Steamers—was an All-American player at St. Thomas Aquinas-Mercy.

Bob Bozada was a versatile player that earned Missouri All-State and All-American honors. After high school, Bob won a NCAA Division I national championship with SIUE. He played professionally on a few teams, including the St. Louis Steamers and Kansas City Comets.

Perry Van der Beck—born in 1959 in Florissant, Missouri—went straight from high school to the Tampa Bay Rowdies in the NASL in

1978. He played for a number of pro teams, including the St. Louis Steamers and St. Louis Ambush. In addition, he played with the USMNT for 23 games (1979-85) in which he scored two goals. Winners of the U.S. Soccer Player of the Year Award have been restricted to one player a year since 1984, including but not limited to Christian Pulisic, Michael Bradley, Clint Dempsey, Landon Donovan, Tab Ramos, Paul Caligiuri, Rick Davis, and in 1985, one Perry Van der Beck. A few of his inspirations growing up were Dave Berwin, Pat Leahy, Bob O'Leary, Pat McBride, and Al Trost.

Greg Koeller subsequently has been a standout coach at St. Dominic High School with five state titles to date for the boys' team.

Mike Sorber, who's known as the MVP of the USMNT during World Cup 1994, was a standout player during his high school days under the direction of Vince Drake. Sorber was part of the 1985 and 1988 state championship squads, and earned the MVP award for the North during the St. Louis North-South High School Senior All-Star game. He was also the assistant coach of the USMNT with Bob Bradley, and in 2017, he began work as director of soccer operations with LAFC. Certainly, down the road, we may expect more coaching news from Mike Sorber and don't be surprised to see him at the helm of the USMNT, perhaps.

On its illustrious 11-title run, St. Thomas Aquinas-Mercy won three titles in a row on two occasions: 1988, 1989, 1990 and 1996, 1997, 1998! In St. Louis, where soccer is king, and in Missouri, arguably the most competitive soccer state in the nation, that is incredible!

CBC High School
Missouri State Championships: 10
1968, 1983, 1984, 1988, 2004, 2005, 2009, 2012, 2016, 2018
Did you know? CBC is short for Christian Brothers College.

CBC kicked things off with the first high school state championship in the 1968-69 season. Coach Terry Michler, a legend, has won eight state championships for CBC to date. In Missouri history, as of 2021, he is second only to Vince Drake for all-time high school state titles as a coach.

Harry Ratican, Jimmy Dunn, Jimmy Roe, and Carl Gentile are a few legendary players from CBC's past. The talented defender Don Droege—a star at SLU and member of the USMNT (1977-79)—played with the Steamers (1983-85) and other pro teams after his time at CBC.

Tommy Howe of the St. Louis Stars went to CBC. Prior to playing for the St. Louis Steamers, Jeff Sendobry—who also played for Florissant Valley Community College and Indiana University—attended CBC.

Mike Freitag left CBC and played defense for the Indiana Hoosiers (in the late 1970s) and eventually the Denver Avalanche of the MISL. Eventually, Freitag traveled back to his alma mater and became a successful head coach at Indiana University in the 2000s.

Daryl Doran—of the St. Louis Steamers, St. Louis Storm, and St. Louis Ambush—went to CBC. Brothers Mark and Chris Santel attended CBC. Both players later represented St. Louis University. Mark eventually represented the USMNT. Jeff DiMaria—who played for the St. Louis Steamers and St. Louis Ambush—attended CBC.

As CBC has set the standard for high-quality high school soccer in St. Louis and nationwide, the list of talent continues with Brandon Barklage, Zach Bauer, and Tom Heinemann.

A.J. Cochran—a high school All-American and recipient of the Missouri Gatorade Soccer Player of the Year award in 2011—was part of a state championship with CBC.

As a leader in high school soccer, CBC is a good example for other schools to follow in terms of "aspirations." As crazy as it sounds, by 1988, CBC had only four state titles. (Only might be the wrong word as four is a lot.) Then from 1988 to 2004 CBC didn't get another state championship! That's a long drought for a powerhouse like CBC. Finally, in 2004, the school got its fifth title and the rest rolled in from there.

Whitfield
Missouri State Championships: 8
2002, 2003, 2004, 2006, 2007, 2009, 2010, 2021
Did you know? Bill Daues coached the team for seven state championships.

A few key players over the years include Todd Wallace, Jay Alberts (who eventually went to Yale before playing professionally), Joe Klosterman, Trevor House, along with goalkeepers, Kyle Clausen, Ted Jocobi, and David Greyhouse.

Many coaches have different approaches to success. Some of those for Coach Daues were based on staying current with the modern game. He was open minded, studying all aspects of the game, both here in the US and in Europe; anything to keep his teams ahead of the curve. According to Coach Daues, a person should look at "what is happening at the highest level and then you look at those trends, and then you see what you can use within the players you have."

In 2004, Whitfield had something special occur, more special than the other state titles and perhaps a little more special than any state title ever won in Missouri or the entire nation, for that matter. As Coach Daues told me, "We won the game 3-2 vs. Pembroke in the final. Our record that year was 18-10-2." That seems innocuous enough, but here's the thing: In the second overtime, shortly before dreaded penalty kicks, the ball somehow wound up in the air around the penalty spot, and Doug Londoff struck a bicycle-kick that won the game and state championship all at once! How often do you hear that? Probably never. Pretty amazing. And yes, the crowd went wild.

Consider the fact that Whitfield isn't the biggest school in the world. Back in 2004-05, under the coaching guidance of Daues and Assistant Coach Michael Quantes, Whitfield pulled off a major 1-0 upset over nationally ranked CBC.

As of 2015, Michael Quantes—a Chaminade grad who played college soccer with Metro East legend Dr. Ryan Seim at Truman State University, formally named Northeast Missouri State University—assumed the position of head coach at Whitfield. Following this, in 2021, Charlie Noonan led the squad as coach to its most recent state championship. Considering the massive success from past years, Whitfield has a lot to build upon as it goes up against rivals John Burroughs, Priory, and Westminster.

Vianney, an old rival of CBC, is another example of a strong program that has endured a state championship drought but that has the capability of mounting an incredible comeback.

Vianney High School

Missouri State Championships: 7

1978, 1980, 1981, 1982, 1987, 1991, 1992

Did you know? Vianney High School (located in the southwestern part of St. Louis) is very close to World Wide Technology Soccer Park (located in Fenton, Missouri). Vianney High School is a proud owner of seven Missouri high school soccer state championships. The good years were definitely the late 1970s and into the early 1990s. There was a strong run in the early 1980s and a final run in the early 1990s. Since then, Vianney hasn't been able to find another title. Don't be surprised, though, to see a resurgence down the road.

Coach Mike Villa won six state championships for Vianney.

Ron Jacober—a legendary voice of the St. Louis Cardinals—had a son, Jeff, a defender that was part of Vianney's state championship glory in the early 1980s. Down the road, Jeff had experience at the famous Top Gun academy as a pilot.

Casey Klipfel—an extremely talented goalie, once a member of Busch Soccer Club—was a key player at Vianney before moving onto SLU. Eventually he played professionally with the Nashville Metros. Unfortunately, Casey—born in 1976—passed away in 2016. His obituary read, in part, "He graduated Vianney High School and St. Louis University with Honors and Academic All America. His degree was in I.T. but his passion was soccer. As a junior in high school his soccer team was voted #1 in Nation, as a senior he was in Parade Magazine as #1 goalie in U.S."[106]

Tony Williams—a crafty defender and midfielder—played at Vianney before landing with Clemson, and the pro team Richmond Kickers.

De Smet

Missouri State Championships: 6

1991, 1993, 1995, 1997, 2011, 2019

Did you know? De Smet standout Sam Bick was a defender and midfielder that eventually played for the hometown St. Louis Steamers and the USMNT.

Eric Delabar was an All-American goalie at De Smet that subsequently was a member of the St. Louis Steamers.

Matt McKeon—a midfielder—earned All-American honors at De Smet before playing for the St. Louis Billikens, Kansas City Wizards, Colorado Rapids, and the USMNT.

Chris Klein was a talented midfielder at De Smet before he went on to play in MLS and for the USMNT. Following his MLS career, Klein became president of the LA Galaxy.

Pat Noonan played at De Smet before moving on to Indiana University, a handful of MLS teams including that of the New England Revolution, and the USMNT.

Will Bruin was a forward that won the Missouri Gatorade Player of the Year at De Smet before suiting up with Indiana University. He also played in MLS and for the USMNT.

A noteworthy state championship for De Smet came in dramatic fashion in the 2019 final game at World Wide Technology Soccer Park. In a tense and lengthy penalty-kick shootout, midfielder Henry Lawlor scored on an important kick. Then the stage was set as De Smet's keeper Connor Mulvaney made a crucial save to capture the title against Lee's Summit. This historic achievement for the school marked the sixth overall title. In doing so it put De Smet in elite company as a school with over five state titles. Surely, in years to come, there will likely be more from this powerhouse program.

St. Mary's (St. Louis)

Missouri State Championships: 6

1969, 1995, 1999, 2000, 2001, 2010

Did you know? John Roeslein was part of the school's first state championship soccer team and he's also a member of the St. Mary's Hall of Fame.

Frank Flesch—who was also a baseball player in his day—played at St. Mary's and won the school's first state championship in soccer. He subsequently competed collegiately at UMSL and won the 1973 NCAA Division II soccer championship.

Denny Vaninger—who played for St. Louis Kutis, St. Louis Stars, St. Louis Steamers, and the USMNT—was an impact player when he attended St. Mary's.

Frank Flesch II played on the St. Mary's state championship soccer team in 2000.

St. Mary's proclaimed its greatness with three state titles in a row: 1999, 2000, and 2001.

The official website of St. Mary's, the Class of '71 Hall of Fame page, has the first state championship for soccer listed as 1969-70, while the Missouri State High School Activities Association has it listed as 1969.[‡]

Rosary High
Missouri State Championships: 5
1970, 1979, 1985, 1987, 1991
Did you know? It appears that Rosary High, which was close to St. Thomas Aquinas-Mercy, later combined with St. Thomas Aquinas-Mercy and turned into Trinity Catholic High School. In 1985, the year Missouri broke into 1A-3A and 4A, both Rosary (1A-3A) and St. Thomas Aquinas-Mercy (4A) won the soccer state championship in their respective classes.

Don Ebert—of the St. Louis Steamers—played at Rosary High, "where he lettered four times and set a record for goals scored in one season, 31."[107]

[‡]   Websites for St. Mary's and the Missouri State High School Activities Association were accessed December 2, 2020 and January 17, 2021.

Greg Makowski—of the St. Louis Steamers and USMNT—played at Rosary High.

St. Dominic
Missouri State Championships: 5
2004, 2008, 2009, 2012, 2013
Legendary coach: Greg Koeller. To date, Greg Koeller has attainted five state titles coaching the boys. (He's had success coaching the girls as well.) Tim Ream attended St. Dominic and eventually played with Bolton Wanderers, Fulham, and the USMNT.

John Burroughs
Missouri State Championships: 4
2008, 2013, 2016, 2018

Chaminade College Prep
Missouri State Championships: 3
2001, 2002, 2006
Did you know? Chaminade's legendary coach: Mike Gauvain. Brad Davis played at Chaminade before representing the USMNT.

Kevin Robson was a major factor in the 2001 and 2002 championships. Robson went on to win two national championships at Indiana University; as of 2020, he was working as an assistant coach and recruiting coordinator for the soccer powerhouse.

Speedy Danny Wynn joined SLU and played with New England Revolution.

The Missouri Gatorade Soccer Player of the Year award has been given to four Chaminade players: Brad Davis, Tim Collico, Mike Roach, and Tommy Barlow.

Priory (Saint Louis Priory School)
Missouri State Championships: 3
2005, 2011, 2017

St. Louis University (High School)
Missouri State Championships: 3
1972, 1990, 2003
Did you know? Bob Kehoe (former USMNT player and coach), Dan Flynn (former CEO of U.S. Soccer Federation), and Ty Keough (former USMNT player) went to SLUH.

Tim Twellman—who was tapped by St. Louis City SC in 2020 to be a sporting community relations consultant for the team—attended SLUH, SIUE, and eventually played in the NASL.

Jeff Cacciatore, "came up through the ranks of the CYC youth soccer program at St. Ambrose,"[108] and, "went on to play at St. Louis University High School under Head Coach Ebbie Dunn and became All-State selection."[109] Jeff also won a NCAA Division I national championship at SIUE, and then played with the St. Louis Steamers as a forward.

Taylor Twellman eventually played for New England Revolution, won the 2005 MLS MVP, and represented the USMNT as a forward.

HIGH SCHOOL TEAMS IN METRO EAST, ILLINOIS

The Illinois side of the Mississippi River is considered an area of St. Louis and is known as the Metro East. In past years, the two best soccer-playing cities of this area have been Granite City and Collinsville. Over the years, these schools, and a few others, have represented the greater St. Louis area in Illinois high school soccer with much success.

To speak of the "Metro East" as part of "St. Louis" is an interesting side note. In athletic competition (and, one could argue, just generally speaking), there's always been a dislike between the Metro East schools and those of St. Louis. Let's put it this way: at its best you could call it "healthy competition"; at its worst you could call it "tribal warfare." Furthermore, in the world of high school soccer, this conversation gets a bit more tantalizing as it includes an interesting connection with Chicago. So let's step back for a second. Over many generations, there's been a major dislike between St. Louis and Chicago. This situation has gone back many years, beginning with the rivalries of the St. Louis Cardinals vs. Chicago Cubs, and the St. Louis Blues vs. Chicago Blackhawks, for instance. Here's how 'Metro East high schools representing St. Louis at large in the overall rivalry with Chicago' comes in to play. Despite tensions between the Metro East and St. Louis, Metro East high schools have represented St. Louis in terms of soccer state championships against the best teams of Chicago. While some from St. Louis may not admit it, the Metro East schools certainly compete on behalf of St. Louis, by proxy if you will. Every Illinois high school state championship won over the years, by Granite City, Collinsville, Edwardsville, and others, has represented yet another 'trophy for the trophy case' in the longstanding rivalry between St. Louis and Chicago. The only thing separating the Metro East from St. Louis is a river. The bottom line is pretty simple: The Metro East—in so many ways—is St. Louis. Furthermore, in the Metro East there has been no other school greater at bringing home championships in the name of St. Louis soccer than Granite City.

In fact, the soccer program of Granite City—previously led by mega-coach, the one, the only, Gene Baker—is legendary. Much of Granite City's past success was thanks to the experience of Gene Baker, who had won an NCAA national soccer championship with SLU as a player. All in all, Granite City gathered up 10 state titles, five of those were in a row. All the while proving to people of Chicago (and around the nation) that St. Louis soccer was king.

From 1972-73 through 1996-97, Illinois had one high school soccer champion. From 1997-98 to 2007-08, Illinois switched to Class A (small schools), and AA (big schools). In the 2008-09 season, Illinois switched to Class 1A, 2A, and 3A ("3A" being the biggest schools).§

---

§   This information was accessed from the IHSA (Illinois High School Association) official website on January 17, 2021.

Granite City High School

(Granite City and Granite City South)

Illinois State Championships: 10

1972, 1976, 1977, 1978, 1979, 1980, 1982, 1987, 1989, 1990

It's scary how good Granite City was. Did you know? Granite City's legendary coach: Gene Baker. Granite City's formidable home field was known as the Gauntlet. Separated by a fence, a city road passed right behind one of the goals. Some of the industrial parts of the town were very close to the field.

Coach Baker held a famous midnight practice to kickoff the season. Fans, who numbered in the hundreds, would purchase a ticket for $1 to view the event. It turned into a big deal. It was the pride of Granite City, and sometimes would bring in as much as $500-700. Baker's practices were highly structured. It would last from 12:00-1:30AM. Coach Baker would have the lights turned off on cue. The idea was to be the first team in the state on the field, and eventually the last (following, of course, a state championship in Chicago). A tradition for Gene after this practice was to get take-out from a local White Castle, go home, and await the next workout.

A legendary run from the Granite City Warriors: the 1970s and 80s. (Granite City's success carried into the 90s as well, but the good times were behind them.)

Granite City was basically a stud factory. The best St. Louis schools on the other side of the river knew they were in for a battle when they saw the red and black uniforms of Granite City get off a bus.

Steve Trittschuh, a former Granite City standout (who, coincidentally, attended Granite City North), was a regular member of the USMNT.

Coach Baker spoke very highly of Dave Fernandez, a juggling phenom.* In terms of all-time greats from Granite City, he's as close to the top of the list as you can get.

---

*   As Gene Baker explained to me, Dave's juggling record was something over 5,000!

John van Buskirk—a state champion and All-American in high school, arguably one of Granite City's best all-time players—ended up playing for Indiana University and professionally in Germany.

Brent Broshow was in goal for Granite City during the 1989 state championship victory.

Jeff Stephens—a crafty dribbler—was part of the 1989 and 1990 state championship squads.

Tim Henson—a talented goalie for Granite City—ended up playing professional indoor soccer.

To date, the last player to win a state title for Granite City High School was Jamey Bridges. He was a freshman on the 1990 squad that won state that year.

Matt Little—a Granite City standout in the 1990s—played for SIUE and the St. Louis Ambush.

Shawn Petroski—a Granite City standout in the 1990s that possessed a hard shot—was a member of the US U20 national team and played professionally in Germany.

Justin McMillian—a former Granite City Warrior—played professional indoor soccer.

Ryan Reeves, a former player at Granite City High School, ended up returning as coach of the team.

Oddly enough, around the same time as that of Collinsville High School, Granite City's state championship success faded away in the 1990s. But the legend continues.

Collinsville High School

Illinois State Championships: 4

1981, 1986, 1991, 1992

Collinsville High School produced a ton of talented teams over the years that eventually earned four Illinois high school state championships. Did you know? In full disclosure, I should admit that I attended CHS. I can tell you with complete certainty that competition with St. Louis schools, such as CBC, helped make Collinsville and Granite City the powerhouses they were. Coincidentally, I was part of the 1991 and 1992 CHS state championship runs, lettered both years and in 1992, which we'll discuss momentarily, I took part in the championship game alongside very talented teammates. But first, let's look back a little, shall we?

Once upon a time, a St. Louis Stars defender and member of the USMNT, Gary Rensing, coached the Kahoks.

For a time, Paul "Whitey" Kapsalis—author of *To Chase a Dream*—landed in Collinsville as a kid and played youth soccer there before eventually moving to Indiana where he walked onto Indiana University's soccer team, and subsequently became captain. If you're thinking: *This isn't how most captains of Indiana's soccer team become captains*, you are correct. After many ups and downs, Whitey made the team and was captain even though he was not a focal point of the lineup. Despite never being a Kahok, Whitey drew on some of his Collinsville experience to guide him down the road.

Craig Stahl played at CHS during the 1970s and then followed up his successful collegiate career at Rockhurst University with a stint in the MISL where he played for the talented Kansas City Comets.

Joe Reiniger followed up his CHS scoring rampage by doing the same at SIUE and then with the St. Louis Ambush (1995 NPSL champions), St. Louis Steamers, Milwaukee Wave, St. Louis Illusion, and Illinois Piasa. Throughout his pro career, he amassed over 600 goals.

The list of great Kahoks goes on and on. A tiny fraction includes Jerry Modglin, Bob Tejada, Tony Ellis, Marc Mahat, Steve VanDyke, Mike Verning, Matt Chandler, Rick Artime, Marty Bub, Brandon Stultz, Kyle Touchette, and CJ Cerna. When you have good players like these, and a powerhouse program, you have exceptional teams. For a good stretch of time, Collinsville was a powerhouse rivaling the great Granite City. Along these lines, there are four special CHS teams—1981, 1986, 1991, and 1992—that won state titles. Are the days of titles over? Like Granite City, Collinsville could jump back in the race at any time. For now though, only four Collinsville teams earned the coveted state trophy, which, to date, is still second best in the state of Illinois.

Incidentally, it's worth mentioning again, the titles Collinsville and Granite City won were attained when there was only one state champion.

Illinois High School Soccer State Champions†

Granite City	10
Collinsville	4
Naperville (North)	4
Waterloo (Gibault Catholic)	4
Peoria (Notre Dame)	4

There's another fascinating point to be made about Collinsville. Between Collinsville and Granite City, CHS is the last Metro East powerhouse to win an Illinois state championship (1992). As such, it's like a long-forgotten vestige from St. Louis' past. Let's take a closer look at the last standing Metro East powerhouse, to date.

The 1981 team was the first from Collinsville to win a soccer state championship. Coached by Jim Stranz, it was a team that had stiff competition in the form of Granite City, the big dog on the block. To somehow come out ahead of Granite City was an achievement in and of itself, but then to knock off elite Chicago talent was yet another milestone.

The 1986 team featured scoring sensation Joe Reiniger. It was a phenomenal season that saw Collinsville earn its second state title. The coach was Jim Stranz. Collinsville won the championship game over Libertyville by a score of 2-1 in 4 OTs.

The 1991 team was something special. For starters, it had to live up to the standards of the 1981 and 1986 teams (not an easy task). It was a legendary squad led by the iron wall in midfield, Steve VanDyke (eventually a standout at Eastern Illinois University and SIUE), Mike Verning, and Kevin Krietemeyer, along with the fleet scoring of Matt

†   This information was gathered at the IHSA (Illinois High School Association) official website, accessed December 16, 2020 and January 17, 2021.

Chandler up front. Behind this midfield iron wall was a defensive iron wall; it was a special group of talent. Most high school teams—regardless of how much talent they have—are boy bands. This was a man band, plain and simple. Oddly enough, the smallest of the starters, Jason Digirolamo, was probably the toughest. It just so happened, starting center midfielders Steve VanDyke and Kevin Krietemeyer were also starting guards on the 1991 basketball team—coached by Bob Bone—that made it to state that year, led by Richard Keene. Such a scenario doesn't happen too often, especially in light of the fact that Illinois is one of the leading states nationwide for both high school soccer and basketball.[‡] For those that witnessed the greatness of the 1991 soccer team, comprised of many seniors by the way, it was a magical march to the championship game which had to go through Gene Baker and Granite City along the way. That was a game for the ages that ended 1-0 in sudden death overtime thanks to a pointblank rifle of a shot from VanDyke which keeper Tim Henson instinctively deflected up into the air, creating a moment of uncertainty on his part which allowed Chandler's tap in. The subsequent championship, which took place in Naperville, Illinois, was a testament to how great the Collinsville team was and a reminder throughout the state that the St. Louis area was still in charge.

On an individual level, during his senior year, Steve VanDyke, my elder by a few years, arguably had perhaps the best single-season performance in Illinois high school history. By the way, back in the day, I don't think he was ever a fan of yours truly, nor am I trying to win anyone's favor; I just call them like I see them. The best four-year high school performance in Illinois history would likely go to Kenny Snow. As for a single season, it's hard to refute the year VanDyke had. Obviously, I and others have not seen every great player down the pike, so it's hard to directly compare. Though when you see a great single-season performance up close, and you compare it to every other great performance at all levels in your

---

[‡]   Around this time, the Kahok basketball program was ranked alongside Centralia, Illinois, as the top-two all-time winning high school teams nationwide.

mind, it's hard for any Illinois high school player to surpass the single-season performance of VanDyke in 1991. Whether this is true or not is debatable, though every touch of the ball and every game played was in league with Dave Fernandez and John van Buskirk of Granite City, Joe Reiniger, Kenny Snow, Steve Snow, Mike Fisher, or Brian McBride. On the St. Louis side of the river, players such as Perry Van der Beck, Daryl Doran, and Mark Santel would stand out, among *hundreds* of others throughout the litany of great St. Louis high school performers. True to form, VanDyke, a center midfield phenom—that scored the big goals and carried his team to a state championship, even going so far as to score the winning goal in the final game—was right there with the best of them.

The following year, in 1992, Collinsville won state again.

Essentially, CHS was full of athletic talent in the early 1990s. It didn't hurt matters that the Athletic Director happened to be Bob Bone, who previously excelled in basketball at UMSL, whose website in 2020 stated: "Bob Bone is the all-time career scoring leader in UMSL history with 2,678 points. He was a three-time All-American during his career and holds numerous UMSL records in addition to the scoring title."[110] Bone was also a former Kahok. His legend was such that when I spoke on the phone with former *St. Louis Post-Dispatch* reporter, Dave Dorr, a member of the Missouri Sports Hall of Fame, he recalled Bone's play with alacrity and hastened to point out the dominant Illinois basketball programs to that of Missouri. Luckily for the Kahoks' athletic program, Bone was on board. Perhaps Bone's storied presence as CHS AD—along with his slow, methodical, basketball swagger—trickled over greatness exuded by multiple athletic teams.

The 1992 soccer team had an impressive roster that included senior leaders Rick Artime (midfielder), Brett Boerm (goalkeeper), Tino Galvan (midfielder), and junior leader Marty Bub (midfielder). It was a team with a number of good defenders, midfielders, and forwards. In midfield and up top, there was a ton of talent, including but not limited to Brandon Stultz (who'd previously made the leap over the river to play for Scott Gallagher), a few Mikes (such as Mike Darnell and Mike Theis), with some help from a youngster, Donnie Smith. The championship game was nothing short of a Metro East team representing St. Louis soccer yet again against the best of Chicago (just as Granite City had successfully done on so many previous occasions). Before the game ended 2-1, Marty Bub—one of the best players I've come across—had a solid game in midfield.[§] In a crucial moment of the game, Rick Artime—who was wearing a pair of Brazilian cleats belonging to yours truly, after he lost his pair—scored an important game-tying penalty-kick. Then, thanks to a miraculous shot from some 40-yards out by one Doug Hartmann, who was about as familiar with scoring as a dog is walking on the moon, the result was another state title for Collinsville, and another notch on the belt for St. Louis soccer at large.

Within the bigger picture of St. Louis soccer, this 1992 Illinois state championship holds a unique significance as it happens to be the last state title for Collinsville. For that matter, Granite City's last state title happened to be in 1990. Both Metro East powerhouses Collinsville and Granite City ran roughshod over northern Chicago teams in the battle for Illinois high school state championships. To date, the combined championships of Granite City and Collinsville equal an astounding 14 titles. Despite the Mississippi River separating both towns from St. Louis, both schools represented the resplendent echo chamber of great teams from the greater St. Louis area.

For both Collinsville and Granite City, high school state championships might be waiting around the corner. For now though, Collinsville's last championship of 1992 represented the end of an era. The dominant Granite City teams of the 1970s and 80s, and the influx of talent from

---

[§]   Bub underwent a kidney transplant shortly after high school which essentially hampered any potential soccer pursuits; he was a quality player at any level. A few years prior, circa 1990, I'd seen Marty carry the heavy underdog Collinsville Untouchables over the highly favored powerhouse Scott Gallagher, stacked with talent left and right including Chris Klein and Craig Corbett, by a score of 3-2 in the championship game of The Southwest Illinois Shoot-Out in Collinsville, Illinois.

Collinsville in the 80s and 90s, had been influenced in one way or another from the St. Louis Stars, the early St. Louis Steamers, St. Louis University, and SIUE. Sometimes the Mississippi River has acted as a boundary that causes inhabitants on either side to forget that both sides are interconnected. The accomplishments of Collinsville and Granite City from this era are (in reality) no different from the achievements of the extraordinary powerhouse programs of St. Thomas Aquinas-Mercy, CBC, Vianney, and a few others. From the 1970s through the early 90s it was a magical time for Metro East soccer, and, somehow or another, the 1992 Collinsville state championship team symbolically represents the end of that time.

Short of listing all the 1992 CHS players, which is out of the scope of this book (we only have so much room to work with here), a list of the names can be found on plaques that were placed around the soccer field at Collinsville High School, which is within view of the Arch and downtown St. Louis.

Feel free to drop by, certainly the city of Collinsville would appreciate that. After all, it's probably why the plaques were erected in the first place. The plaques—which embody the school colors of purple and white— are designed in the shape of Illinois and they also include the overall record from the state championship year in question. Other plaques— commemorating other achievements—are present as well, including the 1981, 1986, and 1991 state championship teams.

In 1993, which happened to be my senior year, we came so close to winning three state titles in a row but eventually placed third. What bitter irony. This plaque is also featured. This is a tale that could go on forever so let's leave it there for now.

The plaques were conceived with good intentions, however, they are a little small and were fastened onto a chain-link fence with some sort of bolt or screw or nail (whatever holds something of that sort up on a fence). So, you tell me: Good idea, bad idea? Very Metro East, you know; come on guys, get it together; geez, this is supposed to be for eternity here, come on now. Perhaps they'll be updated eventually. In fact, if you're so inclined, write a letter; tell them to change the plaques to a larger size, perhaps engraved on a colossal wooden gate entrance similar to the one found just down the road at O'Fallon Family Sports Park in O'Fallon, Illinois (a magnificent facility with numerous turf soccer fields that serves the greater St. Louis area). They got the idea right with a huge gate entrance that honors a former mayor; lo and behold, to the best of my knowledge, the mayor in question wasn't even part of a high school soccer state championship team. Go figure. Until then, until the magical day when well-intentioned Collinsville figures it out, the Collinsville High School plaques represent an interesting piece of Metro East high school history for tourists and sports aficionados alike.

Of further interest, there are large championship team photos of the aforementioned CHS teams inside Hurricanes Bar & Grill, a popular stop in downtown Collinsville that supports soccer. Mike Theis—a skillful player that was part of the 1992 team—can be found there on some nights swinging in a shift or two, always ready to talk soccer.

Of course, the world-famous Cahokia Mounds are right down the road from Collinsville High School. Any tourist interested in such things would have a field day.

Before locating the new MLS soccer-specific stadium in downtown St. Louis, Collinsville, Illinois, was a heavy favorite for the location, given its close proximity to St. Louis, the river, bridges, and interstates. As most know by now, that wasn't meant to be.

OTHER METRO EAST STATE CHAMPIONS

The following Illinois state championship runs took place after Illinois broke up high schools into size categories in 1997-98.

For instance, in the case of Waterloo (Gibault Catholic), four championships is a significant achievement but these were acquired in a multi-class format, as opposed to when things consisted of one champion (which is when Granite City and Collinsville gained their championships).

Waterloo (Gibault Catholic)
Illinois State Championships: 4
2005, 2006, 2007, 2013

Edwardsville High School
Illinois State Championships: 2
2000, 2013
Did you know? Edwardsville's coach for its two championships was
Mark Heiderscheid.

Alton Marquette
Illinois State Championships: 2
2012, 2017

Waterloo H.S.
Illinois State Championships: 1
2015

COLLEGE

COLLEGES IN ST. LOUIS, GENERALLY SPEAKING...

St. Louis University (SLU) is the top soccer-playing college in the area.
However, there are plenty of other local colleges with strong programs.

SIUE is one of the top schools in the Midwest to play soccer. It's also
a top destination nationwide, though, for generations, it has drawn a lot
of its talent from the St. Louis area.

UMSL is a local school with historic national success that typically
will attract talented players from St. Louis.

In addition, there are Webster University, Washington University in St.
Louis, Fontbonne University, St. Louis Community College, McKendree
University, Southwestern Illinois College (SWIC), and Lewis and Clark

Community College. Each school pulls a large number of St. Louis high school grads.

McKendree, a school tucked away in Lebanon, Illinois, for example, has leaned on players from all over the area, and, notably from Granite City and Collinsville, including, Brent Broshow, Matt Chandler, Chris Digirolamo, Jason Digirolamo, Chris Sandrowski, and CJ Cerna, to name a few.

Washington University in St. Louis, has, through no fault of its own, a reputation for inferior talent to that of St. Louis University. Both are strong academic schools but when it comes to soccer, it's an unfair fight. Washington University (AKA WashU), has a reputation for good coaching, such as Ty Keough and Joe Clarke, but weaker talent overall as compared with SLU. When it comes to soccer, SLU is elite. Every player in the area wants to attend this storied university, with all of its championships.

ST. LOUIS COLLEGES IN 1973: THE BIG YEAR!

Somewhere, lost in the archives of American college soccer, is the insanely phenomenal year of 1973. In this year, as crazy as it sounds, St. Louis colleges won each national championship across-the-board!

NCAA Division I
1973 Champs: SLU

NCAA Division II
1973 Champs: UMSL

NCAA Division III
Evidently, the men's soccer championship for NCAA Division III schools started in 1974.

NJCAA Division I
1973 Champs: Florissant Valley Community College

THE MISSOURI ATHLETIC CLUB HERMANN TROPHY

Did you know? St. Louis houses the award for college soccer's best player in the nation. As of 1967, the Hermann Trophy was given to the best collegiate player in the nation, a great honor. Other rival awards have taken shape. *Wikipedia* summed up some of the history behind the award process with the following explanation: "In 1986, the Missouri Athletic Club (MAC) began naming an annual player of the year as a rival to the Hermann Trophy. Then in 1996, the National Soccer Coaches Association of America (NSCAA) initiated its own annual player of the year award. These three competing awards began merging three years later when the NSCAA and MAC agreed to cooperate on naming a combined collegiate player of the year. Finally, beginning in 2002, the MAC/NSCAA and Hermann Trophy organization merged to create a unified trophy for the top college soccer player of the year."[111] Interestingly, greater St. Louis holds the honor of housing the award. "The original Hermann Award Trophy is on display in the Hermann Atrium located in the McDonnell Athletic Center at MICDS in Ladue, Missouri. The original trophy was donated to the school by Hermann in 2003."[112] Furthermore, "The current MAC Hermann Trophy is on display in the lobbies of the Missouri Athletic Club's Downtown and West County Clubhouses."[113]

Now let's take a closer look at two specific colleges, SIUE and SLU.

SIUE

NCAA Championships: 1

1979

Did you know? Legendary coach: Bob Guelker.

John Stremlau—AKA the "Iron Man"—went to SIUE. While he was on the St. Louis Steamers, the team's media guide informed fans that Stremlau "teamed with Ty Keough to form superlative midfield tandem."[114]

Tim Twellman played for SIUE from 1973-76 and went on to play in the NASL and MISL. He also earned a cap with the USMNT in 1982.

Greg Villa—born in 1956 in St. Louis, Missouri—played at SIUE and, additionally, for various professional teams, including the St. Louis Steamers; he also played on the USMNT. At the official website of The St. Louis Soccer Hall of Fame,* Greg, who was inducted in 2016, was featured in a 1979 team photo with the US men's national team—red uniforms for field players, black and yellow jerseys for goalies, and blue track suits for coaches—which included a large number of players with St. Louis roots: Greg Villa, Ty Keough, Tony Bellinger, Perry Van der Beck, Steve Pecher, and Greg Makowski.

Greg Makowski was a very accomplished player. A classic St. Louis Steamers brochure from 1981-82 noted, he "was a three-time 1st team All-American"[115] at SIUE during the 1970s. In addition, he played defender for the St. Louis Steamers and was on the USMNT.

Make way for a goalie? Ed Gettemeier, a St. Louis native who played keeper for the St. Louis Steamers (among other teams), once played for SIUE and helped lead the team to the 1979 NCAA Division I national championship.

Bob Bozada, Jeff Cacciatore, and Don Ebert were part of the famous squad that won the 1979 NCAA Division I championship alongside Ed Gettemeier, other great players, and Coach Bob Guelker. Bozada, Cacciatore, and Ebert—all St. Louis natives—also played for the St. Louis Steamers during the golden era of indoor soccer when a game at the Checkerdome was the place to be.

Don Ebert was also a "collegiate All-American and set a school record scoring 22 goals in one season."[116]

Steve Trittschuh—a former SIUE Cougar—played for the USMNT in the 1990 FIFA World Cup. The Granite City native was well-known as a tough defender.

---

*   Accessed May 22, 2020.

Joe Reiniger—a former SIUE Cougar—was an outstanding scorer during his time in professional indoor soccer, and comes from Collinsville, Illinois, the man with a left-footed blast. Practically anyone that saw Reiniger play would agree that few could shoot the ball quite as hard and true as he could.

Tom Stone, who grew up in Alton, Illinois, played for Scott Gallagher and was a midfielder and captain for the SIUE Cougars in the late 1980s.

Matt Little, a Granite City product that played for the Granite City Elks, Granite City High School, and eventually the St. Louis Ambush, was an All-American during his time at SIUE.

A few standout players in the 2000s include Justin McMillian, Kevin Thibodeau, Greg Crook, and Zach Bauer.

Kevin Kalish gets a double mention in both the SLU section and here. Kalish, who assumed the role of head coach at SLU in 2018, is also a former head coach at SIUE.

SIUE PRO PLAYERS BONUS LIST

Quick note to readers: The following list was taken verbatim from the SIUE official website. As you may notice, for a few players, just a city or state was listed and it's unclear which team, exactly, the player was with. For example:

Chris Damico   Kansas City

Take "Kansas City" for example. It just says "Kansas City" and there is no team associated with it. Kansas City has had a few different pro teams, such as the Kansas City Comets and Kansas City Wizards, etc. Investigating each player's exact location is out of the scope of this book. The observation of how some players were listed in this fashion should not negate any accomplishments. Please direct any related question(s) to SIUE. I'm sure they'll be glad to hear from you.

Here is SIUE's impressive list of former players that reached the pro level:

Player	Played for or Drafted By
Mike Jones	Sporting Kansas City
Mike Banner	Chicago Fire
Zach Bauer	AC St. Louis
Bruce Bellinger	Minnesota (MISL)
Rick Benben	Atlanta
John Berner	Colorado Rapids
Justin Bilyeu	New York Red Bulls (MLS)
Bob Bozada	Minnesota
Chris Cacciatore	Rochester
Jeff Cacciatore	Ft. Lauderdale
Steve Cacciatore	Rochester
Chris Carenza	San Antonio
John Carenza	St. Louis
Tim Clark	Minnesota
Greg Crook	St. Louis Ambush
Chris Damico	Kansas City
John Deinowski	St. Louis Stars
Dave Delphus	Minnesota
Mark Downar	St. Louis Stars
Don Ebert	New York
Lewis Ellis	Bodens BK (Sweden)
Vince Fassi	Dallas
Tom Galati	Philadelphia
Ed Gettemeier	Kansas City (MISL) and Montreal (NASL)
Brian Groark	St. Louis Ambush
Tim Groark	St. Louis (MISL)
Tim Guelker	Buffalo
Tom Henson	St. Louis Stars
Brian Higgins	Indianapolis
Joe Howe	Atlanta
Kevin Howe	Atlanta

Tom Howe	St. Louis Stars
Dave Hummert	Los Angeles
Chris Hundelt	St. Louis Steamers
Dave Hundelt	Houston
Kevin Hundelt	St. Louis Steamers
Devyn Jambga	Portland Timbers 2 (USL)
Mike Kelley	Dallas
Peter Kelly	Saint Louis FC
Andrew Kendall-Moullin	Atlanta United 2 (USL)
Bobby Kessen	Dallas
Kent Kobernus	Saint Louis FC
Andy Korbesmeyer	St. Louis Ambush
Chester Kowalewski	Denver
Brett Lane	F.C. Linkoping (Sweden)
Todd Lauer	St. Louis Ambush
Austin Ledbetter	Saint Louis FC (USL)
Tim Loughman	Louisville Thunder (AISA)
Matt Little	St. Louis Ambush
Greg Makowski	Colorado
Scott Marty	St. Louis Ambush
Matt Malloy	Phoenix (MISL)
Dan McManemy	St. Louis Knights
Justin McMillian	St. Louis Ambush
Gene Mishalow	Washington
Mark Moran	Kicks
Sean Mulqueeny	St. Louis Steamers
Dan O'Keefe	Kansas City (MISL)
Matt Polster	Chicago Fire
Joe Reiniger	St. Louis Ambush
Addae Rique	St. Louis Steamers
Bob Robson	Atlanta
Darren Snyder	St. Louis Ambush
Bill Stallings	St. Louis Ambush (MISL)

John Stone	Wichita (MISL)
Tom Stone	St. Louis Knights (USISL Pro)
John Stremlau	Dallas
Cal Thomas	St. Louis Steamers
Steve Trittschuh	St. Louis (MISL)
Jason Turkington	Lafayette Swampcats (EISL)
Mike Twellman	St. Louis (MISL)
Tim Twellman	Stars
Tom Twellman	Stars
Greg Villa	Kicks
Christian Volesky	Rochester Rhinos/Saint Louis FC (USL)
John Zacheis	Detroit Express (NASL)[117]

SLU

NCAA Championships: 10

1959, 1960, 1962, 1963, 1965, 1967, 1969, 1970, 1972, 1973

Now we're ready for the legendary collegiate success of SLU. Now we're talking! I figured we'd wait a little bit and save the best for last. (Relax SLU guys—you can't always go ahead of SIUE.)

Such is the legend of SLU that even to this day, no other university has gathered more national championships. That's right: SLU leads all universities in NCAA Division I men's national soccer championships. It has 10. In second place is Indiana University with 8. In third place is Virginia with 7. Did you know? Legendary coaches: Bob Guelker (1959-66) and Harry Keough (1967-82).

Between 1969-73, three St. Louis University players won the Hermann Trophy award for the best collegiate player in the country. Those players were Al Trost, Mike Seerey, and Dan Counce, listed below. It was a glorious time for SLU soccer.

1969

Hermann Trophy

Al Trost (SLU)

1970

Hermann Trophy

Al Trost (SLU)

1971

Hermann Trophy

Mike Seerey (SLU)

1972

Hermann Trophy

Mike Seerey (SLU)

1973

Hermann Trophy

Dan Counce (SLU)

Gene Baker, the legendary coach of Granite City High School, with the most high school state titles as coach in Illinois, was a national champion on SLU's NCAA soccer team as an outside defender.

Vince Drake, the legendary coach of St. Thomas Aquinas-Mercy, with the most high school state titles as coach in Missouri, was a national champion on SLU's NCAA soccer team as an outside defender. (Sound familiar? Something about those outside defenders!)

Don Ceresia won two national championships at SLU and also became an All-American. At St. Philip Neri, Bill McDermott and others looked up to Ceresia, a schoolyard legend. After SLU, Ceresia played for the St. Louis Stars in the late 1960s.

Pat McBride—born in 1943 in St. Louis, Missouri—was an All-American player at SLU and a national champion there as well. He went on to have a distinguished career playing midfield for the St. Louis Stars (1967-76). He also represented St. Louis and the nation as a member of the USMNT. Later, he coached the illustrious St. Louis Steamers.

Carl Gentile, a prolific forward in his day, played for SLU, the St. Louis Stars, and the USMNT.

Bill McDermott, the one and only Mr. Soccer, was part of SLU's championship runs in 1967 and 1969 and later became a longtime PA announcer for SLU soccer games while also setting trends in the broadcasting field for various pro and World Cup games.

Jim Leeker, an All-American collegiate forward from St. Louis, Missouri, was a national champion on SLU's NCAA soccer team. He went on to play for the St. Louis Stars and was Rookie of the Year in the NASL (1970). In addition, for many years, he's been President of the St. Louis Soccer Hall of Fame.

The quick and versatile John Pisani was a midfielder with SLU before turning pro with the St. Louis Stars.

Gary Rensing took the field with SLU as a standout defender. He subsequently was a key figure with the St. Louis Stars while he also represented the USMNT.

Steve Frank was a Billiken midfielder before a solid career with the St. Louis Stars. He also got a cap with the USMNT in 1973.

Gene Geimer was a talented forward that played for SLU, the St. Louis Stars, and the USMNT.

Al Trost—born in 1949 in St. Louis, Missouri—won the Hermann Trophy two years in a row at SLU (1969, 1970) and was an NCAA national champion. His professional career included playing with the St. Louis Stars, California Surf, Seattle Sounders, and New York Arrows. In addition, Trost, a midfielder, served as captain of the USMNT. Following his playing career, Trost coached the St. Louis Steamers from 1981-83 during the golden era of pro indoor soccer.

Mike Seerey—a forward at SLU—immediately followed in Al Trost's footsteps by winning the Hermann Trophy two years in a row (1971,

1972). Seerey—who was born in 1950 in St. Louis, Missouri—played professionally with the Miami Toros and St. Louis Stars.

Dan Counce—born in 1951 in St. Louis, Missouri—was a forward for SLU who won the Hermann Trophy on one occasion (1973). Subsequently, he played on a number of teams, including Boston Minutemen, San Jose Earthquakes, San Antonio Thunder, Team Hawaii, California Surf, Philadelphia Fever, Toronto Blizzard, St. Louis Steamers, Baltimore Blast, and the USMNT (1974-76).

Jim Bokern—born in 1952 in St. Louis, Missouri—played forward for St. Louis University and then for the St. Louis Stars.

According to a classic St. Louis Steamers brochure from 1981-82, Joe Clarke, "...Played for the 1972 and 1973 St. Louis University NCAA Division I National Champions."[118] He was also, "First Team All-American in 1975 and was a teammate of Steamer Ty Keough on that club."[119] Later, Clarke played professionally for the St. Louis Stars, California Surf, and St. Louis Steamers. In his post-playing career, Clarke has been a head coach for many years at SLU, then Washington University in St. Louis.

Dan Flynn, the longtime CEO and Secretary General of the U.S. Soccer Federation, was a defender with the Billikens from 1973-77.

Don Droege was a talented defender that eventually played for a number of pro teams including the St. Louis Steamers. He also played for the USMNT.

The great Ty Keough played for SLU, Cincinnati Kids, San Diego Sockers, St. Louis Steamers, Kansas City Comets, and the USMNT. He also had a distinguished career as a TV announcer for international soccer matches. "From 1990 until 2002, Keough covered four World Cups for TNT, ESPN and ABC."[120]

Larry Hulcer—born in 1957—played for SLU and a few other teams including the Los Angeles Aztecs, New York Cosmos, St. Louis Steamers, and USMNT.

Steve Sullivan—born in 1958 in St. Louis, Missouri—played forward at SLU and with the St. Louis Steamers.

John Hayes—born in 1960—was a forward at SLU. According to a St. Louis Steamers brochure from 1982-83, Hayes was a "three-time All American at St. Louis University."[121] He also played for the St. Louis Steamers and Kansas City Comets.

Daryl Doran—a pro indoor soccer icon—played for SLU in 1981.

Mark Santel, who eventually played in MLS, along with the USMNT, was a member of Scott Gallagher and a midfielder at SLU. A skillful player that was very quick, Santel was said to have multiple gears in his arsenal.

Steve Kuntz—born in 1970 in St. Louis, Missouri—played defender for St. Louis University and then for the St. Louis Ambush in the 1990s.

Mike Sorber—born in 1971 in St. Louis, Missouri—was a midfielder at SLU before he played in MLS and for the USMNT. As a member of the US men's national team, Sorber competed in the 1994 FIFA World Cup. To date, that tournament, which was hosted by the United States, holds records for World Cup attendance.

Shane Battelle—born in 1971 in St. Louis, Missouri—played for SLU and eventually landed with Columbus Crew in MLS.

Matt McKeon played midfield with SLU from 1992-95 before moving on to the Kansas City Wizards, Colorado Rapids, and USMNT.

Tim Leonard was a very talented midfielder that led SLU in the 1990s. Eventually he played professionally with the St. Louis Ambush and coached Saint Louis FC.

Kevin Quigley—who played youth soccer for Johnny Mac—was a talented player for SLU that eventually played with the St. Louis Steamers as well. From Signature Medical Group online (circa March 22, 2020) a portion of Quigley's impressive achievements stated: "Kevin Quigley, MD, is an orthopedic surgeon and sports medicine physician, board-certified by the American Academy of Orthopedic Surgeons." In addition, "Dr. Quigley graduated from Saint Louis University School of Medicine and completed his orthopedic surgery residency at Saint Louis University Hospital." How many former athletes end up achieving such ranks? Not many. Certainly, he's a graduate making SLU proud.

Kevin Kalish is an experienced St. Louis product who began coaching the men's soccer team at SLU in 2018. Kalish is a former Scott Gallagher standout, who also played professionally with the St. Louis Ambush, and, not to mention, he's a former player at SLU.

Mike and Pat Moriarty, who had previously attended CBC, were highly skilled defenders at SLU in the 1990s.

Jeff DiMaria—born in 1977—was a talented, crafty, possession-oriented, midfielder that played for SLU, the Colorado Rapids, St. Louis Steamers, St. Louis Ambush, and the U.S. Futsal team.

Jack Jewsbury was a Billiken before playing extensively with the Kansas City Wizards and Portland Timbers.

Brad Davis was at SLU before flourishing in MLS and with the USMNT where he ultimately played in the 2014 FIFA World Cup.

John DiRaimondo attended SLU before joining the Colorado Rapids and D.C. United.

Brandon Barklage played at SLU and then graduated to a handful of teams including D.C. United, New York Red Bulls, and San Jose Earthquakes.

Tim Ream, arguably the best possession-oriented central defender the USMNT has put forth, started out as a Billiken (2006-09). Since then he's represented the USMNT as captain and landed with Fulham.

Forward Mike Roach played for St. Louis University (2009-11) and then moved onto the St. Louis Ambush and Saint Louis FC.

Last but not least, Jim Kavanaugh, a co-owner of St. Louis City SC (the ultimate destination of St. Louis soccer), once played at SLU and eventually sported a uniform with the original St. Louis Steamers.

SLU PRO PLAYERS BONUS LIST

Quick note to readers: This list below was taken verbatim from the Saint Louis Billikens official website. As you may notice, for a few players, just a city or state was listed and it's unclear which team, exactly, the player was with. For example:

Kevin Handlan
Tulsa, San Jose, St. Louis, Chicago, Kansas City

Bob O'Leary
St. Louis, California
Take "St. Louis" for example. It just says "St. Louis" and there is no team associated with it. St. Louis has had many different pro teams, such as the St. Louis Steamers, St. Louis Storm, St. Louis Ambush, and so on. Similarly, "Kansas City" has had the Kansas City Comets, Kansas City Wizards, and so on. Investigating each player's exact location is outside the scope of this book. The observation of how some players were listed in this fashion should not negate any accomplishments. Please direct any related question(s) to Saint Louis University. I'm sure they'll be glad to hear from you. Here is Saint Louis University's impressive list of Billiken players that reached the pro level:

Calum Angus
Wilmington Hammerheads, GAIS (Sweden), Pune, Dempo, East Bengal (India)

Pat Baker
Tacoma Stars, St. Louis Steamers

Brandon Barklage
D.C. United, NY Red Bulls, Saint Louis FC

Shane Battelle
Columbus Crew

Mo Benne
Chicago Storm

Jim Bokern
St. Louis Stars

Brett Branan
Minnesota (A League)

David Brcic
NY Cosmos, Wichita Wings, L.A. Lazers

Kingsley Bryce
Chicago Fire, Saint Louis FC

Derek Carroll
St. Louis Ambush

Don Ceresia
St. Louis Stars

Joe Clarke
St. Louis Stars, California Surf, St. Louis Steamers

Jason Cole
Syracuse FC, Cincinnati (A League)

Pete Collico
St. Louis Steamers

Craig Corbett
Lafayette Swampcats

Ken Costello
St. Louis Steamers

Dan Counce
Boston, San Antonio, Hawaii, California, Toronto, St. Louis Steamers

Brad Davis
NY/NJ Metrostars, Dallas Burn, San Jose Earthquakes, Houston Dynamo

Jeff Davis
Colorado Foxes, St. Louis Steamers, Kansas City Comets

Mark Demling
San Jose, San Diego, San Francisco

Jeff DiMaria
Colorado Rapids, St. Louis Steamers

John DiRaimondo
Colorado Rapids, D.C. United

Daryl Doran
St. Louis Steamers, St. Louis Storm, St. Louis Ambush

Jim Draude
St. Louis Steamers

Don Droege
Rochester, Washington, Atlanta, Tulsa, Tampa Bay, St. Louis Steamers

Steve Eise
St. Louis Steamers

Dave Fernandez
L.A. Lazers, Louisville Thunder

Joe Filla
Kansas City Comets

Steve Frank
St. Louis Stars

Mark Frederickson
Kansas City Comets, St. Louis Steamers, St. Louis Storm

Adnan Gabeljic
Sporting Kansas City, Sacramento Republic

Jack Galmiche
St. Louis Stars

Gene Geimer
St. Louis, Boston, Chicago

Carl Gentile
St. Louis Stars

Brian Grazier
Colorado Rapids

Denny Hadican
Seattle Sounders

Joe Hammes
Milwaukee Wave

Dado Hamzagic
FK Sarajevo (Bosnia)

Kevin Handlan
Tulsa, San Jose, St. Louis, Chicago, Kansas City

John Hayes
St. Louis Steamers

Tom Hayes
St. Louis Steamers, Louisville Thunder

Don Huber
Minnesota, Tulsa, Baltimore

Bruce Hudson
St. Louis Stars

Larry Hulcer
Los Angeles, New York, St. Louis Steamers

Steve Hunsicker
St. Louis Steamers

Martin Hutton
Kansas City Wizards, Houston Dynamo

Vedad Ibisevic
Paris St. Germain, Alemania Achenn, 1899 Hoffenheim, VfB Stuttgart, Hertha BSC

Jack Jewsbury
Kansas City Wizards, Portland Timbers

Will John
Chicago Fire, Kansas City Wizards, Randers FC

Johnny Johnson
St. Louis Steamers

Kevin Kalish
Kansas City Wizards, St. Louis Ambush

Jim Kavanaugh
L.A. Lazers, St. Louis Steamers

Chris Kenny
Chicago, St. Louis Steamers

Ty Keough
Cincinnati, San Diego, St. Louis Steamers

Jack Kinealy
St. Louis Stars

Mike Kirchhoff
St. Louis Steamers

Casey Klipfel
Nashville Metros

Robert Kristo
Columbus Crew, Spezia Calcio, North Carolina FC

Steve Kuntz
St. Louis Ambush, Milwaukee Rampage

Tom Layton
St. Louis Stars

Raymond Lee
Philadelphia Union, Tulsa Roughnecks

Jim Leeker
St. Louis Stars

Tim Leonard
Nashville Metros, Hershey (A League)

Tim Logush
St. Louis, New Jersey, Indianapolis

Scott MacDonald
St. Louis Steamers

Anthony Manning
Portland Timbers

Bob Matteson
St. Louis Stars

Steve Maurer
Cleveland, Canton

Brian McBride
Milwaukee Rampage, Wolfsvurg, Germany, Columbus Crew, Fulham
FC, Chicago Fire

Pat McBride
St. Louis Stars

Scott McDoniel
St. Louis Ambush, Milwaukee Rampage, St. Louis Steamers

Bill McKeon
Kansas City

Matt McKeon
Kansas City Wizards, Colorado Rapids

Jay Moore
Dallas

Ed Nuesel
St. Louis Stars

Bob O'Leary
St. Louis, California

Mike O'Meara
St. Louis Steamers

Mark Pais
Saint Louis FC, Miami FC

Kyle Patterson
Los Angeles Galaxy, Tamworth

Ed Pinon
Colorado Foxes, Kansas City Attack

John Pisani
St. Louis Stars

Kevin Quigley
Nashville Metros, St. Louis Steamers

Don Range
St. Louis Stars

Tim Ream
NY Red Bulls, Bolton Wanderers, Fulham FC

Gary Rensing
St. Louis Stars, Chicago

Mike Roach
New England Revolution, Saint Louis FC

John Roselein
New Jersey, Indianapolis

Bruce Rudroff
Seattle, Hartford, Memphis

Tanner Rupp
L.A. Zodiac

Mark Santel
St. Louis Storm, Colorado Foxes, Dallas Burn, Kansas City Wizards

Dave Schlitt
St. Louis

Frank Schuler
St. Louis Steamers

Mike Seerey
Miami, St. Louis Stars

Dipsy Selolwane
Chicago Fire, Real Salt Lake, Ajax Cape Town, Supersport United, Pretoria

Mike Sorber
Kansas City Wizards, NY/NJ MetroStars, Chicago Fire

Tom Strunk
St. Louis Steamers

Steve Sullivan
St. Louis Steamers

Jacob Thomas
Braunschweig, Germany, Columbus Crew

Jim Tietjens
Ft. Lauderdale, Kansas City

Al Trost
St. Louis Stars, Seattle, California Surf

Chad Vandegriffe
Saint Louis FC

Scott Vorst
Los Angeles, St. Louis Steamers

Nick Walls
Milwaukee Wave, Chicago Fire

Tim Ward
NY/NJ MetroStars, Columbus Crew, Colorado Rapids

Denny Werner
Indianapolis

Ryan Wileman
Rochester Raging Rhinos

Brad Wilson
L.A. Galaxy

Danny Wynn
New England Revolution

Chuck Zorumski
St. Louis Stars[122]

For generations, SLU has been elite. Many players have applied. Many players, trying to validate how good they think they are, have asked to play. They were turned away. Then they dealt with a glaringly stark reality: You cannot play for SLU because you're not good enough. Your heart starts fluttering like a paper tiger, dreams of glorious moments in a SLU uniform flicker away into the world of reality. Excuses are made; a false sense of reality is built up; anything to stop the truth. Everything on your resume is likely based on previous political moves to try to give yourself a leg up in your delusional dream to play at SLU. News flash: You were never that good in the first place. That's the thing about SLU, weak talent is not allowed; not everyone can join the team. Only the best players can enter. The others, who tried and failed, land elsewhere, perhaps WashU. This couldn't be truer than at goalie. So you're a goalie and you want to play at SLU? Chances are you won't. You'll try, you'll fail, and inevitably end up at—I don't know—WashU. Same old story. Only one keeper takes the field, and for SLU that person has to be special. By special I mean a true, one of a kind, talent. Over the years, a select handful of goalies have adorned the gloves and guarded the Billiken net. A few would include: Patrick Schulte (a recent keeper that has experience with the United States U20 national team), Casey Klipfel, Kevin Johnston, Pat Baker, and Chuck Zorumski. The Mount Rushmore of SLU keepers.

For aficionados, SLU is soccer royalty. For the average fan, SLU is something they've heard of before. All in all, as a university at the forefront of college soccer, it's a force to be reckoned with.

The prestige of SLU lingers on like impending rain. A well-known alum, Brian McBride, got promoted to General Manager of the USMNT circa January 11, 2020. Despite originally coming from Chicago-land, he distinguished himself collegiately as a Billiken. The *St. Louis Post-Dispatch* pointed out, "McBride, who played at St. Louis University, had 30 goals in 95 appearances for the U.S. from 1993-2006. He played for Wolfsburg, Columbus, Preston North End, Everton, Fulham and Chicago. He was so popular in London that Fulham named a bar at Craven Cottage after him. (AP)"[123]

From Billiken forward, to USMNT forward, to USMNT General Manager, Brian McBride—thought by some, such as Bill McDermott, to be perhaps the best striker in the history of the USMNT—now adds to the multifaceted trophy case of honors that SLU holds with pride.

For the future of soccer in America, SLU is a cornerstone; it's done so much for the sport and it continues to hold a prominent place within the lexicon of collegiate soccer.

UMSL (University of Missouri-St. Louis)
Did you know? UMSL won the 1973 NCAA Division II soccer championship. Regarding the 1973 championship run, Don Dallas, the team's head coach, was quoted at the official UMSL Tritons website: "'Pick out an individual hero? How can I? Everyone did his job superlatively and that's what it took to win it.'"[124] UMSL honored the team with a photo and description of the accomplishment online. The following was gathered from UMSL's official website:

"1973 Men's Soccer Championship Team at the 2004 UMSL Sports Hall of Fame

Front Row (Left to Right): Chris Werstein, Steve Stockmann, Jim Creamer, Mark LeGrand, Frank Flesch, Pat Reagan, Tim Kersting, Mark Dorsey.

Back Row (Left to Right): Don Schmidt, Luke Wientge, Rick Anselm, Pat Hogan, Mike Caraffa, Ed Fleming, Frank Tusinski, Don Deason, Tim Fitzsimmons, Al Rudruff, John Kroll, Jim McKenna."[125]

Dan Muesenfechter played forward at UMSL (an All-American) before playing with the Denver Avalanche and St. Louis Steamers.

Dan King—a St. Louis native that played professional soccer, won two national championships as a player at Indiana University, and was a member of a US youth national team—has been head soccer coach at UMSL for many years. In fact, as of May 20, 2020, the UMSL Tritons website posted, "Dan King enters his 20th season in 2020 as head coach for the UMSL men's soccer program and is the fourth head coach in the storied history of the Tritons soccer program."[126]

Florissant Valley Community College

Did you know? Florissant Valley Community College won the 1973 NJCAA Division I soccer championship. Legendary coach: Pete Sorber.

Pete Sorber—father of soccer-great, Mike Sorber (who played for the US in the 1994 FIFA World Cup)—was coach at Florissant Valley Community College from 1967-97.

His overall record: 415-85-22. His teams won 10 NJCAA championships. On five occasions Sorber earned NJCAA Coach of the Year honors. He is in the St. Louis Sports Hall of Fame and the St. Louis Soccer Hall of Fame.

Denny Vaninger, an ultra-talented forward, was a national champion with Florissant Valley Community College and, as featured in a St. Louis Steamers brochure from 1981-82, "was a two-time All American."[127] In addition to playing for the St. Louis Stars and St. Louis Steamers, he played for the USMNT in the 1970s.

262

Steve Pecher...heard of him? He was All-State in Missouri at Normandy High School, an All-American at Florissant Valley Community College (where he also won the NJCAA championship), the "1976 NASL Rookie-of-the-Year,"[128] an NASL All-Star, captain of the St. Louis Steamers, an MISL All-Star, and captain of the USMNT. Now you have.

Jeff Sendobry—who played for the St. Louis Steamers—attended Florissant Valley Community College.

Steve Sullivan played for Florissant Valley Community College and St. Louis University before joining the St. Louis Steamers.

Before playing pro, and prior to playing for UMSL, a St. Louis Steamers brochure from 1981-82 mentioned for fans that Dan Muesenfechter suited up at, "Florissant Valley Community College under Pete Sorber and named to the NJCAA All American squad in 1978."[129]

The Indiana Factor

Indiana University is second all-time with 8 NCAA Division I national championships for soccer. Of course, siting number one is St. Louis University, with 10 NCAA Division I national championships.

Here's how it currently looks:

St. Louis University:	10
Indiana:	8
Virginia:	7
Maryland:	4
UCLA:	4
San Francisco:	4
Clemson:	3
Stanford:	3

Indiana University's soccer program has been so strong, for so long that many people might not know that Indiana has recruited heavily from St. Louis talent to help make its program so successful. In fact, St. Louis has served as a goldmine for Indiana, dating back to the 1970s. Some St. Louis area talent that has played for Indiana University includes:

Jeff Sendobry	Mike Ambersley
Tim Walters	Mike Roach
Mike Freitag	Harry Weiss
Dan King	Will Bruin
Joel Shanker	Jack Maher
Kenny Godat	AJ Palazzolo
John van Buskirk	Austin Panchot
Chris Klein	Daniel Munie
Pat Noonan	Kyle Barks
Kevin Robson	

PROFESSIONAL SOCCER IN ST. LOUIS: A BUILDUP TO MLS

St. Leo's
1902-1918[†]
St. Louis Association Foot Ball League
St. Louis Soccer League
(Outdoor)

Perhaps you haven't heard of St. Leo's. Well, most people haven't. It was a long time ago. According to an article from *Wikipedia*: "The St. Louis Soccer League, founded in 1907, was the country's only fully professional soccer league of its day. St. Leo's, the league's only fully professional squad, dominated the standings for seven years."[130]

A few players from the team, by way of 1910, included Jimmy Donohue, William Tallman, Chuck O'Berta, Richard "Bull" Brannigan, Joe Mason, Dave Miller, Joe Flynn, Johnny Miller, and Jack Tully.[131]

St. Leo's competed at various levels from 1902-1918. St. Leo's, in all likelihood, was not a professional team as we know professional sports

---

[†] In 1918, St. Leo's changed names to St. Louis Screws.

today. In other words, players were likely paid by the owners of the team in some capacity; however, pro soccer in the US during this time was a far cry from what pro soccer is today. You must remember, during the 1960s, the player's union in Major League Baseball—with help from Marvin Miller of the United Steel Workers of America—was fighting for better pay. This was many years after St. Leo's, and would heavily suggest that payment to St. Leo's players (for soccer, a non-popular sport) was less than satisfactory. In 1906, Upton Sinclair published his book *The Jungle,* which depicted the true—and very alarming—reality of the food and labor industry in parts of the US. (The book, in a broad sense, represented many facets of life in America back then.) Put it this way: Safe, good-quality food was not a guarantee during that time, and, humane working conditions were not a high priority. By this measure (without sounding insensitive, not to ruin the mood here), I seriously doubt the players of St. Leo's were riding high with financial success in the early days of soccer and playing pro was probably nothing more than a meager stipend accompanied by a glorious title to carry around.

St. Louis Stars
1967
NPSL
(Outdoor)
The St. Louis Stars kicked-off in 1967. This team, this effort, in a sense, is a little like the godfather of outdoor pro soccer in St. Louis. Notwithstanding St. Leo's, the Stars were essentially the original pro soccer experience in St. Louis, and it set the pace for the rest that followed.

(The following team information, from 1967, was acquired online from *Stats Crew*, while the roster was from *Just Sports Stats*, circa March 2020.)

1967 St. Louis Stars
National Professional Soccer League (NPSL)

Team Record: 14-11-7 in the NPSL's Western Division
Coach: George Mihaljevic (14-11-7)
Location: St. Louis, Missouri
Attendance: 121,719, Avg. 7,607 in 16 home dates

Roster

Tomis Basic	Pat McBride
Thor Beck	Allie McNab
Donald Ceresia	Marcel Nowak
Edward Clear	Norbert Pogrzeba
Miguel DeLima	Don Popovic
Kazimierz Frankiewicz	Joe Puls
Joe Fuhrmann	Gauntlett Rowe
Carl Gentile	Carl Schwarzen
Eric Hahn	Dragoslav Sekularac
Milonja Kalicanin	Harry Smits
Rudi Kolbl	Ilija Tojacic
Bora Kostic	Branco Topalovic
Tihomir Markovic	Tabka Toufik
Ratislav Matic	

St. Louis Stars
1968-1977
NASL
(Outdoor)

The Stars—who played outdoor and some indoor—represented St. Louis in the NPSL and NASL long before MLS came to fruition. Former SLU Billikens Al Trost and Pat McBride, among others, were featured players. This was back in the day when soccer was gaining momentum around the country. The journey of the Stars (along with subsequent efforts of the Steamers and others) laid down the groundwork for the eventual arrival of an MLS team in St. Louis.

During a time that seems long ago, when the Stars were testing the grounds of US soccer, as Jim Leeker explained, a small handful of games were played indoors at the St. Louis Arena (AKA the Checkerdome), but it didn't last. First and foremost, the Stars were a professional outdoor team. Leeker—a talented forward who was named NASL Rookie of the Year in 1970—set himself apart during a game in Atlanta when he scored a hat-trick, one of his career highlights. In this era, the pay wasn't what it is today. Many of the players, such as Trost, McBride, and Leeker, were in it for the glory. One of Leeker's coaches, Bob Kehoe, was a St. Louis native, and, if you didn't know already, Kehoe was sort of a legend from the area. After all, Kehoe played for the Stars and coached the Stars. He was also captain of the USMNT, and coach of the USMNT. Unfortunately, Kehoe, who was living in the south St. Louis area, passed away in 2017 at the age of 89 and was unable to see the formation of St. Louis City SC. Though he certainly had a significant role in this long, ongoing, tradition of soccer in St. Louis. According to Leeker, one of Kehoe's proudest moments was walking onto the field for the US as captain and fielding an all-St. Louis team as coach of the Stars. This was a unique element of the team; it relied strongly on local St. Louis talent.

In their day, the Stars had adversaries, exciting games, and exciting players. In a game against the Atlanta Chiefs in 1970, Frank Hyland of *The Atlanta Journal* wrote: "In the first game of the season, Leeker had three goals and had another in the last outing. Four of his five goals for the year, in other words, have come against the Chiefs. The leading scorer for the Stars, however, is another former St. Louis U. All-American, Pat McBride. McBride has six goals and an assist for the season."[132] Regardless the opponent, Pat McBride—a key figure with the Stars—was often a leading force in the attack, along with Tommy Ferguson, Steve Frank, Gene Geimer, Carl Gentile, Jim Leeker, John Pisani, Gary Rensing, Willy Roy, Al Trost, Dennis Vaninger, Chris Werstein, and others. McBride was among a large group of local players putting St. Louis soccer front and center, nationwide. It was certainly a unique period in American soccer.

While the Stars remain a distant memory to some, it was a team that was making history and providing excitement along the way. Back in 1970, from a game between the St. Louis Stars and Kansas City Spurs, covered by Charles Gould for the *St. Louis Globe-Democrat*, there appeared the following quote: "Tim Tyebo, at fullback for the injured Mike Kalicanin, showed good soccer sense and a fine right hand."[133] At first glance I was wondering what in the world this writer meant. Was soccer so foreign to American writers back in 1970 that they thought right hands played an important role in the game? Well, shortly after, it became evident what he meant. "Late in the first half Tyebo and Saccone got into a fracas down the left side in St. Louis territory. Tyebo figured Saccone had fouled him and gave him a push. Ademar kicked the ball at Tyebo and this earned him a sock in the jaw that stretched the Kansas City inside left flat on his back."[134] Ah-ha. Got it. "Incredibly, Tyebo was not thrown out of the game. Perhaps referee Mike Wuertz didn't see it, but most of the fans saw Tim land the right with devastating effect."[135] It was, after all, 1970. And what a beautiful time it was.

Unfortunately, in 1977, the Stars folded operations.

Bob Hermann, the team's owner, played a large role in getting soccer off the ground in a country that, back then, preferred baseball, basketball, football, and even bowling. His influence touched many areas of the greater soccer landscape. According to *Wikipedia*: "Hermann is the founder and former owner of the St. Louis Stars soccer team, and a former president of the National Professional Soccer League. Hermann was one of the founders of the North American Soccer League and was the chairman of the executive committee of NASL. The soccer stadium of the St. Louis Billiken's soccer team, Hermann Stadium, was named after him."[136]

While the Stars eventually took a backseat to history, the legacy of its venture lives on to this day in the form of memories along with a great wealth of soccer-knowledge which has been passed on from retired players to new generations of St. Louis talent.

It could be said: Without the Stars there wouldn't be a St. Louis City SC. Let's take a closer look at the Stars of the NASL.

(The following team information, from 1968-77, was acquired online from *Stats Crew*, while the rosters were from *Just Sports Stats*, circa March 2020.)

1968 St. Louis Stars

North American Soccer League (NASL)
Team Record: 12-14-6 in the NASL's Gulf Division
Coach: Rudi Gutendorf (12-14-6)
Location: St. Louis, Missouri
Attendance: 86,212, Avg. 5,388 in 16 home dates

Roster

Oscar Black
Manfred Bundschoks
Donald Ceresia
Cheung Chi-Doy
Hipolito Chilinque
Edward Clear
Eli Durante
Kazimierz Frankiewicz
Gernot Fraydl
Joe Fuhrmann
Carl Gentile
Rudi Gutendorf
Milonja Kalicanin
Laszlo Kaszas
Waldemar Kaszubski
Bob Kehoe
Jack Kinealy
Rudi Kolbl
Nick Krat
Branco Kubala
Odd Lindberg
Tihomir Markovic
Pat McBride
Jan Ohman
Norbert Pogrzeba
Don Popovic
Joe Puls
Milenko Rus
Blagoje Vidinic
Kay-Arne Wiestal
Wilhelm Wrenger

1969 St. Louis Stars

North American Soccer League (NASL)

Team Record: 3-11-2 in the NASL

Coach: Bob Kehoe (3-11-2)

Location: St. Louis, Missouri

Attendance: 18,192, Avg. 2,274 in 8 home dates

Roster

Tom Bokern	Lombardo
Edward Clear	Pat McBride
Miguel DeLima	Jay Moore
Tommy Ferguson	Jerry Mueller
Frank Fischer	Paul Pisani
Kazimierz Frankiewicz	Don Popovic
Larry Hausmann	Joe Puls
Dave Jokerst	Don Range
Milonja Kalicanin	Dave Schlitt
Tom Layton	Chris Werstein‡

1970 St. Louis Stars

North American Soccer League (NASL)

Team Record: 5-17-2 in the NASL's North Division

Coach: Bob Kehoe (5-17-2)

Location: St. Louis, Missouri

Attendance: 38,424, Avg. 2,745 in 14 home dates

---

‡   At *Just Sports Stats*, Chris Werstein's name was spelled "Wernstein" for the 1969, 1970, and 1971 St. Louis Stars seasons. The spelling of "Werstein" was chosen to reflect information at the St. Louis Soccer Hall of Fame.

Roster

Tom Bokern

Calderon

Miguel DeLima

Frank Fischer

Steve Frank

Kazimierz Frankiewicz

Jack Galmiche

Jose Gonzales

Larry Hausmann

Bogdan Hiblovic

Dave Jokerst

Milonja Kalicanin

Jim Leeker

Pat McBride

Jerry Mueller

John Pisani

Paul Pisani

Don Popovic

Joe Puls

Don Range

Gary Rensing

Joe Right

Darrell Smith

Tim Tyebo

Chris Werstein

1971 St. Louis Stars

North American Soccer League (NASL)

Team Record: 6-13-5 in the NASL's South Division

Coach: George Meyer (1-5-2)

Coach: Kazimierz Frankiewicz (5-8-3)

Location: St. Louis, Missouri

Attendance: 50,103, Avg. 3,579 in 14 home dates

Roster

Orest Banach

Joe Baum

Tom Bokern

Steve Frank

Kazimierz Frankiewicz

Jack Galmiche

Gene Geimer

Carl Gentile

Jose Gonzales

Larry Hausmann

Milonja Kalicanin

Jim Leeker

Pat McBride

Ed Neusel

John Pisani

Paul Pisani

Don Popovic

Joe Puls

Gary Rensing

Joe Right

Willy Roy

Darrell Smith

Walter Spiewak

Bert Uhlander

Chris Werstein

1972 St. Louis Stars
North American Soccer League (NASL)
Team Record: 7-4-3 in the NASL's South Division
Lost Championship
Coach: Kazimierz Frankiewicz (7-4-3)
Location: St. Louis, Missouri
Attendance: 54,409, Avg. 7,773 in 7 home dates

Roster
Orest Banach

Robert Baylis

Edmundo Camacho

Jim Draude

Steve Frank

Kazimierz Frankiewicz

Gene Geimer

Larry Hausmann

Stan Horne

Tom Howe

Yeo Kankam

Jim Leeker

Pat McBride

John Pisani

Paul Pisani

Joe Puls

Gary Rensing

Willy Roy

John Sewell

Wilf Tranter

Bert Uhlander

Kazimierz Uranin

Mike Winter

1973 St. Louis Stars

North American Soccer League (NASL)
Team Record: 7-7-5 in the NASL's South Division
Coach: Kazimierz Frankiewicz (7-7-5)
Location: St. Louis, Missouri
Attendance: 63,367, Avg. 6,337 in 10 home dates

Roster

John Carenza
Buzz Demling
Steve Frank
Kazimierz Frankiewicz
Gene Geimer
Larry Hausmann
Tom Howe
Dave Jokerst
Yeo Kankam

Pat McBride
Joe Puls
Gary Rensing
Willy Roy
John Sewell
Al Trost
Dennis Vaninger
Mike Winter

1974 St. Louis Stars

North American Soccer League (NASL)
Team Record: 4-15-1 in the NASL's Central Division
Coach: John Sewell (4-15-1)
Location: St. Louis, Missouri
Attendance: 71,891, Avg. 7,189 in 10 home dates

Roster

Jim Bokern
John Carenza
Steve Frank
John Garland
Gene Geimer

Denny Hadican
Larry Hausmann
Tom Howe
Dave Jokerst
Bob Matteson

Pat McBride	John Sewell
Bob O'Leary	Al Trost
John Pisani	Dennis Vaninger
Gary Rensing	Mike Winter
Mike Seerey	

1975 St. Louis Stars
North American Soccer League (NASL)
Team Record: 13-9 in the NASL's Central Division
Lost Semifinal
Coach: John Sewell (13-9)
Location: St. Louis, Missouri
Attendance: 66,777, Avg. 6,071 in 11 home dates

Roster
Jim Bokern	Pat McBride
Peter Bonetti	Bob O'Leary
Dennis Burnett	Don Popovic
John Carenza	Gary Rensing
Steve Frank	Mike Seerey
Gene Geimer	John Sewell
Larry Hausmann	Al Trost
John Hawley	Dennis Vaninger
Dave Jokerst	Roger Verdi
Bob Matteson	

1976 St. Louis Stars
North American Soccer League (NASL)
Team Record: 5-19 in the NASL's Western Division

Coach: John Sewell (5-19)
Location: St. Louis, Missouri
Attendance: 73,795, Avg. 6,150 in 12 home dates

Roster

Jim Bokern	Dave Jokerst
Len Bond	Bob Matteson
John Carenza	Pat McBride
Joe Clarke	Bob O'Leary
Mark Dorsey	Gary Rensing
Keith Fear	Mike Seerey
Larry Hausmann	Al Trost
John Hawley	Dennis Vaninger
Bruce Hudson	Roger Verdi
Carl Humphreys	

1977 St. Louis Stars

North American Soccer League (NASL)
Team Record: 12-14 in the NASL's North Division
Lost First Round
Coach: John Sewell (12-14)
Location: St. Louis, Missouri
Attendance: 118,635, Avg. 9,126 in 13 home dates

Roster

Peter Bennett	Joe Clarke
Fred Binney	Terry Daly
Dennis Bozesky	Len Dudkowski
Steve Buckley	Ray Evans
Dennis Burnett	Bill Glazier
Steve Cacciatore	John Jackson

Dave Jokerst

Bob Matteson

Steve Moyers

Bob O'Leary

Gary Rensing

Barry Salvage

John Stremlau

Len Toedebusch

Al Trost

Dennis Vaninger

Roger Verdi

Peter Wall

Attendance

The actual attendance figures for the Stars were interesting. Let's take a closer look. The following attendance information for the St. Louis Stars (1967-77) was acquired online from *Stats Crew*, accessed circa February 2020.

1967 St. Louis Stars
Attendance: 121,719, Avg. 7,607 in 16 home dates

1968 St. Louis Stars
Attendance: 86,212, Avg. 5,388 in 16 home dates

1969 St. Louis Stars
Attendance: 18,192, Avg. 2,274 in 8 home dates

1970 St. Louis Stars
Attendance: 38,424, Avg. 2,745 in 14 home dates

1971 St. Louis Stars
Attendance: 50,103, Avg. 3,579 in 14 home dates

1972 St. Louis Stars
Attendance: 54,409, Avg. 7,773 in 7 home dates

1973 St. Louis Stars

Attendance: 63,367, Avg. 6,337 in 10 home dates

1974 St. Louis Stars

Attendance: 71,891, Avg. 7,189 in 10 home dates

1975 St. Louis Stars

Attendance: 66,777, Avg. 6,071 in 11 home dates

1976 St. Louis Stars

Attendance: 73,795, Avg. 6,150 in 12 home dates

1977 St. Louis Stars

Attendance: 118,635, Avg. 9,126 in 13 home dates

The attendance for the Stars—who played plenty of games at Busch Memorial Stadium—went on a downswing, then upswing, then sort of back-and-forth before ending on a good note. Essentially, following the first season in 1967, the attendance went: Down, down. Up, up, up. Down, up, down. Up, up. The best average attendance numbers were in 1977, the last year for the Stars.

In 1979, as the Stars ended, the Steamers took the mantel, thus building on the momentum generated by the Stars. One unfortunate thing outdoor soccer frequently does is draw a decent-sized crowd into a huge stadium, the end result being that it looks as if no one is there. This, in fact, has been a hindrance for American soccer over the years. (This was an issue MLS grappled with in the early days of the league and subsequently 'soccer specific stadiums' were erected.) What the original Steamers inherited from the Stars, in part, consisted of fans. When these fans entered a cozy arena, where the noise reverberated off the walls and ceiling, whether there were 5,000 or 17,000 present, it carried with it the sound of electric thunder!

St. Louis Steamers

1979-1988

MISL

(Indoor)

The Steamers, a classic all-time great Major Indoor Soccer League team, drew heavy crowds during a time when indoor soccer was the craze. Players like Sam Bick, Tony Bellinger, Steve Pecher, Jeff Cacciatore, Don Ebert, Carl Rose, Ty Keough, Slobo, and Daryl Doran led the way. Fans wore the jerseys, concession stands sold food and drink; the player introductions—accompanied by music, smoke, lights, and a booming announcer—had a rock star feel about it, a party atmosphere. There was a new wave of excitement in St. Louis and around the country in cities that hosted MISL teams.

The following information highlights the first run of the Steamers. (From 1979 to present day, the order of professional indoor soccer in St. Louis has gone as follows: St. Louis Steamers, St. Louis Storm, St. Louis Ambush, St. Louis Steamers, St. Louis Illusion, Illinois Piasa, and St. Louis Ambush.) It's important we take a close look at the original St. Louis Steamers—in all its white, green, and blue glory—because it was the golden era of pro indoor soccer in St. Louis.

General Information

St. Louis Steamers (1979-88)

One word to describe this era: Electric! (The following team information for the St. Louis Steamers, from 1979-88, was acquired online from *Stats Crew*, while the rosters were from *Just Sports Stats*, circa February-March 2020.)

1979-80 St. Louis Steamers

Major Indoor Soccer League (MISL)

Team Record: 12-20 in the MISL's Western Division

Coach: Pat McBride (12-20)

Location: St. Louis, Missouri

Attendance: 224,959, Avg. 14,060 in 16 home dates

Roster

Tony Bellinger

Sam Bick

Pete Collico

Dan Counce

Hugh Creaney

Manuel Cuenca

Eric Delabar

Don Doran

Tom Galati

Tony Graham

Kevin Handlan

Emilio John

Mike Kelley

Ty Keough

Dusan Lukic

Greg Makowski

Mark Mathis

Danny McDonnell

Stojan Nikolic

Steve Pecher

Njego Pesa

Bob Robson

Emilio Romero

Carl Rose

Frank Schuler

Paul Turin

Scott Vorst

1980-81 St. Louis Steamers

Major Indoor Soccer League (MISL)

Team Record: 25-15 in the MISL's Central Division

Postseason: 3-1

Lost Championship

Coach: Pat McBride (25-15)

Location: St. Louis, Missouri

Attendance: 304,377, Avg. 15,219 in 20 home dates

Roster

Tony Bellinger

Sam Bick

Bob Bozada

Hugh Creaney

Manuel Cuenca

Eric Delabar

Don Ebert

Tony Glavin

Winston Hackett

Slobodan Ilijevski

Emilio John

Ty Keough

Greg Makowski

Danny McDonnell

Bob O'Leary

Damian Ogunsuyi

Yilmaz Orhan

Steve Pecher

Mal Roche

Emilio Romero

Carl Rose

Manny Schwartz

Jeff Sendobry

John Stremlau

Steve Sullivan

Paul Turin

Dennis Vaninger

Greg Villa

1981-82 St. Louis Steamers

Major Indoor Soccer League (MISL)

Team Record: 28-16 in the MISL's Western Division

Postseason: 6-4

Lost Championship

Coach: Al Trost (28-16)

Location: St. Louis, Missouri

Attendance: 376,349, Avg. 17,107 in 22 home dates

Roster

Tony Bellinger

Sam Bick

Bob Bozada

Jeff Cacciatore

Joe Clarke

Eric Delabar

Don Ebert

Tony Glavin

Winston Hackett

John Hayes

Larry Hulcer

Slobodan Ilijevski

Ty Keough

Redmond Lane

Greg Makowski

Dan Muesenfechter

Steve Pecher

Emilio Romero

Carl Rose
Manny Schwartz
Jeff Sendobry
John Stremlau

Paul Turin
Dennis Vaninger
Greg Villa

1982-83 St. Louis Steamers
Major Indoor Soccer League (MISL)
Team Record: 26-22 in the MISL's Western Division
Postseason: 1-2
Lost Division Semifinal
Coach: Al Trost (5-9)
Coach: Dave Clements (21-13)
Location: St. Louis, Missouri
Attendance: 352,620, Avg. 14,693 in 24 home dates

Roster

Ian Anderson
Tony Bellinger
Sam Bick
Jeff Cacciatore
Neil Cohen
Daryl Doran
Don Ebert
Tony Glavin
John Hayes
Larry Hulcer
Slobodan Ilijevski
Ty Keough

Redmond Lane
Dan Muesenfechter
Steve Pecher
Carl Rose
Dale Russell
Craig Scarpelli
Manny Schwartz
Jeff Sendobry
John Stremlau
Dennis Vaninger
Tim Walters

1983-84 St. Louis Steamers
Major Indoor Soccer League (MISL)
Team Record: 26-22 in the MISL's Western Division
Postseason: 7-6
Lost Championship
Coach: Dave Clements (26-22)
Location: St. Louis, Missouri
Attendance: 335,805, Avg. 13,992 in 24 home dates

Roster

Tony Bellinger	Slobodan Ilijevski
Sam Bick	Ty Keough
Jeff Cacciatore	Redmond Lane
Neil Cohen	Duncan MacEwan
Ricky Davis	Ken McDonald
Eric Delabar	Sean Mulqueeny
Daryl Doran	Mike O'Mara
Don Droege	Steve Pecher
Don Ebert	Njego Pesa
Tony Glavin	Billy Phillips
John Houska	Carl Rose
Larry Hulcer	Tim Walters

1984-85 St. Louis Steamers
Major Indoor Soccer League (MISL)
Team Record: 24-24 in the MISL's Eastern Division
Postseason: 0-2
Lost Wild Card
Coach: Dave Clements (24-24)
Location: St. Louis, Missouri
Attendance: 305,054, Avg. 12,711 in 24 home dates

Roster

Tony Bellinger

Armando Betancourt

Sam Bick

Jeff Cacciatore

Ricky Davis

Daryl Doran

Don Droege

Don Ebert

Sepp Gantenhammer

Ed Gettemeier

Tony Glavin

Larry Hulcer

Slobodan Ilijevski

Greg Kennedy

Ty Keough

Redmond Lane

Duncan MacEwan

Ken McDonald

Steve Moyers

Njego Pesa

Billy Phillips

Carl Rose

Tim Schulz

Jim Tietjens

Tim Walters

1985-86 St. Louis Steamers

Major Indoor Soccer League (MISL)

Team Record: 23-25 in the MISL's Western Division

Postseason: 1-3

Lost Division Semifinal

Coach: Pat McBride (23-25)

Location: St. Louis, Missouri

Attendance: 244,543, Avg. 10,189 in 24 home dates

Roster

Pat Baker

Nebo Bandovic

Tony Bellinger

Armando Betancourt

Sam Bick

Jeff Cacciatore

Ricky Davis

Daryl Doran

Don Ebert

Mark Frederickson

Ed Gettemeier

Mike Hylla

Slobodan Ilijevski
Chris Kenny
Redmond Lane
Stuart Lee
Duncan MacEwan
Greg Makowski

Steve Pecher
Njego Pesa
Carl Rose
Bill Stallings
Greg Villa

1986-87 St. Louis Steamers
Major Indoor Soccer League (MISL)
Team Record: 19-33 in the MISL's Western Division
Coach: Pat McBride (9-18)
Coach: Tony Glavin (10-15)
Location: St. Louis, Missouri
Attendance: 182,984, Avg. 7,038 in 26 home dates

Roster
Albert Adade
John Bain
Pat Baker
Boki Bandovic
Nebo Bandovic
Tony Bellinger
Sam Bick
Jeff Cacciatore
Ade Coker
Angelo DiBernardo
Daryl Doran
Don Ebert
Charlie Falzon
Mark Frederickson
Poli Garcia

Ron Glavin
Tony Glavin
Mike Hylla
Slobodan Ilijevski
Jim Kavanaugh
Chris Kenny
Redmond Lane
Louie Nanchoff
Steve Pecher
Tim Schulz
Bill Stallings
Lou Stojanovic

1987-88 St. Louis Steamers

Major Indoor Soccer League (MISL)
Team Record: 18-38 in the MISL's Western Division
Coach: Tony Glavin (**18-38**)
Location: St. Louis, Missouri
Attendance: 180,318, Avg. 6,440 in 28 home dates

Roster

Albert Adade	Poli Garcia
John Bain	Gerry Gray
Pat Baker	Kevin Hundelt
Boki Bandovic	Slobodan Ilijevski
Nebo Bandovic	Godfrey Ingram
Tony Bellinger	Jim Kavanaugh
Ade Coker	Chris Kenny
Daryl Doran	Redmond Lane
Ivor Evans	Tim Schulz
Charlie Falzon	Steve Trittschuh
Ken Fogarty	Perry Van der Beck

What's interesting about the first run of the Steamers are the attendance levels. Below, I've laid out the attendance, year by year, and you'll see a culmination in the 1981-82 season, as the team reached its highest attendance levels ever; then a steady decline followed, year after year. By the 1987-88 season, attendance essentially plummeted. Why is this important? Why are the attendance figures from this era worth looking at with such scrutiny? The answer is simple: This was the golden era of pro soccer in St. Louis. The first run of the Steamers might not have produced a championship, like the St. Louis Ambush of 1994-95, but it was a team that got second a few times, and, most importantly, it was a magical time for St. Louis soccer.

Attendance

The following attendance information for the St. Louis Steamers (1979-88) was acquired online from *Stats Crew*, accessed February 22, 2020.

1979-80 St. Louis Steamers
Attendance: 224,959, Avg. 14,060 in 16 home dates

1980-81 St. Louis Steamers
Attendance: 304,377, Avg. 15,219 in 20 home dates

1981-82 St. Louis Steamers
Attendance: 376,349, Avg. 17,107 in 22 home dates
(Incredible! This was a leader nationwide in the MISL!)

1982-83 St. Louis Steamers
Attendance: 352,620, Avg. 14,693 in 24 home dates

1983-84 St. Louis Steamers
Attendance: 335,805, Avg. 13,992 in 24 home dates

1984-85 St. Louis Steamers
Attendance: 305,054, Avg. 12,711 in 24 home dates

1985-86 St. Louis Steamers
Attendance: 244,543, Avg. 10,189 in 24 home dates

1986-87 St. Louis Steamers
Attendance: 182,984, Avg. 7,038 in 26 home dates

1987-88 St. Louis Steamers
Attendance: 180,318, Avg. 6,440 in 28 home dates

St. Louis Storm
1989-1992
MISL
(Indoor)

The Storm rocked the house in the Major Indoor Soccer League. Though, as a team, the rocking didn't last too long. However, Preki, a future MLS MVP winner, would light up the scoreboard with plenty of goals, including a walloping 68 in the 1990-91 season, followed by 45 in the 1991-92 season. (The following team information, from 1989-92, was acquired online from *Stats Crew*, while the rosters were from *Just Sports Stats*, circa February-March 2020.)

1989-90 St. Louis Storm
Major Indoor Soccer League (MISL)
Team Record: 24-28 in the MISL's Western Division
Postseason: 1-3
Lost Division Semifinal
Coach: Don Popovic (24-28)
Location: St. Louis, Missouri
Attendance: 178,036, Avg. 6,848 in 26 home dates

Roster

Zoran Bojovic
David Brcic
Terry Brown
Fernando Clavijo
Michael Collins
Claudio DeOliveira
Daniel Donigan
Daryl Doran
Emil Dragicevic
David Eise

Mark Frederickson
Gary Heale
Slobodan Ilijevski
Godfrey Ingram
John Klein
Marcio Leite
Diego Mandagaran
Gus Mokalis
Stan Terlecki
Thompson Usiyan

1990-91 St. Louis Storm
Major Indoor Soccer League (MISL)
Team Record: 32-20 in the MISL's Western Division
Postseason: 3-5
Lost Division Final
Coach: Don Popovic (32-20)
Location: St. Louis, Missouri
Attendance: 200,769, Avg. 7,722 in 26 home dates

Roster

David Brcic	Slobodan Ilijevski
Terry Brown	Godfrey Ingram
Fernando Clavijo	Kevin Koetters
Claudio DeOliveira	Marcio Leite
Gino DiFlorio	Bobo Lucic
Daniel Donigan	Mark Moser
Daryl Doran	Greg Muhr
Emil Dragicevic	Preki
David Eise	Brian Schmetzer
Mike Fox	Zoltan Toth
Mark Frederickson	Thompson Usiyan

1991-92 St. Louis Storm
Major Indoor Soccer League (MISL)
Team Record: 17-23 in the MISL
Coach: Don Popovic (12-20)
Coach: Fernando Clavijo (5-3)
Location: St. Louis, Missouri
Attendance: 205,323, Avg. 10,266 in 20 home dates

Roster

Scott Biason

Terry Brown

Mirko Castillo

Fernando Clavijo

Claudio DeOliveira

Daryl Doran

Ted Eck

Mark Frederickson

Jim Gorsek

Waad Hirmez

Kevin Hundelt

Slobodan Ilijevski

Godfrey Ingram

John Klein

Greg Muhr

George Pastor

Preki

Mark Santel

Branko Segota

Zoltan Toth

Thompson Usiyan

Attendance

Let's take a closer look at the St. Louis Storm's attendance levels, shall we? As opposed to the preceding Steamers (1979-88), the Storm's attendance grew each year. Take a look.

The following attendance information for the St. Louis Storm (1989-92) was acquired online from *Stats Crew*, accessed circa February 2020.

1989-90 St. Louis Storm
Attendance: 178,036, Avg. 6,848 in 26 home dates

1990-91 St. Louis Storm
Attendance: 200,769, Avg. 7,722 in 26 home dates

1991-92 St. Louis Storm
Attendance: 205,323, Avg. 10,266 in 20 home dates

The St. Louis Storm—perhaps because of the Preki factor—laid down a path of attendance growth that was inherited by the St. Louis Ambush. Also, a long awaited championship season was around the corner.

St. Louis Ambush

1992-2000

NPSL (National Professional Soccer League)

(Indoor)

Following the Steamers and Storm, the Ambush represented professional indoor soccer in St. Louis during the 1990s and a lot of excitement ensued. Daryl Doran, Kevin Hundelt, Steve Kuntz, Mark Moser, Joe Reiniger, and Mark Santel—all local products—were among many players that stood out for the team. A few 'cameos' came in the form of Eric Eichmann, Steve Ralston, Kenny Snow, Branko Segota, Steve Trittschuh, and Perry Van der Beck.

In 1995, the Ambush won the NPSL championship with a strong roster that included a significant amount of local talent. For the team and owner Abe Hawatmeh, this championship represented the highest achievement for pro soccer in St. Louis to that point. And for many years to follow it remained as such. Perhaps down the road, St. Louis City SC will tally up a few more. Though, for the history books, the 1995 pro soccer title the Ambush brought home was St. Louis' first.

Here's a list of champions leading up to when the Ambush finally earned a championship.[§]

League	Season	Champions	Series	Runners-Up
MISL	1978-79	New York Arrows	2-0	Philadelphia Fever
MISL	1979-80*	New York Arrows	7-4	Houston Summit
MISL	1980-81*	New York Arrows	6-5	St. Louis Steamers
MISL	1981-82	New York Arrows	3-2	St. Louis Steamers

[§]   According to the *Wikipedia* page entitled "Division 1 Professional Indoor Soccer Championships" on December 15, 2019.

MISL	1982-83	San Diego Sockers	3-2	Baltimore Blast
MISL	1983-84	Baltimore Blast	4-1	St. Louis Steamers
MISL	1984-85	San Diego Sockers	4-1	Baltimore Blast
MISL	1985-86	San Diego Sockers	4-3	Minnesota Strikers
MISL	1986-87	Dallas Sidekicks	4-3	Tacoma Stars
MISL	1987-88	San Diego Sockers	4-0	Cleveland Force
MISL	1988-89	San Diego Sockers	4-3	Baltimore Blast
MISL	1989-90	San Diego Sockers	4-2	Baltimore Blast
MISL	1990-91	San Diego Sockers	4-2	Cleveland Crunch
MISL	1991-92	San Diego Sockers	4-2	Dallas Sidekicks
NPSL	1992-93	Kansas City Attack	3-2	Cleveland Crunch
NPSL	1993-94	Cleveland Crunch	3-1	St. Louis Ambush
NPSL	1994-95	St. Louis Ambush	4-0	Harrisburg Heat

* *Single-game championship*

(The following St. Louis Ambush team information, from 1992-2000, was acquired online from *Stats Crew*, while the rosters were from *Just Sports Stats*, circa February-March 2020.)

1992-93 St. Louis Ambush
National Professional Soccer League (NPSL)
Team Record: 19-21 in the NPSL's National Division
Postseason: 3-2
Lost Semifinal
Coach: Steve Pecher (7-9)
Coach: Daryl Doran (12-12)
Location: St. Louis, Missouri
Attendance: 154,351, Avg. 7,718 in 20 home dates

Roster

Alan Adams	Douglas Kriska
Scott Biason	Steve Maurer
Terry Brown	Kirk Moser
Roger Chavez	Mark Moser
Bill Cowie	Dan O'Keefe
Daryl Doran	Dev Reeves
David Doyle	Jeff Robben
Gary Heale	Mark Santel
Kevin Hundelt	Thompson Usiyan
Slobodan Ilijevski	Tim Walters
Chris Kenny	Pat Zarky
John Klein	

1993-94 St. Louis Ambush
National Professional Soccer League (NPSL)
Team Record: 25-15 in the NPSL's National Conference
Postseason: 5-4
Lost Championship
Coach: Daryl Doran (25-15)
Location: St. Louis, Missouri
Attendance: 162,861, Avg. 8,143 in 20 home dates

Roster

Terry Brown
Tim Collie
Bill Cowie
Jeff Davis
Daryl Doran
David Doyle
Ted Eck
Craig Frederking
Scott Gaither
John Gates
Kevin Groark
Kevin Hundelt

Chris Kenny
John Klein
Steve Kuntz
Mike Laposha
Scott Marty
Steve Maurer
Scott McDoniel
Mark Moser
Ted Powers
Dev Reeves
Joe Reiniger
Jeff Robben

1994-95 St. Louis Ambush

National Professional Soccer League (NPSL)
Team Record: 30-10 in the NPSL's National Conference
Postseason: 9-2
Won Championship
Coach: Daryl Doran (30-10)
Location: St. Louis, Missouri
Attendance: 157,621, Avg. 7,881 in 20 home dates

Roster

Shane Battelle
Terry Brown
Bill Cowie
Jeff Davis
Ryan Degrand
Daryl Doran
Eric Eichmann

Craig Frederking
John Gates
Kevin Groark
Kevin Hundelt
Chris Kenny
John Klein
Steve Kuntz

Mike Laposha
Todd Lauer
Scott Marty
Steve Maurer
Scott McDoniel
Mark Moser

Dan O'Donnell
Joe Reiniger
Rich Reiniger
Greg Sczurek
Jamie Swanner
Steve Trittschuh

1995-96 St. Louis Ambush
National Professional Soccer League (NPSL)
Team Record: 24-16 in the NPSL's National Division
Postseason: 4-4
Lost Division Final
Coach: Daryl Doran (24-16)
Location: St. Louis, Missouri
Attendance: 182,043, Avg. 9,102 in 20 home dates

Roster

Jeff Bannister
Erik Barbieri
Bill Cowie
Jeff Davis
Ryan Degrand
Daryl Doran
Eric Eichmann
John Gates
Kevin Groark
Kevin Hundelt
Kris Kelderman
Chris Kenny
Joey Kirk
John Klein

Scott Kreitmeyer
Steve Kuntz
Mike Laposha
Pat Mann
Scott Marty
Steve Maurer
Matt McAvin
Scott McDoniel
Mark Moser
Greg Muhr
Steve Ralston
Dev Reeves
Joe Reiniger
Rich Reiniger

Mark Santel
Greg Sczurek
Joel Shanker

Jamie Swanner
Simon Weiss

1996-97 St. Louis Ambush

National Professional Soccer League (NPSL)
Team Record: 27-13 in the NPSL's Midwest Division
Postseason: 3-4
Lost Conference Final
Coach: Daryl Doran (27-13)
Location: St. Louis, Missouri
Attendance: 181,435, Avg. 9,072 in 20 home dates

Roster

David Banks
Jeff Bannister
Derek Carroll
Bill Cowie
Daryl Doran
Juvenal Dos Santos
Noah Epstein
Ben Erickson
Willy Giummarra
Kevin Groark
Tim Hardy
Kevin Hundelt
John Johnson
Chris Kenny
Steve Kuntz
Mike Laposha

Pat Mann
Steve Maurer
Matt McAvin
Scott McDoniel
Mark Moser
Mitar Mrkela
Rob Nichols
Shawn O'Fallon
Joe Reiniger
Jamie Swanner
Perry Van der Beck
Brandon Ward
Harry Weiss
Simon Weiss
Jeff Yenzer

1997-98 St. Louis Ambush
National Professional Soccer League (NPSL)
Team Record: 27-13 in the NPSL's Midwest Division
Postseason: 6-5
Lost Championship
Coach: Daryl Doran (27-13)
Location: St. Louis, Missouri
Attendance: 164,069, Avg. 8,203 in 20 home dates

Roster

Ian Carter	Franklin McIntosh
Daniel Donigan	Dan McManemy
Daryl Doran	Byron Mitchell
Noah Epstein	Mark Moser
Abraham Francois	Brian Negrete
Jesse Haddix	Joe Reiniger
Nando Hernandez	Joel Shanker
Kevin Hundelt	Toni Siikala
Chris Kenny	Darren Snyder
Steve Kuntz	Curtis Stelzer
Mike Laposha	Jamie Swanner
Pat Mann	Brandon Ward
Matt McAvin	Simon Weiss
Scott McDoniel	Jeff Yenzer

1998-99 St. Louis Ambush
National Professional Soccer League (NPSL)
Team Record: 21-19 in the NPSL's Midwest Division
Postseason: 6-4
Lost Championship
Coach: Daryl Doran (21-19)
Location: St. Louis, Missouri
Attendance: 169,439, Avg. 8,472 in 20 home dates

Roster

Mariano Bollella

Ian Carter	Scott McDoniel
Daniel Donigan	Mark Moser
Daryl Doran	Dan Radke
Tim Henson	Joe Reiniger
Nando Hernandez	Travis Roy
Kevin Hundelt	Joel Shanker
Chris Kenny	Ken Snow
Steve Kuntz	Darren Snyder
Mike Laposha	Aaron Susi
Tim Leonard	Jamie Swanner
Pat Mann	Lee Tschantret
Matt McAvin	Carlton Williams

1999-00 St. Louis Ambush

National Professional Soccer League (NPSL)
Team Record: 11-33 in the NPSL's Midwest Division
Coach: Jamie Swanner (10-19)
Coach: Joe Reiniger (1-5)
Coach: Jorge Espinoza (0-9)
Location: St. Louis, Missouri
Attendance: 102,687, Avg. 4,668 in 22 home dates

Roster

Rafael Amaya	Ian Carter
Ricky Andrews	Mirko Castillo
Jeremy Ballenger	Matt Caution
Bill Becher	Diego Cerro
David Beck	Ian Clarke
Marcelo Carrera	Savo Djurica

Derek Garrambone	Dan Radke
Kevin Groark	Joe Reiniger
Nando Hernandez	Eloy Salgado
Todd Hunter	Darren Snyder
Kevin Kalish	Aaron Susi
Ted Kaminski	Jamie Swanner
Andy Korbesmeyer	Maxi Viera
Mike Laposha	Simon Weiss
Tim Leonard	Carlton Williams
Matt Little	

Attendance

The following attendance information for the St. Louis Ambush (1992-00) was acquired online from *Stats Crew*, accessed circa February-March 2020.

1992-93 St. Louis Ambush
Attendance: 154,351, Avg. 7,718 in 20 home dates

1993-94 St. Louis Ambush
Attendance: 162,861, Avg. 8,143 in 20 home dates

1994-95 St. Louis Ambush
Attendance: 157,621, Avg. 7,881 in 20 home dates

1995-96 St. Louis Ambush
Attendance: 182,043, Avg. 9,102 in 20 home dates

1996-97 St. Louis Ambush
Attendance: 181,435, Avg. 9,072 in 20 home dates

1997-98 St. Louis Ambush
Attendance: 164,069, Avg. 8,203 in 20 home dates

1998-99 St. Louis Ambush
Attendance: 169,439, Avg. 8,472 in 20 home dates

1999-00 St. Louis Ambush
Attendance: 102,687, Avg. 4,668 in 22 home dates

The attendance, as you can see, oscillated around 7-9,000 per game with a huge decline in the last season of 1999-2000. The two big years in attendance for the Ambush, 1995-96 and 1996-97, coincidentally coincide with the emergence of MLS in 1996. Perhaps call it a spillover of excitement on the St. Louis scene. Not to mention, the 1994-95 season was the championship run for the Ambush which certainly produced some box-office momentum for the next few years.

St. Louis Steamers
1998-2006*
WISL/MISL
(Indoor)
The second attempt of the St. Louis Steamers occurred between 1998-2006. The team was founded—or "Re-founded"—in 1998. Though, evidently, the second incarnation of the Steamers more or less represented St. Louis on the field from 2000-2006.[137]

As such, the Steamers made a comeback in the World Indoor Soccer League and the Major Indoor Soccer League. (The following team information, from 2000-2006, was acquired online from *Stats Crew*, while the rosters were from *Just Sports Stats*, circa February-March 2020.)

---

*   Technically, the second run of the St. Louis Steamers saw the field from 2000-2006.

2000 St. Louis Steamers

World Indoor Soccer League (WISL)
Team Record: 9-15 in the WISL
Postseason: 1-1
Lost Semifinal
Coach: Daryl Doran (9-15)
Location: St. Louis, Missouri
Attendance: 64,697, Avg. 5,391 in 12 home dates

Roster

Pat Barry	Pat Mann
Ken Costello	Scott McDoniel
Jeff Davis	Kirk Moser
Jeff DiMaria	Mark Moser
Daniel Donigan	D.J. Newsom
Daryl Doran	Mike Payne
Kevin Groark	Brett Phillips
Brad Hansmann	Kevin Quigley
Dan Harvatin	Joe Reiniger
Kevin Hundelt	John Ryan
John Johnson	Steve Siebert
Brad Jordan	Chris Smith
Chris Kenny	Joe Smugala
Kevin Koetters	Curtis Stelzer
	Tim Walters

2001 St. Louis Steamers

World Indoor Soccer League (WISL)
Team Record: 11-13 in the WISL
Postseason: 1-2
Lost Semifinal
Coach: Daryl Doran (11-13)
Location: St. Louis, Missouri
Attendance: 57,747, Avg. 4,812 in 12 home dates

Roster

Ken Costello

Jeff Davis

Jeff DiMaria

Daryl Doran

Fernando Errecalde

Brandon Gibbs

Kevin Groark

Kevin Hundelt

Kevin Koetters

Kirk Moser

Mark Moser

D.J. Newsom

Brett Phillips

Kevin Quigley

Clint Regier

Clovis Simas

Chris Smith

Joe Smugala

Tim Tedoni

Bojan Vuckovic

Harry Weiss

Carlton Williams

2002 St. Louis Steamers

There was a year off for the St. Louis Steamers.

2003-04 St. Louis Steamers

Major Indoor Soccer League (MISL)

Team Record: 14-22 in the MISL's Central Division

Coach: Daryl Doran (13-23)

Location: St. Louis, Missouri

Attendance: 62,702, Avg. 3,483 in 18 home dates

Roster

Michael Apple

Jake Bleyenberg

Steve Butcher

Matt Caution

Jason Cole

Jeff DiMaria

Daryl Doran

Fernando Errecalde

Ryan Ferguson

Nando Hernandez

Mike Kirchhoff

Erik Kuster

Franck M'bemba

Joe Morelli

D.J. Newsom
Brett Phillips
Addae Rique
Dan Santoro
Craig Scheer
Carl Schmitt
Sipho Sibiya

Aaron Susi
Tim Tedoni
Cal Thomas
Mark Thomas
Mali Walton
Sterling Wescott
Carlton Williams

2004-05 St. Louis Steamers
Major Indoor Soccer League (MISL)
Team Record: 20-20
Currently 4th in the MISL
Postseason: 0-2
Lost Semifinal
Coach: Daryl Doran (20-20)
Location: St. Louis, Missouri
Attendance: 95,882, Avg. 4,794 in 20 home dates

Roster
Michael Apple
Kellon Baptiste
Mariano Bollella
Matt Caution
Nino da Silva
Shaun David
Jeff Davis
Jeff DiMaria
Daryl Doran
Jesse Elmore
Fernando Errecalde
Carlos Farias

Bob Graeff
Nate Houser
Elvir Kafedzic
Daouda Kante
Ibrahim Kante
Lindsay Kennedy
Mike Kirchhoff
Marco Lopez
Justin McMillian
D.J. Newsom
Brett Phillips
Joe Reiniger

Bret Richardson
Addae Rique
Craig Scheer
Chris Smith
Randy Soderman

Aaron Susi
Riley Swift
Cal Thomas
Mali Walton
Sterling Wescott

2005-06 St. Louis Steamers
Major Indoor Soccer League (MISL)
Team Record: 23-7
Currently 1st in the MISL
Postseason: 3-2
Lost Championship
Coach: Omid Namazi (23-7)
Location: St. Louis, Missouri
Attendance: 85,131, Avg. 5,675 in 15 home dates

Roster

Michael Apple
Jamar Beasley
Mariano Bollella
Marcos Chantel
Shaun David
Jeff DiMaria
Bayard Elfvin
Jesse Elmore
Carlos Farias
Elvir Kafedzic
Mike Kirchhoff
James Koehler

Genoni Martinez
Rey Martinez
Justin McMillian
Omid Namazi
Sandre Naumoski
D.J. Newsom
Brett Phillips
Damien Pottinger
Joe Reiniger
Randy Soderman
Mali Walton
Sterling Wescott

Attendance

The following attendance information for the St. Louis Steamers (2000-06) was acquired online from *Stats Crew*, accessed circa February-March 2020. Let's take a closer look.

2000 St. Louis Steamers
Attendance: 64,697, Avg. 5,391 in 12 home dates

2001 St. Louis Steamers
Attendance: 57,747, Avg. 4,812 in 12 home dates

2002 St. Louis Steamers
There was a year off for the St. Louis Steamers.

2003-04 St. Louis Steamers
Attendance: 62,702, Avg. 3,483 in 18 home dates

2004-05 St. Louis Steamers
Attendance: 95,882, Avg. 4,794 in 20 home dates

2005-06 St. Louis Steamers
Attendance: 85,131, Avg. 5,675 in 15 home dates

Interestingly, the attendance numbers started out at a little over 5,000 people per game, then declined, then grew again. Yet, the numbers, in contrast with the original Steamers run, were too low to sustain a team. In fact, even during the last 2005-06 season, in which the team had a great year and placed second in the championship, the average attendance was listed at 5,675. It would seem this was cause for the team to end its run. Next up were the St. Louis Illusion.

St. Louis Illusion
2008-2010
Professional Arena Soccer League (PASL-Pro)
(Indoor)
Following the decline of the St. Louis Steamers, the St. Louis Illusion
filled in the gap for professional indoor soccer. (The following team
information, from 2008-2010, was acquired online from *Stats Crew*, while
the rosters were from *Just Sports Stats*, circa February-March 2020.)

2008-09 St. Louis Illusion
Professional Arena Soccer League (PASL)
Team Record: 8-8
Currently 2nd in the PASL's Eastern Division
Location: St. Louis, Missouri

Roster

Vedad Alagic	Shane Hanson
Ricky Andrews	Dan Hilson
Cal Angus	Senad Hot
John Anzalone	Rich Hutchinson
Mike Banner	Anel Ibricic
Ross Beverige	Justin Judiscak
Brad Boyer	Elvir Kafedzic
Pat Brazzil	Mike Kirchoff
Peter Christofilakos	Chris Knopp
Greg Crook	Damir Kordic
Shaun David	Ilfan Kudic
Taib Dedic	Adam Lanter
Daryl Doran	Matt Little
Roger Gemoules	Justin McMillian
Joe Genovese	Eric Modeer
Brandon Gibbs	Harry Nelson

D.J. Newsom
Jason Norsic
Joe Reiniger
Dominic Schell
Darren Snyder

Kevin Thibodeau
Daniel Ulloa
Mike Utley
Mali Walton
Mike Zaegel

2009-10 St. Louis Illusion
Professional Arena Soccer League (PASL)
Team Record: 6-10
Currently 5th in the PASL's Eastern Division
Location: St. Louis, Missouri

Roster

Miles Abel
Vedad Alagic
Ricky Andrews
John Anzalone
Josh Boyd
Allen Bradaric
Brad Campbell
Brock Chatman
Jerry Chavez
Peter Christofilakos
Taib Dedic
RJ Dougherty
Jesse Elmore
Marco Florez
John Fridal
Sam Gelvin
Roger Gemoules
Anel Ibricic

Justin Judiscak
Elvir Kafedzic
Ahmo Karahasanovic
Sammy Keomanivane
Ilfan Kudic
Jerry Lakin
Justin Maddock
Chris Mattingly
Justin McMillian
Dan Muesenfechter
Steven Neira
D.J. Newsom
Jason Norsic
Jensel Olascoaga
Lawrence Olum
Georgi Petrov
Neil Pilla
Joe Reiniger

Lucas Rodrigues Alvez

Andrew Sandheinrich

Matt Segal

Mike Utley

John Van Buskirk

Mali Walton

Adam Wiedenhoffer

Ben Zemanski

AC St. Louis

2010

NASL

USSF Division 2 Professional League

(Outdoor)

AC St. Louis—coached by St. Louis area native Dale Schilly—had a run in the lower ranks of professional outdoor soccer, though it didn't last long. Sometimes, in American soccer, the names of teams and leagues can get confusing. *Wikipedia* described the attempt of AC St. Louis in pro outdoor soccer in the following way: "AC St. Louis was an American professional soccer team based in St. Louis, Missouri, United States. Founded in December 2009, the team played its first and only season the next year in the NASL Conference of the temporary USSF D2 Pro League, the second tier of the American Soccer Pyramid. With plans to join the new North American Soccer League the following season, the club folded in January 2011 under unmanageable financial strain."[138]

A highlight of the team arrived in the form of the U.S. Open Cup where coach Schilly found himself in LA, on LA Galaxy's home turf, coaching opposite Bruce Arena. The game ended 2-0 in favor of the LA Galaxy. (The following AC St. Louis roster was acquired from the *Wikipedia* page "AC St. Louis" on March 16, 2020.)

Roster

Alec Dufty

Zach Bauer

Troy Cole

Tim Velten

Jack Traynor

John Lesko

Luke Kreamalmeyer
Anthony O'Garro
Elvir Kafedzic
Hagop Chirishian
Chris Salvaggione Gilbert
Pogosyan
Gauchinho
Mike Ambersley

Brad Stisser
Jeff Cosgriff
Mark Bloom
Chad Becker
Ryan Moore
Alex Titton
Dillon Barna
Michael Videira

Illinois Piasa
2010-2014 (*Stats Crew* online)
Professional Arena Soccer League (PASL-Pro)
(Indoor)
Following the collapse of the St. Louis Illusion, Illinois Piasa—with some association to FC Adrenaline—carried the torch for professional indoor soccer in St. Louis. (The following team information, from 2010-2014, was acquired online from *Stats Crew*, while the rosters were from *Just Sports Stats*, circa March 2020.)

2010-11 Illinois Piasa
Professional Arena Soccer League (PASL)
Team Record: 9-3
Currently 1st in the PASL's Frontier Division
Postseason: 0-1
Location: Granite City, Illinois

Roster
Miles Abel
Chris Anzalone
John Anzalone

Roshan Bassett
Brad Boyer
James Chambers

Greg Crook

Jared Eden

Marco Flores

Jon Fridal

Roger Gemoules

Kevin Jacobsmeyer

Dave Kane

Pat Kane

Joe Kelly

Sammy Keomanivane

Chris Mattingly

Paul McKee

Jason Norsic

Eric Polka

Matt Reeb

Aaron Reuther

Andrew Sandheinrich

Brian Towery

Mike Utley

2011-12 Illinois Piasa

Professional Arena Soccer League (PASL)

Team Record: 6-10

Currently 4th in the PASL's Eastern Division

Postseason: 0-1

Lost Divisional Playoff

Location: Glen Carbon, Illinois

Roster

Miles Abel

Ricky Andrews

Chris Anzalone

Dustin Attarian

Jeff Baker

Mike Banner

Zach Bauer

Josh Boyd

Alen Bradaric

Peter Christofilakos

Greg Crook

Brian Donnelly

Jared Embick

Jon Fridal

Roger Gemoules

Richard Henderson

Kevin Jacobsmeyer

Mychel Jones

Justin Judiscak
Elvir Kafedzic
Chris Mattingly
Justin McMillian
D.J. Newsom

Blake Ordell
Joe Reiniger
Muriz Smajic
Tim Vance
Matt Williams

2012-13 Illinois Piasa
Professional Arena Soccer League (PASL)
Team Record: 4-12
Currently 4th in the PASL's Eastern Division
Location: Glen Carbon, Illinois

Roster

Sami Abu-Douleh
Ricky Andrews
Sam Arnsby
Zach Bauer
Josh Boyd
Alen Bradaric
Taylor Brophy
Spencer Brown
Dana Byquist
Greg Crook
Joe Daise
Saliou Diop
Jesse Elmore
Gregory Ermold
Pat Fagen
Julio Falconi
Marco Flores
Jon Fridal

Roger Gemoules
Alan Hagerty
Denaldin Hamzagic
Matt Harris
Gary Henderson
Kevin Jacobsmeyer
Justin Judiscak
Elvir Kafedzic
Gabriel Kleinert
Ilfan Kudic
Brad Land
Malcolm LeBourne
Chris Mattingly
Matt Mattingly
Justin McMillian
Pat McSheehy
D.J. Newsom
Jason Norsic

Shadrack Ondinga
Blake Ordell
Victor Pacheco
Matt Poole
Wes Rasdorf
Azeem Razwan
Joe Reiniger
Frank Rojas
Jason Rust

Jesse Semnacher
Muriz Smajic
Brett Smith
Jeff Stepan
Drew Sullivan
Tim Vance
Micah Wangia
Hezekiah Weiss

2013-14 Illinois Piasa

Professional Arena Soccer League (PASL)
Team Record: 2-13
Currently 6th in the PASL's Eastern Division
Location: Glen Carbon, Illinois

Roster

Miles Abel
Andres Acosta
Eric Addison
Ricky Andrews
Chris Anzalone
John Anzalone
Adam Balbi
Matt Bearley
JJ Bilyeu
Alen Bradaric
Ernad Cavka
Senad Cavka
Cody Costakis
Greg Crook

Jarid Faulkerson
Garnet Ferron
Marco Flores
Jon Fridal
Steven Frierdich
Roger Gemoules
Selver Germic
Jake Grote
Aaron Guzman
Alan Hagerty
Denis Hamzabegovic
Nate Heryford
Anel Ibricic
Andy Jones

Mychel Jones
Zachary Kittrell
Damir Kordic
Mirza Kovacevic
Greg Kranz
Doug Lampert
Corey Loberg
Ross MacGregor
Bryan McCausland
Doug Montroy
Nilber Nativo
Steven Neira
Chris Nicholson

John Niebruegge
Blake Ordell
Azeem Razwan
Brad Reibold
Ed Rulo
Almin Sabotic
Richard Schmermund
Cory Scott
Tarik Sehovic
Muriz Smajic
Jaime Toro
Tomas Tostado

St. Louis Ambush
2013-Present
MISL/MASL
(Indoor)

Competing out of St. Charles, Missouri, the St. Louis Ambush have been a part of the Major Indoor Soccer League and the Major Arena Soccer League. Throughout the duration of the Ambush's second incarnation, the team has struggled to keep up with the legacy of the 1990s. (The following St. Louis Ambush team information, from 2013-2020, was acquired online from *Stats Crew*, while the rosters were from *Just Sports Stats*, circa March 2020.)

Special note: The roster for the 2019-20 team was accessed January 22, 2021, from *Just Sports Stats*. The team information and roster for the 2020-21 campaign was accessed January 22, 2021, from the official St. Louis Ambush website in conjunction with the MASL. The team information and roster for the 2021-22 campaign was accessed April 19, 2022, from *Stats Crew* and the official St. Louis Ambush website in conjunction with the MASL.

2013-14 St. Louis Ambush

Major Indoor Soccer League (MISL)
Team Record: 4-16
Currently 6th in the MISL
Location: St. Louis, Missouri
Attendance: 56,361, Avg. 5,636 in 10 home dates

Roster

Andres Acosta	Matthew Kimball
Corey Adamson	Brandon Manzonelli
Nick Aguilar	Chris Mattingly
Dan Antoniuk	Pat McSheehy
Jamar Beasley	Michael Mesle
Jake Bleyenberg	Nicholas Pollard
Greg Crook	Jeff Richey
Jeff DiMaria	Michael Roach
Kory Dowell	Richard Schmermund
Tim Findall	Odaine Sinclair
Brian Groark	Brian Soell
Kyle Hopson	Tim Vance
Elvir Kafedzic	Chad Vandegriffe

2014-15 St. Louis Ambush

Major Arena Soccer League (MASL)
Team Record: 8-12 in the MASL's Central Division
Location: St. Louis, Missouri
Attendance: 61,106, Avg. 6,111 in 10 home dates

Roster

Corey Adamson	Cody Costakis
Anthony Arrico	Greg Crook
Jamar Beasley	Jeff DiMaria
Kevin Corby	Kory Dowell

Axel Duarte
Manny Forbes
Adnan Gabeljic
Gordy Gurson
Alan Hagerty
Elvir Kafedzic
Tim Kelly
Greg Kranz
Ross MacGregor

Chris Mattingly
Pat McSheehy
Blake Ordell
David Paul
Nicholas Pollard
Richard Schmermund
Odaine Sinclair
Stefan St. Louis
Chad Vandegriffe

2015-16 St. Louis Ambush
Major Arena Soccer League (MASL)
Team Record: 5-15
Currently 4th in the MASL's Central Division
Location: St. Louis, Missouri
Attendance: 53,017, Avg. 5,302 in 10 home dates

Roster
Lucas Almeida
Anthony Arrico
Daniel Berko
Cody Costakis
Jeff DiMaria
Manny Forbes
Victor France
Ian Garrett
Gordy Gurson
Andre Hayne
Dylan Hundelt
Bobby Hurwitz
Elvir Kafedzic

Ross MacGregor
Chris Mattingly
Freddy Moojen
Marcelo Moreira
Luiz Mota
Blake Ordell
David Paul
Richard Schmermund
Cory Scott
Odaine Sinclair
Piotr Sliwa
Kentaro Takada
Chad Vandegriffe

2016-17 St. Louis Ambush
Major Arena Soccer League (MASL)
Team Record: 1-19
Currently 5th in the MASL's Central Division
Location: St. Louis, Missouri
Attendance: 25,736, Avg. 2,574 in 10 home dates

Roster

Corey Adamson	Nathaniel Kast
Lucas Almeida	Nick Kolarac
Daniel Berko	Greg Kranz
Cody Blentlinger	Ross MacGregor
Casey Clark	Nikola Marojevic
Vadim Cojocov	Chris Mattingly
Carlos Contreras	Carson Pryor
Cody Costakis	Jonathan Ramos
Kory Dowell	Richard Schmermund
Victor France	Cory Scott
Mitch Garcia	Stefan St. Louis
Ian Garrett	Kentaro Takada
Dylan Hundelt	JT Thomas
Joao Junqueira	

2017-18 St. Louis Ambush
Major Arena Soccer League (MASL)
Team Record: 3-19
Currently 4th in the MASL's Central Division
Location: St. Louis, Missouri
Attendance: 28,659, Avg. 2,605 in 11 home dates

Roster

Robert Acosta

Corey Adamson

Antonio Aguilar

Lucas Almeida

Daniel Berko

Cody Blentlinger

Diego Bobadilla

Jake Cawsey

Casey Clark

Vadim Cojocov

Carlos Contreras

Cody Costakis

Pablo da Silva

Kory Dowell

Axel Duarte

Victor France

Jerjer Gibson

Nestor Hernandez

Dylan Hundelt

Joao Junqueira

Greg Kranz

Ross MacGregor

Nikola Marojevic

Clayton Matheus

Chris Mattingly

Hewerton Moreira

Paulo Nascimento

Raphael Nascimento

Zachary Reget

Richard Schmermund

Stefan St. Louis

Justin Stinson

James Thomas

Alex Tozer

2018-19 St. Louis Ambush

Major Arena Soccer League (MASL)

Team Record: 10-14

Currently 3rd in the MASL's South Central Division

Location: St. Louis, Missouri

Roster

Robert Acosta

Corey Adamson

Lucas Almeida

Diego Bobadilla

Edin Campara

Jake Cawsey

Casey Clark

Vadim Cojocov

Douglas Dos Santos

Axel Duarte

Jerjer Gibson
Joao Junqueira
Greg Kranz
Jowayne Laidley
Ross MacGregor
Eduardo Maia
Antonio Manfut
Mario Marcos
Clayton Matheus
Chris Mattingly
Howard Miller

Hewerton Moreira
Paulo Nascimento
Nic Powers
Zachary Reget
Mike Scharf
Felipe Silva
Magui Souza
Stefan St. Louis
Justin Stinson
JT Thomas
Alex Tozer

2019-20 St. Louis Ambush
Major Arena Soccer League (MASL)
Team Record: 9-12
Currently in the MASL's South Central Division
Location: St. Louis, Missouri

Roster
Corey Adamson
Lucas Almeida
Diego Bobadilla
Andre Braithwaite
Duduca Carvalho
Jake Cawsey
Vadim Cojocov
Pablo Da Silva
Oitomeia de Souza
Douglas Dos Santos
Axel Duarte
Anthony Grant

Ado Jahic
Joao Junqueira
Niko Karidis
Greg Kranz
Qudus Lawal
Ross MacGregor
Mario Marcos
Paulo Nascimento
Jason Norsic
Wil Nyamsi
Jonnathan Pachar
Adrian Porcayo

Saphir Salvador	Magui Souza
Jonatan Santos	Stefan St. Louis
Mike Scharf	JT Thomas
Felipe Silva	Tony Walls

This particular 2019-20 season for the St. Louis Ambush did not completely finish thanks to the coronavirus of 2020. As Joe Lyons of the *St. Louis Post-Dispatch* pointed out, "On March 12, the MASL Board of Directors met and voted unanimously to shut down the 2019-20 season because of the new coronavirus, acting in the best interests of players, staff and fans."[139] (Other leagues—such as the NBA and MLS—had to shut down as well.) Lyons wrote, "At the time, the St. Louis Ambush of the Major Arena Soccer League had just two games remaining and had already been eliminated from the playoffs."[140]

The team record of 9-12 was the record at the time the MASL shut down because of the 2020 coronavirus. While writing this portion of the book (circa March 2020), it was unclear if the St. Louis Ambush would eventually play its remaining games.

A few key players included JT Thomas, Duduca Carvalho, Tony Walls, Oitomeia de Souza, Lucas Almeida, Pablo Da Silva, Felipe Silva, Jonatan Santos, Axel Duarte, and Paulo Nascimento.

2020-21 St. Louis Ambush
Major Arena Soccer League (MASL)
Team Record: 8-7
Coach: Hewerton Moreira
Location: St. Louis, Missouri

Roster
Corey Adamson	Duduca Carvalho
Lucas Almeida	Vadim Cojocov

Axel Duarte	Paulo Nascimento
Max Ferdinand	Wil Nyamsi
Sam Guernsey	Brett Petricek
Ado Jahic	Alexis Robles
Pepe Junqueira	Mike Scharf
Niko Karidis	Richard Schmermund
Greg Kranz	Felipe Silva
Mario Marcos	Magui Souza
Stefan Mijatovic	JT Thomas
Howard Miller Jr.	Tony Walls

Inactive Player List

Diego Bobadilla	Jonatan Santos
Douglas Dos Santos	Oitomeia de Souza

For the St. Louis Ambush, the 2020-21 season began on January 2, 2021, due to the COVID-19 pandemic and all the delays that came with it.

The team finished the 2020-21 regular season with a record of 8-7. From the official website of the St. Louis Ambush, on April 10, 2022, it read: "Several of the league teams were unable to play due to COVID-19 restrictions in their home cities. The Ambush also made their first playoff appearance since returning to indoor soccer in 2013. The Ambush lost both games of a 2 game series to the Kansas City Comets in March 2021." With two playoff losses, the team finished with an 8-9 record, overall.

2021-22 St. Louis Ambush
Major Arena Soccer League (MASL)
Team Record: -
In the MASL's Eastern Conference
Location: St. Louis, Missouri
(The regular season record was 10-14; with the playoffs it was 10-16.)

Roster

Eduardo "Pollo" Cortes

Chris "Tito" Favela

Tony Walls

Christian Briggs

Triston Austin

Wyatt Fowler

Vadim Cojocov

Mohamed Ndiaye

Lucas Almeida

Kyle Swanner

Curtis Kirby

William Eskay

Chris Mattingly

Sam Guernsey

Wil Nyamsi

Greg Kranz

JT Thomas

Robert Kristo

Jeff Michaud

Marcel Berry

Stefan Mijatovic

Axel Duarte

Josue Mazon

Pepe Junqueira

Jose Resendiz

Niko Karidis

Duduca Carvalho

Ado Jahic

Inactive Player List

Paulo Nascimento

Rafael Dias

For the 2021-22 season, the Ambush earned a 10-16 overall record (playoffs included).

Attendance

Attendance figures were not available for the 2018-21 seasons. Leading up to that point, the average attendance for the first few seasons was around 5-6,000 per game and then from 2016-18 it descended to around 2,500 per game.

In the years ahead, the Ambush will likely get a boost from the presence of St. Louis City SC.

Saint Louis FC
2015-2020
USL Championship
(Outdoor)
Saint Louis FC took the lead for St. Louis pro outdoor soccer before the magical announcement of St. Louis City SC came about.

Some local players included Emir Alihodzic, Mike Ambersley, Brandon Barklage, Jake Bond, John Berner, AJ Cochran, Sam Fink, Austin Ledbetter, Jack Maher, Mark Pais, Alex Riggs, Michael Roach, Seth Rudolph, Aedan Stanley, and Chad Vandegriffe. (The following Saint Louis FC team information, from 2015-2020, was acquired online from *Stats Crew*, circa March 2020 and February 2021.)

2015 Saint Louis FC (8-11-9)
2016 Saint Louis FC (8-12-10)
2017 Saint Louis FC (9-14-9)
2018 Saint Louis FC (14-9-11)
2019 Saint Louis FC (11-14-9)
2020 Saint Louis FC (7-5-4)

2015 Saint Louis FC
United Soccer League Championship (USL)
Team Record: 8-11-9
Finishing 9th in the USL
Location: St. Louis, Missouri

2016 Saint Louis FC
United Soccer League Championship (USL)
Team Record: 8-12-10 in the USL
Location: St. Louis, Missouri

2017 Saint Louis FC
United Soccer League Championship (USL)

Team Record: 9-14-9
Finishing 12th in the USL
Location: St. Louis, Missouri

2018 Saint Louis FC
United Soccer League Championship (USL)
Team Record: 14-9-11
Finishing 8th in the USL
Location: St. Louis, Missouri

2019 Saint Louis FC
United Soccer League Championship (USL)
Team Record: 11-14-9 in the USL
Location: St. Louis, Missouri

2020 Saint Louis FC
United Soccer League Championship (USL)
Team Record: (7-5-4)
Finishing 2nd in the USL
Location: St. Louis, Missouri

In 2020, Steve Trittschuh—a Granite City native who represented the USMNT for a number of years—took over as Saint Louis FC coach. Though, the season was interrupted by the worldwide coronavirus. In fact, the NBA, MLS, and other sporting organizations suspended play because of the coronavirus. Eventually, Saint Louis FC resumed games. Unfortunately, this was the final season for Saint Louis FC.

St. Louis City SC
2023-
Major League Soccer
(Outdoor)
In 2019 the team was made official.

In 2022 the opening season was planned.

In 2023 the opening season took off due to the 2020 COVID-19 pandemic.

St. Louis is finally in Major League Soccer! It was a long wait. Though, it's an exciting time for St. Louisans. (The following reflects the first signings for St. Louis City SC's initial team. Things were moving fast as everything was coming together. These first few names are historic signings for a team that should have a long, lucrative, future in store. Stay tuned. Many more names will follow!)

Roster[†]

Selmir Pidro

João Klauss

Tomas Ostrak

Roman Burki

Joakim Nilsson[‡]

Coach: Bradley Carnell

Sporting Director: Lutz Pfannenstiel

Director of Coaching: John Hackworth

Owners: Carolyn Kindle Betz, Jo Ann Taylor Kindle, Jim Kavanaugh

Stadium: Centene Stadium

The stadium has a capacity of 22,500 and it's located in the Downtown West neighborhood. The architectural firm was HOK. Construction started in 2020. The cost was $457.8 million, give or take. The previous name for the stadium was St. Louis City Stadium. The field is grass.

St. Louis City SC 2

2022-

(Outdoor)

[†] At the publication of this book, the official roster was still being formed.

[‡] As this book was getting close to publication, this player was in the process of signing.

(The following is the roster of the reserve squad known as St. Louis City SC 2. It was made known at the official St. Louis City SC website under the title "Unveiling STL CITY2's MLS NEXT Pro Roster," published February 7, 2022, accessed April 19, 2022. This, of course, was before the first team arrived.)

Roster

Dida Armstrong
Ezra Armstrong
Michael Creek
Josh Dolling
Anthony Faupel
Nathan Ferguson
Karson Gibbs
Ryley Gibbs
Aaron Heard
Kyle Hiebert
Josh Maher
Célio Pompeu Martins
Alex Palazzolo

Miguel Perez
Sergio Rivas
Max Schneider
Fritz Volmar
Jack Wagoner
Wan Kuzain Wan Kamal
Akil Watts
Joshua Yaro
Kwame Awuah
Vitor Dias
Ben Di Rosa
Eric Walker

ST. LOUIS CITY SC CARRYING THE TORCH OF THE FIRST STEAMERS

For some, the first run of the St. Louis Steamers—1979-88—might just be the most magical time in the history of St. Louis soccer. It was the golden era. Perhaps the players back then knew how cool the whole thing was. Will the campaign of St. Louis City SC be similarly as epic? Yes, without doubt. Will the players know how significant the whole thing is? Likely so. Just as the first Steamers run, St. Louis City SC is about to embark on a *new* golden era of St. Louis soccer. It's an era that is strengthened by the firm standing of MLS. Since 1996, the league and all its employees active behind the scenes have worked hard to reach this grand stage. As a result, St. Louis should be a successful recipient of the progress.

Will St. Louis be able to successfully lean on its historical cachet in the opening five years in MLS?

Somehow, the franchise will have to balance filling seats with wins on the field while reaching for (what all involved will hope to be) an MLS Cup championship.

Considering all St. Louis attendance figures from past pro indoor teams (both highs and lows), St. Louis City SC will have a lot to juggle in regard to keeping people in seats over the long haul. If the front office can keep these numbers up then good things should follow, regardless of the team's record. Though, at the same time, if the team on the field can provide wins, then getting people in seats—along with season ticket holders—should not be an extremely difficult task. The St. Louis Rams—of the NFL, of course—dealt with this issue, and, subsequently, it was partly why the team left town. Go figure. St. Louis had an actual NFL team, which is huge when you think about it; after all, given it's the NFL, the nation's most popular league, you'd think that attendance in St. Louis would've been a no-brainer. But in fact, there were challenges. Hence, the MLS experience in St. Louis might eventually face the same.

Regarding the big crowds around MLS these days, such as the case with Atlanta where 70,000 fans is normal, former General Manager of the St. Louis Ambush, Ed Gettemeier, remarked that "in terms of how that must feel for the young players" it's got to be "mind boggling." Gettemeier pointed out that when he was GM of the Ambush in the 1990s it was about getting people in seats, which was a day-to-day concern. As such, regarding MLS today, which is on an upward climb with continued expansion, Gettemeier said, "It's long overdue."

CLOSING WORDS

Pierre Teilhard de Chardin, a French philosopher, proposed a theory known as Eternal Spirit. It was a theory summed up briefly by Giorgio Tsoukalos on *Ancient Aliens*, a popular show on the History channel. The theory suggests that every particle in the universe has within it the history of the universe (and knowledge thereof). It's such an interesting theory—one that has merit beyond our knowledge and experience—that goes beyond the known and into the unknown albeit on a latent level just waiting to be discovered. Regardless, this book has cornered a piece of St. Louis soccer history; it has laid out as much salient information about St. Louis soccer as is humanly possible. Well, from one human that is. I suppose if I had had a team of other humans, each working diligently on a task, we could've added a few more pages here and there, with possibly a few more dinners with Jim Leeker. Who knows...the point is, this book has set out to capture the St. Louis soccer experience, its enticing history, topped with the arrival of MLS for the world to see just how interesting this story of MLS reaching St. Louis really is. Appropriately, *The New York Times* reminded an international audience, "The new soccer club will join the Stanley Cup champion St. Louis Blues and the 11-time World Series champion Cardinals as the city's major sports teams."[141]

As for MLS, it is destined to be the world's next super league; St. Louis has been, and will continue to be, a significant actor in that progression down the road. As time rolls on, and as people look back on this amazing bellwether of soccer, it will become even more clear to future generations just how significant St. Louis has been in the big picture of American soccer, and, hence, world soccer.

NOTE FROM THE AUTHOR

One might call this entire piece of work a love letter to St. Louis soccer. My response: You're not far off! I'd be flattered by such a statement. There's no other way with St. Louis soccer. At the same time, if you have seen St. Louis soccer as I have you'd understand if I refute such a claim, as one should just look at the facts to realize that a grand symphony of über-amazing records exist within the realm of St. Louis that (when reported correctly) will come across as nothing less than a love letter. Prior to this book, I knew a ton about St. Louis soccer (more than is legal) but as I went along, researching this, that, and the other, I was impressed more and more. Essentially, if anyone were to write a book about St. Louis soccer, they'd quickly realize it might be misconstrued as a love letter. This is basically irrefutable. Sure, there have been some ups and downs; no soccer-city is perfect. I kept a critical eye, though when a city is this good at soccer over the long haul it's hard to present arguments against it. There's really no negative way to look at St. Louis soccer (unless you're an anti-Scott Gallagher type that's screaming "monopoly!"). And after you really research it, you realize just how amazing it actually is!

Regarding pro teams in St. Louis, some information was acquired online from *Stats Crew* and *Just Sports Stats*. Without checking every last minute detail, with fastidious attention, it seems like both sites share the same information. *Just Sports Stats* was used for the listing of rosters because the formatting of its online site was easier to work with. Pretty easy answer, wouldn't you say? Though, both sites were used for accessing rosters and team records.

Furthermore, when it comes to the year or years that such and such player spent with a team, there was, at times, conflicting information online. (There's a shocker.) Online resources, such as *Stats Crew* and *Just Sports Stats*—which are the most trustworthy—might vary with other sources. In such a case, I likely went with the information from

Stats Crew and/or *Just Sports Stats*. In addition to online sources, I also relied on printed information which varied in nature, including but not limited to old game-day programs lent to me by Jim Leeker and Al Trost from which I gleaned valuable information; these programs were fantastic as a matter of fact. It might seem like a superfluous point to be made, but nonetheless I went to great lengths to confirm the best, most reliable information out there. For example, Angelo DiBernardo, a former member of the USMNT and St. Louis Steamers, had varying information online listed about his playing career in terms of when he played for the St. Louis Steamers. (One online location said he played for the Steamers in 1986-87 while another listed it as 1987-88. I went with the former.) I made the best choice possible based on a variety of factors. So before someone out there looks up his stats and sees a discrepancy regarding the time he played for the Steamers, just know that a lot of time went into getting this minute information as accurate as possible. This goes for him and others. And also know that when I discovered this interesting little online difference regarding when he played for the Steamers, I was not the least bit excited. And, short of calling such people up personally, which would've taken an exorbitant amount of time, certain online resources have to be utilized. It's all done right for posterity's sake.

Toward the tail end of this book, more St. Louis news came about in the form of Steve Ralston making the list of MLS's top 25 players (for its first 25 years in existence). Great news but I thought: *C'mon St. Louis, again? More research for me? I'm tapped out!* My office was piling up like a room in the Library of Congress. Incidentally, Preki, who has a ton of St. Louis experience, also made the list. It just kept piling up— another newspaper article to read! And for all intents and purposes it's not going to stop. The talent of St. Louis soccer has forever in the past been prominent and will forever in the future remain the same.

At dinner on December 2, 2019, on a cold St. Louis night on the Hill, Jim Leeker presented me with his scrapbook collection from years past, something to make the soccer version of *American Pickers* light up like a classic pinball machine reaching a record score administered by Frank.

Then, within his treasure of memories, Leeker showed me a unique flyer from SLU's dinner banquet to celebrate the 1969 NCAA men's soccer national championship. The team—related school staff, along with invited guests—wound up in Stan Musial's old restaurant, which was near Forest Park. A story in the newspaper by Bob Broeg, *St. Louis Post-Dispatch* Sports Editor, read: "The seniors and the rest of the Billikens' newest title team will be honored at a dinner Thursday night at Stan Musial and Biggie's restaurant. Tickets at $10 each can be reserved" by calling the St. Louis University athletic department. The story also illuminated some concerns of the St. Louis pro team at the time: "Meanwhile, [Ted] Martin and associates, all of whom suffered financially the first two years when soaring into flights of pro soccer fancy, now are making realistic plans for a fourth season." Ted Martin was President of the St. Louis Stars at the time. The Stars, despite navigating through testy financial waters, were relying heavily on St. Louis players and this SLU team was rich with talent. As Broeg pointed out in his story: "[Ted] Martin said he hoped the Stars' 1970 roster would include some of the graduating seniors at St. Louis U. Among them are Steve Frank, Jack Galmiche, Gene Geimer, Jim Leeker, Billy McDermott, John Pisani, Gary Rensing and Chuck Zoeller." This was part of the legacy of talent that Leeker was showing me. And impressive it was.

As for the banquet, all the players and coaching staff—including legends Bob Kehoe and Harry Keough—had signed the flyer. Lo and behold, somewhere in the mix, there was Stan Musial's actual signature. Leeker stressed how valuable this scrapbook collection was to him, and (as I could gather based on a few signatures) to mankind. Let's put it this way, very few—if any—St. Louisans would allow a signed autograph of Stan Musial to go out of their sight. To think that Leeker entrusted me enough to take this off his hands for what turned out to be a few months for research was an honor. In a nano-second, my head raced with things to say and not to say. I certainly didn't want to screw this transaction up. The stuff in his collection was invaluable.

While researching a book like this you'll come across many programs, brochures, and the like which are poorly written, ridden with grammatical errors, boring, and, frankly, not funny in the least. One such story, by Gib Twyman of *The K.C. Star* (from way back in 1970) was somewhat different. I came across it while researching the St. Louis Stars. I found it humorous and well done. So much so that I looked Gib up, with the idea of telling him I liked his story and to see if he had any input on the world of soccer today. Well, unfortunately, Gib died of a heart attack in 2001. He was 57. For what it's worth, he had an interesting story that was featured in the 1970 Kansas City Spurs program.

During my journey of research, without knowing their full backgrounds, I came across Jim Thebeau (a co-founder of the St. Louis Steamers SC which competes in SLYSA) and D.J. Newsom (a former member of the St. Louis Steamers pro indoor team). I spoke with both by phone in 2020. By pure chance, I realized something peculiar was going on. Thebeau, born in 1975, was a center mid for Busch. I was born in 1976, and was a center mid for Busch. Newsom, born in 1977, was a center mid for Busch. Talk about a coincidence.

For a book about St. Louis soccer, there are so many people—past and present—to thank. For starters, there were many experienced people I spoke to that shared valuable information about the history of St. Louis soccer. A special thanks to

Gene Baker, Dave Berwin, Pete Collico, Sam Cosner, Dave Dorr, Bill Daus, Vince Drake, Frank Flesch, Abe Hawatmeh, Tommy Howe, Ron Jacober, Dan King, Jim Leeker, Bill McDermott, John Moad, D.J. Newsom, Pat McBride, Mike Quante, Kevin Robson, Brian Roth, Dale Schilly, Don Schmidt, Jim Thebeau, Steve Trittschuh, Al Trost, along with Mayor Michelle Harris of Clayton, Missouri, and Mayor Herb Roach of O'Fallon, Illinois.

Thanks to George Mishalow and Ed Gettemeier, both of which were youth coaches of mine. Both, as a matter of fact, played at SIUE.

George, who has since passed, was my coach at Busch and we gained a Missouri State Cup together; I had a great experience with him. Ed was my coach for a Metro East team that won the Holland Cup with only two practices before departing for Europe. We won, in large part, due to Ed's keen understanding of the sport. As it turns out, both coaches played a fundamental role in shaping my experiences with the sport, which, by the way, somehow, years later, has led to this book. Go figure. For a book like this I'd also like to thank Tom Stone (going way back) who was captain at SIUE when I met him at the age of 13, and, at that young age, he was urging me to go there; his confidence in me resonated as the years went on, and, thanks to him and others, despite encountering ups and downs (which everyone will do), I realized that maybe, just maybe, I belonged with this game that I had drifted in and out of during stints of my life. Eventually I decided to get back in the game—perhaps a story for another time. Though, in a roundabout way, it led to this interesting point in time with regard to St. Louis soccer.

Many thanks to them and thanks also to Meyer & Meyer Sport and Cardinal Publishers Group for bringing this book to fruition.

A QUICK WORD ON GENE BAKER

As I was preparing this book (doing research, calling people, setting up dinners), I came across the former coach of Granite City High School who owns the title of most state championships in Illinois high school history, Gene Baker, who, by the way, coached against me in high school. This would be the early 1990s. Apparently at my high school I set a record for total red cards received: four. One for each year, actually. I was told this some time later. My fourth red card coincidentally arrived against Baker in Granite City in a playoff game; a huge fight broke out that game, with fans on the field, perhaps an arrest or two; it made the papers. Oh the memories! (Nothing like getting kicked out of a game!) Regarding Baker, I recall this larger than life figure, intense and passionate, yelling, keeping things in order, essentially—in my eyes—owning the referees as best he could. (Who doesn't, right?) I looked up to him then, and to this day. It was remarkable, and somewhat amazing to me, that I was on the phone interviewing him for this story. We talked for around two hours; he was very insightful and extremely professional, never a bad word to say about anyone. A month or so later, I caught up with him at The St. Louis Sports Hall of Fame of Southern Illinois Sports Legends induction ceremony—a jam-packed event co-hosted by former Cardinals announcer Ron Jacober, held in O'Fallon, Illinois—that featured Gene, Steve Trittschuh, and other inductees. Gene, as he asked me to call him, had a strong Granite City following, as usual, some 75 strong, hooping and hollering. A day or so later, I touched base with him about a dinner with Jim Leeker and others in St. Louis which he'd been interested in attending. He told me there were some appointments that he would have to move around schedule-wise, but he'd call me the next day. True to form, he gave a call and regretfully said he couldn't change his schedule. He suggested the following week. I'll say this, even when he couldn't make it, somehow he made it feel like a compliment... truly a professional, one of a kind guy.

If future archaeologists—from a primitive society on the brink of enlightenment—were to stumble across a stream of tape from a cassette tape of, let's say, for the sake of argument, Led Zeppelin, the future researchers would have a hard time figuring out what it was for. Without the actual tape enclosure, along with a stereo to play it on, along with electricity, a stream of Led Zeppelin tape only looks like *flimsy tape*. The people looking at it couldn't possibly conceive what its original function actually was. Perhaps they could, with a stroke of pure genius. Though, likely, it would remain a mystery. National Geographic, BBC, the History channel, and other outlets have explored the intriguing world of lost civilizations that delineate various possibilities of advanced cultures reaching back thousands of years. Whatever the case may be, there are records left all around the world—from Gobekli Tepe, Egypt,

Stonehenge, Angkor Wat, Easter Island, Teotihuacan, and elsewhere—that point to mysterious undertakings of the highest order.

Records—so I've been reminded of in writing this book—are the key.

While different forms of soccer—however rudimentary they may have been—have roots in games played around the ancient world, including the Mayans, Egyptians, Chinese, and Romans, it was the English, to the delight of everyone, that eventually refined the sport of soccer as we know it today.

As such, the international community of soccer has reached a new milestone with the addition of St. Louis City SC.

Many people in the St. Louis soccer family have stressed to me the importance of keeping the St. Louis soccer story alive—all the names, teams, and accomplishments of the past. Sports, as we have seen in our modern global society, are the engine that keeps humanity sane, so to speak. Sports bring hope and ignite passion.

The story of St. Louis soccer is an important one as it illustrates not just a city standing by itself, but one that is intertwined with American soccer, the USMNT, and international soccer at large.

America, a latecomer to soccer, will someday finally conquer it. In fact, as I've said many times before: Soccer is America's last athletic frontier. The only thing standing in the way is a men's FIFA World Cup championship.[§] The US has reached the highest levels in every other sport. In fact, the US leads the world in Olympic gold medals. But not soccer. It may take a little time, but one day the USMNT will conquer soccer. When this occurs, when the USMNT finally reaches the Holy Land of a men's World Cup championship, fans and historians alike will look back and be reminded that St. Louis has been the cradle of soccer in America for as long as anyone can remember. Philadelphia, D.C., cities in New Jersey, Chicago, Dallas, Seattle, Portland, San Francisco, LA, and others, will deserve some of the fame as well. But, all along, in terms of

---

[§]   And, technically speaking, an Olympic gold medal in men's soccer. However, the FIFA World Cup is more coveted in the realm of soccer.

soccer across-the-board—club, high school, college, and professional—St. Louis has consistently been the leader.

The relationship between St. Louis and other cities with the ongoing development of the USMNT is intriguing, there's no doubt.

Specifically regarding the MLS front, St. Louis has joined an American league and the international soccer community. It now has a golden opportunity to distinguish itself just as Buenos Aires, Rio de Janeiro, Sao Paulo, Barcelona, Madrid, Turin, Milan, Rome, Munich, Paris, London, Manchester, and Liverpool have made a name in their own right.

The future has arrived and things will never be the same. For St. Louis soccer, there's so much history behind it, and it's only getting started.

Down the road, when it's all said and done, when St. Louis racks up championship after championship, with perhaps an all-St. Louis lineup, this book might just be the opening chapter to the greatest sports story ever told.

ABOUT THE AUTHOR

SHANE STAY is a bestselling author whose books include *THE World Cup 2022 Book, The Euro 2020 Book, European Soccer Leagues 2019, Major League Soccer 2019, THE Women's World Cup 2019 Book, THE World Cup 2018 Book, Why American Soccer Isn't There Yet*, and *The Cairo Project*. In 2008, he played professional soccer, co-authored a print book, published a magazine story, bottled Leaf Dressing, worked clubs as a comedian, was a restaurateur, and received a Master of Arts from Southern Illinois University. In 1999, he founded the first online Current Events Game (CE Game). He has appeared on TV and has featured on numerous radio broadcasts including ESPN and NPR.

ENDNOTES

1   Maggie Mckee, "Fast-spinning neutron star smashes speed limit," *New Scientist*, published January 12, 2006, accessed March 27, 2020, https://www.newscientist.com/article/dn8576-fast-spinning-neutron-star-smashes-speed-limit/

2   Ibid.

3   Martin Rees, *Our Cosmic Habitat*, Phoenix, an imprint of Orion Books Ltd, London, 2003, p. 25.

4   *KSDK News*. "Mr. St. Louis soccer, Bill McDermott, talks MLS announcement." YouTube video, 01:31. Posted [August 20, 2019]. Accessed [April 4, 2020]. https://www.youtube.com/watch?v=irFd19cLAUI

5   Joe Lyons, "Maher reaps soccer honors at Indiana," *St. Louis Post-Dispatch*, SPORTS, published December 28, 2019, p. B3.

6   Sarah E. Baires, Zócalo Public Square, "White Settlers Buried the Truth About the Midwest's Mysterious Mound Cities," "Pioneers and early archaeologists credited distant civilizations, not Native Americans, with building these sophisticated complexes," *Smithsonian Magazine*, published February 23, 2018, accessed June 15, 2020, https://www.smithsonianmag.com/history/white-settlers-buried-truth-about-midwests-mysterious-mound-cities-180968246/

7   Ibid.

8   *Wikipedia, The Free Encyclopedia*, s.vv. "St. Louis," accessed December 15, 2019, https://en.wikipedia.org/wiki/St._Louis

9   *Wikipedia, The Free Encyclopedia*, s.vv. "St. Louis," accessed September 8, 2020, https://en.wikipedia.org/wiki/St._Louis

10   Sarah E. Baires, Zócalo Public Square, "White Settlers Buried the Truth About the Midwest's Mysterious Mound Cities," "Pioneers and early archaeologists credited distant civilizations, not Native Americans, with building these sophisticated complexes," *Smithsonian Magazine*, published February 23, 2018, accessed June 15, 2020, https://www.smithsonianmag.com/history/white-settlers-buried-truth-about-midwests-mysterious-mound-cities-180968246/

11   Jane Smiley, "Jane Smiley on What St. Louis Tells Us About America," *The New York Times*, published October 14, 2019, updated October 24, 2019, accessed September 9, 2020, https://www.nytimes.com/2019/10/14/travel/14StLouis-Jane-Smiley-tourism.html

12   *Wikipedia, The Free Encyclopedia*, s.vv. "The Hill, St. Louis," accessed September 9, 2020, https://en.wikipedia.org/wiki/The_Hill,_St._Louis

13   Stefene Russell, "Of Cabbages and Kings," *St. Louis Magazine*, published July 24, 2014, accessed September 10, 2020, https://www.stlmag.com/history/of-cabbages-and-kings/

14   Ibid.

15   Ibid.

16   Ibid.

17   Ibid.

18   Ibid.

19   Ibid.

20   Ibid.

21   *Wikipedia, The Free Encyclopedia*, s.vv. "Lemp Mansion," accessed April 24, 2020, https://en.wikipedia.org/wiki/Lemp_Mansion

22   Ibid.

23   Ibid.

24   Ibid.

25   *Wikipedia,The Free Encyclopedia*,s.vv."Anheuser-Busch,"accessed April 27, 2020, https://en.wikipedia.org/wiki/Anheuser-Busch

26   Ibid.

27   Ibid.

28   Ibid.

29   Kerry A. Dolan, "Billion-Dollar Clans: America's 25 Richest Families 2016," *Forbes*, published June 29, 2016, accessed June 19, 2020, https://www.forbes.com/profile/busch/#66395ded3b08

30   *Wikipedia, The Free Encyclopedia*, s.vv. "World Wide Technology Soccer Park," accessed June 19, 2020, https://en.wikipedia.org/wiki/World_Wide_Technology_Soccer_Park#cite_note-MacIntosh2011-3

31   *Wikipedia, The Free Encyclopedia*, s.vv. "August Busch IV," accessed June 19, 2020, https://en.wikipedia.org/wiki/August_Busch_IV

32 Kerry A. Dolan, "Billion-Dollar Clans: America's 25 Richest Families 2016," *Forbes*, published June 29, 2016, accessed June 19, 2020, https://www.forbes.com/profile/busch/#66395ded3b08

33 Ashley Cole, "Kräftig beer line to shut down," *KSDK 5 On Your Side*, published July 10, 2019, updated July 10, 2019, accessed September 24 2020, https://www.ksdk.com/article/entertainment/dining/whats-cookin-in-the-lou/kraftig-beer-line-to-shut-down/63-f3c364bd-9b2f-4075-b3b6-136e6a8bca3e

34 *Wikipedia, The Free Encyclopedia*, s.vv. "St. Leo's (soccer team)," accessed May 6, 2020, https://en.wikipedia.org/wiki/St._Leo%27s_(soccer_team)#1910_roster

35 *Wikipedia, The Free Encyclopedia*, s.vv. "Harry Keough," accessed January 29, 2021, https://en.wikipedia.org/wiki/Harry_Keough

36 Ibid.

37 St. Louis Scott Gallagher Soccer Club, "HISTORY OF ST. LOUIS SCOTT GALLAGHER," accessed June 21, 2020, http://www.slsgsoccer.com/about-us/history

38 Ibid.

39 Ibid.

40 Ibid.

41 Tom Timmermann, "Davis comes full circle," "St. Louisan returning to lead SLSG club here," *St. Louis Post-Dispatch*, STL TODAY SPORTS, published May 13, 2020, p. B1, B4.

42 Ibid.

43 Joe Lyons | Post-Dispatch Special Correspondent, "U.S. OLYMPIC FESTIVAL '94," "Chance Sighting Leads Ralston To Festival," *St. Louis Post-Dispatch*, published July 2, 1994, p. 7C.

44 Tom Timmermann, "Davis comes full circle," "St. Louisan returning to lead SLSG club here," *St. Louis Post-Dispatch*, STL TODAY SPORTS, published May 13, 2020, p. B1, B4.

45 Al Trost (Mike Kavanaugh | Editor), "1981-82 Steamers' Outlook," *St. Louis Steamers, 1981-1982 Media Guide*, Creative Printing Services, Inc., St. Louis, MO, published circa 1981-82, p. 8.

46 *SIUE official website*, "SIUE Cougars Athletics," "MEN'S SOCCER," "Tim Collico," accessed September 18, 2020, https://www.siuecougars.com/sports/m-soccer/2005-06/bios/collico_tim

47 *Wikipedia, The Free Encyclopedia*, s.vv. "John DiRaimondo," accessed December 24, 2020, https://en.wikipedia.org/wiki/John_DiRaimondo

48 *Wikipedia, The Free Encyclopedia*, s.vv. "Taylor Twellman," accessed May 22, 2020, https://en.wikipedia.org/wiki/Taylor_Twellman

49 *Wikipedia, The Free Encyclopedia*, s.vv. "Intercollegiate Soccer Football Association," accessed September 25, 2020, https://en.wikipedia.org/wiki/Intercollegiate_Soccer_Football_Association

50 Ibid.

51 By Alex Yannis Special to The New York Times, *"St. Louis U. Retains Soccer Title," The New York Times*, published January 5, 1974, accessed June 13, 2020, https://www.nytimes.com/1974/01/05/archives/st-louis-u-retains-soccer-title-fullbacks-aid-goalie.html

52 Josh Sellmeyer, "Billiken Athletics," "Bill McDermott: Mr. Soccer, Mr. Saint Louis," *Saint Louis University Billikens official website*, published June 11, 2014, accessed December 27, 2020, https://slubillikens.com/news/2014/6/11/209520008.aspx

53 Ibid.

54 Ibid.

55 Ibid.

56 Ibid.

57 Ibid.

58 Ibid.

59 *SIUE official website*, "SIUE Cougars Athletics," "1979 SIUE Men's Soccer - Hall of Fame," accessed October 4, 2020, https://www.siuecougars.com/hallfame/team/79msoc

60 Leo Robson, "GOAL-ORIENTED, How we watch soccer now.," *The New Yorker*, June 25, 2018.

61 Ibid.

62 "CHRONOLOGICAL HISTORY OF MISL, 1978—THE MISL BLASTS OFF," *MISL, Major Indoor Soccer League* (official brochure), Bala Cynwyd, PA, published circa 1981-82, p. 62.

63 Ibid.

64 Ibid.

65 Tom Timmermann, "St. Louis City SC tabs diverse trio," *St. Louis Post-Dispatch*, SPORTS, published November 13, 2020, p. B4.

66 Dave Luecking | *St. Louis Post-Dispatch*, "NEBO And BOKI BANDOVIC Soccer's Odd Couple," *Soccer Digest*, published April/May, 1988.

67 Mark Zeigler, "The game that changed everything for US soccer," *The San Diego Union-Tribune*, published October 9, 2017, accessed December 11, 2019, https://www.sandiegouniontribune.com/sports/sd-sp-us-soccer-trinidad-1989-story.html

68 Ibid.

69 Joe Lyons, "Everything came together the year Ambush seized the title," *St. Louis Post-Dispatch*, STL TODAY SPORTS, published April 25, 2020, p. B, B4.

70 Ibid.

71 *Wikipedia, The Free Encyclopedia*, s.vv. "AC St. Louis," accessed November 12, 2019, https://en.wikipedia.org/wiki/AC_St._Louis

72 *Just Sports Stats*, "2016 St. Louis Ambush Roster and Results on JustSportsStats," accessed December, 1, 2020, https://www.justsportsstats.com/soccerroster.php?team=M3SLS&year=2016

73 Joe Lyons, "Trittschuh is new coach for STLFC," *St. Louis Post-Dispatch*, SPORTS, published January 25, 2020, p. B4.

74 Joe Lyons, "STLFC set to play at Indy Eleven in a must-win game down stretch," *St. Louis Post-Dispatch*, SPORTS, published September 23 2020, p. B2.

75 Nathan Rubbelke, "Saint Louis FC to cease operations after 2020 season," *St. Louis Business Journal*, published August 25, 2020, updated August 25, 2020, accessed November 21, 2020, https://www.bizjournals.com/stlouis/news/2020/08/25/saint-louis-fc-to-cease-operations.html

76 Nathan Rubbelke, "In a big week for St. Louis pro soccer, the region's biggest supporters' group hits its own landmark," *St. Louis Business Journal*, published August 14, 2020, accessed November 19, 2020, https://www.bizjournals.com/stlouis/news/2020/08/14/st-louis-pro-soccer-supporters-group-now-nonprofit.html

77 Leo Robson, "GOAL-ORIENTED, How we watch soccer now.," *The New Yorker*, June 25, 2018.

78 Richard P. Feynman, *QED: The Strange Theory of Light and Matter*, Princeton University Press, Princeton, New Jersey, 1985 (copyright Feynman), 1988 (first Princeton paperback printing), p. 9.

79 Morgan Phillips, "America's top 5 deadliest cities," *Fox News*, published January 28, 2020, accessed October 13, 2020, https://www.foxnews.com/us/deadliest-u-s-cities

80 *CBS News*, "Murder map: Deadliest U.S. cities," *CBS*, *KMOV-TV*, published October 7, 2019, accessed October 13, 2020, https://www.cbsnews.com/pictures/murder-map-deadliest-u-s-cities/66/

81 Dave Skretta | AP, "It's official, St. Louis: We're MLS' newest expansion franchise," *Fox Sports*, published August 20, 2019, accessed November 15, 2019, https://www.foxsports.com/midwest/story/its-official-st-louis-were-mls-newest-expansion-franchise-082019

82 Ibid.

83 Kurt Erickson, "State balks at $30M in public money for stadium," "Smaller request for soccer funding to be considered in 2020," *St. Louis Post-Dispatch*, published December 18, 2019, p. A10.

84 Ben Frederickson, "Parson is a soccer blocker," "Governor seems to have bailed on supporting MLS ownership group," *St. Louis Post-Dispatch*, STL TODAY SPORTS, published December 20, 2019, p. B7.

85 Ibid.

86 Ibid.

87 Dave Skretta | AP, "It's official, St. Louis: We're MLS' newest expansion franchise," *Fox Sports*, published August 20, 2019, accessed November 15, 2019, https://www.foxsports.com/midwest/story/its-official-st-louis-were-mls-newest-expansion-franchise-082019

88 Ibid.

89 Ibid.

90 Ibid.

91 Marianne Martinez, "MLS4TheLou releases new renderings of proposed stadium," "Architects said the newest designs are 'more open, accessible and inclusive,'" *KSDK 5 On Your Side*, published March 4, 2020, updated March 4, 2020, accessed November 26, 2020, https://www.ksdk.com/article/sports/soccer/mls4thelou-new-renderings-proposed-soccer-stadium/63-ebe32f3b-1e01-48fe-b1ef-8e4bc987f258#:_:text=The%20stadium%20was%20designed%20by,Snow%20of%20Snow%20Kreilich%20Architects.

92 Ben Frederickson, "BENDING PRIORITIES," "St. Louis MLS club moves forward in some areas, pauses in others," *St. Louis Post-Dispatch*, STL TODAY SPORTS, published April 14, 2020, p. B4.

93 Tim Booth and Anne M. Peterson | Associated Press, "MLS welcomes players back to training fields," *St. Louis Post-Dispatch*, SPORTS, published May 7, 2020, p. B4.

94 Ibid.

95 Ibid.

96 Ibid.

97 Ibid.

98 Daniel Neman, "Philanthropist, soccer owner Bob Hermann dies," *St. Louis Post-Dispatch*, published April 13, 2020, p. Front Page (A1).

99 Ben Frederickson, "Can St. Louis go MLS crazy like Seattle?" *St. Louis Post-Dispatch*, STL TODAY SPORTS, published November 9, 2019, p. B.

100 Ibid.

101 Ibid.

102 Tom Timmermann, "St. Louis City SC tabs diverse trio," *St. Louis Post-Dispatch*, SPORTS, published November 13, 2020, p. B4.

103 Ibid.

104 *Wikipedia, The Free Encyclopedia*, s.vv. "United States v England (1950 FIFA World Cup)," accessed December 14, 2019, https://en.wikipedia.org/wiki/United_States_v_England_(1950_FIFA_World_Cup)

105 *Wikipedia, The Free Encyclopedia*, s.vv. "St. Louis Kutis S.C.," accessed May 22, 2020, https://en.wikipedia.org/wiki/St._Louis_Kutis_S.C.

106 *St. Louis Post-Dispatch* | powered by Legacy, "Casey J. Klipfel," published June 17, 2016, accessed May 30, 2020, https://www.legacy.com/obituaries/stltoday/obituary.aspx?n=casey-j-klipfel&pid=180360162&fhid=12331

107 Mike Kavanaugh I Editor, "THE PLAYERS," *St. Louis Steamers, 1981-1982 Media Guide*, Creative Printing Services, Inc., St. Louis, MO, published circa 1981-82, p. 13.

108 Ibid., p. 11.

109 Ibid.

110 *UMSL Tritons official website*, "UMSL Sports Hall of Fame," "Bob Bone," accessed May 25, 2020, https://www.umsltritons.com/honors/umsl-sports-hall-of-fame/bob-bone/2

111 *Wikipedia, The Free Encyclopedia*, s.vv. "Hermann Trophy," accessed November 8, 2019, https://en.wikipedia.org/wiki/Hermann_Trophy

112 Ibid.

113 Ibid.

114 Mike Kavanaugh I Editor, "THE PLAYERS," *St. Louis Steamers, 1981-1982 Media Guide*, Creative Printing Services, Inc., St. Louis, MO, published circa 1981-82, p. 22.

115 Ibid., p. 17.

116 Ibid., p. 13.

117 *SIUE official website*, "SIUE Cougars Athletics," "MEN'S SOCCER," "SIUE Men's Soccer Players in the Professional Ranks," accessed June 7, 2020, https://www.siuecougars.com/sports/m-soccer/archive/pros

118 Mike Kavanaugh I Editor, "THE PLAYERS," *St. Louis Steamers, 1981-1982 Media Guide*, Creative Printing Services, Inc., St. Louis, MO, published circa 1981-82, p. 11-12.

119 Ibid., p. 12.

120 *Wikipedia, The Free Encyclopedia*, s.vv. "Ty Keough," accessed May 18, 2020, https://en.wikipedia.org/wiki/Ty_Keough

121 Mike Kavanaugh I Editor, "THE PLAYERS," *St. Louis Steamers, 1982-1983 Media Guide*, Creative Printing Services, Inc., St. Louis, MO, published circa 1982-83, p. 22.

122 *Saint Louis University Billikens official website*, "St. Louis Billikens," "Men's Soccer," "Billikens in the Pros," published August 22, 2011, accessed May 27, 2020, https://slubillikens.com/news/2011/8/22/205245800.aspx

123 (AP), "McBride to be GM of U.S. soccer team," *St. Louis Post-Dispatch*, STL TODAY SPORTS, published January 11, 2020, p. B2.

124 *UMSL Tritons official website,* "UMSL Sports Hall of Fame," "(TEAM) 1973 MEN'S SOCCER," accessed May 25, 2020, https://www.umsltritons.com/honors/umsl-sports-hall-of-fame/-team-1973-mens-soccer/66

125 Ibid.

126 *UMSL Tritons official website,* "Men's Soccer," "Dan King," accessed May 20, 2020, https://umsltritons.com/sports/mens-soccer/roster/coaches/dan-king/377

127 Mike Kavanaugh | Editor, "THE PLAYERS," *St. Louis Steamers, 1981-1982 Media Guide*, Creative Printing Services, Inc., St. Louis, MO, published circa 1981-82, p. 23.

128 Ibid., p. 18.

129 Ibid.

130 *Wikipedia, The Free Encyclopedia,* s.vv. "Soccer in St. Louis," accessed November 12, 2019, https://en.wikipedia.org/wiki/Soccer_in_St._Louis

131 *Wikipedia, The Free Encyclopedia,* s.vv. "St. Leo's (soccer team)," accessed May 6, 2020, https://en.wikipedia.org/wiki/St._Leo%27s_(soccer_team)#1910_roster

132 Frank Hyland, *The Atlanta Journal*, published July 25, 1970, p. 3-B.

133 Charles Gould, *St. Louis Globe-Democrat,* published August 24, 1970, p. 5B.

134 Ibid.

135 Ibid.

136 *Wikipedia, The Free Encyclopedia,* s.vv. "Bob Hermann," accessed December 11, 2019, https://en.wikipedia.org/wiki/Bob_Hermann

137 *Wikipedia, The Free Encyclopedia,* s.vv. "St. Louis Steamers (1998-2006)," accessed March 3, 2020, https://en.wikipedia.org/wiki/St._Louis_Steamers_(1998%E2%80%932006)

138 *Wikipedia, The Free Encyclopedia,* s.vv. "AC St. Louis," accessed November 12, 2019, https://en.wikipedia.org/wiki/AC_St._Louis

139 Joe Lyons, "Ambush caught by surprise by cancellation of season," "Despite 9-12 record, team had positives," *St. Louis Post-Dispatch*, STL TODAY SPORTS, published March 27, 2020, p. B.

140 Ibid.

141 By Reuters, *"M.L.S. Adds St. Louis as League's 28th Team," The New York Times*, published August 20, 2019, accessed January 24, 2021, https://www.nytimes.com/2019/08/20/sports/soccer/mls-st-louis-expansion.html